Personnel Policies in Libraries

Personnel Policies in Libraries

Edited by Nancy Patton Van Zant

Neal-Schuman Publishers, Inc.

Published by Neal-Schuman Publishers, Inc.
23 Cornelia Street
New York, New York 10014

Published outside North America by Mansell Publishing, 3 Bloomsbury Place, London WC1A2QA, England.

Printed and bound in the United States of America.

Library of Congress Cataloging in Publication Data

Main entry under title:

Personnel policies in libraries.

Includes index.
1.   Library personnel management.   2.   Libraries, University and college—Personnel management.
3.   Public libraries—Personnel management.
I.   Van Zant, Nancy Patton.
Z682.P3994   023'.068'3   80-11734
ISBN 0-918212-26-X

Contents

Preface

Personnel Policies in Libraries originated in the minds of many librarians who have been faced with the formidable task of writing a personnel policy in the absence of good examples. Such a compilation has occurred to others who have been frustrated because no policy existed for their particular working situations.

This compilation is not a substitute for writing a comprehensive personnel policy tailored to local conditions. It does, however, go a step further than the *Library Personnel Manual: An Outline for Libraries* (American Library Association, 1977), an indispensable outline which recommends detailed and complete information on virtually every dimension of personnel management in libraries. *Personnel Policies in Libraries* assumes that examples of a variety of policy statements are also useful in the construction of a personnel policy. A word of caution here is important because this compilation does not endorse any policy in particular. Furthermore, it is not enough for a library to simply copy another's policy. Policies reprinted here were selected because they speak to one or more areas of personnel conditions, and not because a judgment has been made about the desirability of the resulting procedures or practices. It is important that a group of people in each library in question study the parameters of personnel management and write statements of application for their specific institutions. Except as noted, the compilation aimed to include policies regarding the conditions of employment for professional librarians.

Policies for this book were selected from responses to a letter mailed to 560 public and 550 academic libraries in the United States, February 1979. Over 600 replies to this letter and 325 personnel policies or parts of policies were received. The letter requested copies of policies which would be reviewed for possible inclusion in this book, and suggested that if the library's personnel policy was a composite of various statements, documents of particular interest would be those addressing affirmative action, appointments, position classification, promotion and transfer, terminations, working conditions, and benefits. The request also solicited those policies of the county, city, college, or university that applied to library personnel procedures. The letter stated that the material would not be used without written consent of the librarian, and finally, that a questionnaire would follow.

Many libraries answered that they had no written policy or that they were in the process of writing one. The compiler received numerous letters of support for the work undertaken and encouragement for its conclusion.

Three public library policies and one academic library policy have been reprinted here in full. These four policies are examples of personnel statements which provide reasonably thorough coverage of issues associated with the particular type and size of library. Because of the length of these complete policies, the best way to achieve broad representation by size, geographic location, content, and type of library is to concentrate on reprinting particular *sections* of policies. These selections are organized by major categories of personnel management, and contain parts of policies from 26 public and 20 academic libraries. Minimal editing has been exercised for purposes of standardization, although at least one inconsistency remains: Many documents use only male pronouns. No attempt has been made to write in nonsexist language.

Much care was taken to include policy statements from small public libraries, and the mailing targeted them in a greater proportion than the reprints attest. Similarly, few comprehensive college library policies were received. In most cases, reprints are not from policy manuals of larger jurisdictions such as cities, counties, states, universities, or colleges, unless those statements adequately define or provide important examples of the conditions of employment governing librarians. The compiler recognizes that the personnel manual of the Columbia University Libraries may not appear to be a representative selection in the eyes of other academic librarians. However, regardless of size and geography, all academic libraries can benefit from the organization and thoroughness found in the Columbia University *Handbook for Librarians*. The form of that policy manual, the categories it covers, its ambience, and the commitments it makes to its employees are universally desirable features of personnel policies.

There are at least two distinguishable styles of policy-making, theoretical and operational, both often present in the same document. Ideally the theoretical provides the philosophical framework for the detail and interpretation which emerge from the operational. The interplay of these styles is the key to responding to borderline questions and exceptions.

The results of the questionnaire, mailed in May 1979, are discussed in the "Survey" section. The questionnaire was sent to a larger group, (over 1300 public and 1000 academic libraries) than the group which received the request for copies of personnel policies.

The book provides the reader samples of personnel policies from a cross-section of institutions. It also enlightens one as to the status of and trends in policy-making throughout libraries in the United States by the data summarized from questionnaires. Every effort has been made by the editor and publishers to produce an accurate volume. They have no legal responsibility for errors or omissions.

ACKNOWLEDGMENTS

I wish to thank all libraries which so generously cooperated with me, allowing their policies to be reprinted in full or in part, and answering the questionnaire. I also appreciate the special letters of advice and support which many offered.

Special thanks are due Patricia Glass Schuman and Patsy Read who saw the idea to completion and to many people at Earlham College who are long-suffering where library-based projects are concerned.

Finally, Elizabeth Futas, editor of *Library Acquisition Policies and Procedures*, must be recognized because her initiative and the organization of that work are the prototypes for *Personnel Policies in Libraries*.

Nancy Patton Van Zant
January 1980

Introduction

The literature of librarianship has traditionally been firm yet low-keyed in its assertion that all libraries need a written personnel policy and that although some higher administrative body has the authority to establish such a policy, it is the responsibility of librarians to write the policy and to keep it current. Yet the need for a written statement is often not felt to be imperative until a difficult situation arises between employee and employer, staff member and supervisor, librarian and board, etc. At best, written personnel policies, updated as changes require, provide a theoretical framework in which to observe conditions of employment, are specific in interpretation of regulations, and are descriptive about the expectations and responsibilities of the employees' operation of the library. A good personnel policy helps orient new employees to the library and serves as a guide to board members or institutional administrators.

Although the profession has traditionally recognized the need for written personnel manuals, the importance and complexity of this issue came into sharp focus during the 1960s and '70s when a plethora of new rules and conditions affecting personnel policies and procedures emerged. The need for current and well-articulated policy would have been dramatically underscored even if the only factor considered was the tremendous increase in governmental regulations regarding personnel. Among the most significant federal laws defining fair employment today are the following: Title VII of the Civil Rights Act, enforced by the Equal Employment Opportunity Commission; Equal Pay Act, enforced by the Wage and Hour Division, Department of Labor; Age Discrimination in Employment Act of 1967 and ADEA Amendments of 1978, enforced by the Wage and Hour Division; the Rehabilitation Act of 1973, enforced by the Office of Federal Contract Compliance; Vietnam-Era Veterans Readjustment Act of 1974, enforced by the Assistant Director for Employment Standards, Department of Labor; Executive Order 11246, enforced by the Office of Federal Contract Compliance; the Revenue Sharing Act of 1972, enforced by the Secretary of the Treasury; and Title IX of the Education Amendments of 1972, enforced by the Department of Education.

In addition to the strictures of the federal government, several other key factors affecting library personnel developed: a shrinking job market, tightened library budgets, collective bargaining, and issues of professionalism. To some extent in response to these challenges, dramatic changes have emerged in the areas of performance evaluation and staff development. All of the resulting conditions and programs militate the need for personnel manuals to protect the employee and the employer.

The correspondence generated by the mailings required to produce this compilation registered overwhelming support of the need. A sampling follows:

"I'm not really sure what personnel policy is, though I understand what policy is regarding concrete situations, e.g., hiring, evaluation, and other such matters."

"We are revising the policy handbook."

"Our policy is in the process of revision and is in a million literal pieces right now."

"We don't have a written personnel policy at the present time, but would like to develop one."

"Sorry, but I have only been here for several months and want to rewrite the Personnel Manual, which is in bad shape right now."

"We do not have a detailed written policy for personnel. Sorry; we would like to have a copy of one."

"Your questionnaire caught me at a time when it created several thoughts relative to our new staff manual. May I thank you for this and for your efforts in trying to smooth over a rough spot in personnel relations?"

"We are a city library and function under the City's personnel rules and regulations."

"We follow a 50-page employees' handbook which is produced by our city's Personnel Officer."

"We are a small library—1½ employees and open only 30 hours per week. We do not need a policy."

"At the present time the library does not have any written statement of policy regarding personnel policies, rank and tenure. Criteria for rank and tenure, etc., are presently being established."

"Our librarians' manual is badly out-of-date."

"The Library is, of course, subject to the College policies, and unfortunately these have over the years been various, often conflicting, and always puzzling."

"We are only in draft stages of policy formulation. Topics in process include staff development, retention of staff who receive MLS degree, travel guidelines, peer evaluation for library faculty, philosophy of service. University policies exist but are not very different from run of the mill."

"This library works within the general framework of University-wide personnel policies and with the advice of the EEO office. While we have often felt that personnel policies more appropriate to the library situation would be useful, that project is still on a list of things to be accomplished."

Librarians have also responded by calling attention to studies underway in the area of personnel management. Two of interest are "Survey of Procedures and Criteria for Promotion and Continuing Appointment Used by Libraries of the State University of New York: Part I," compiled by Anne McCartt, with the assistance of Carolyn McBride, Personnel Policies Committee, State University of New York Librarians Association, May 1, 1979 (Part II will deal with community college practices) and "The Status of Status—The Status of Librarians in Texas Academic Libraries," compiled by Carol Burlinson, Denise Karimkhani, Keith Russell, and Jo Anne Hawkins (Chair), Academic Status Committee, College and University Libraries Division, Texas Library Association, 1979.

The four personnel policies reprinted in full provide sample formats and modes of thought. The sections which follow reprint selections from the manuals of various other libraries. The organization for those sections is roughly along the lines of chapters or categories designated in personnel manuals.

Some overlap is found across sections. This happens because some institutions refer to affirmative action implementation as a separate policy while others treat this issue in those portions of their policy dealing with the selection of staff. Part-time employees may be defined under benefits, absences, or position classification. Sabbaticals may be included under staff development or absences. For these and other similar organizational peculiarities, the Index will also guide the user. In addition, sometimes a library policy will be reprinted in a section because it is applicable to a subdivision of that section but is not necessarily the entire policy of the library on the larger subject. For example, the grievance procedures section of one library's policy is reprinted in the section on evaluation and promotion, but not the entire documents defining evaluation and promotion procedures of that institution.

Affirmative action policy statements vary from statements of the position of the institution to detailed procedures supported by data recording progress. The Office for Library Personnel Resources, American Library Association, provides a special reviewing service for the improvement of affirmative action plans, a service established by the Equal Employment Opportunity Policy, ALA, in 1974. In addition to maintaining a functional affirmative action statement, it is important to incorporate *procedure* into other personnel statements where the implementation of affirmative action is called for.

A methodology of evaluation and performance appraisal has developed as librarians have increasingly sought faculty status, tenure, or opted for collective bargaining. Administration of employee evaluation is in a state of transition, as librarians move away from an inventory of characteristics such as punctuality, attitude, and dependability to systems which are better able to communicate to employees expectations made of them, standards of performance, and progress made in these areas.

Many public libraries, and a few academic libraries, include variations of a statement on standards of conduct, either personal or professional. Some refer to basic rules of etiquette, others deal with ethical standards, and some speak to professional standards and activities. Codes of personal and professional ethics, however rigorous, must be explicitly clear to employees. Similarly, there is a category of policy called "Employee Relations to Each Other, to the Community, to the Institution," etc. In those two sections reprinted here, there may be occasional combination or overlap.

Library staff development covers a broad range of activities, including orientation and on-the-job training, skills-building programs, and the emphasis on developing capabilities among current staff members that may be applied to current problems. Staff development programs, organized locally, regionally, or nationally, may support individual or organizational development. The policy selections reprinted in this section include a wide range of support for the encouragement and growth of library staff. Topics which dominate staff development interests are management techniques and areas of librarianship in which change occurs most rapidly. The crucial element in responding to these demands is a growing and stimulating library staff.

Personnel classification and library organization are more critical in larger institutions. Smaller groups of employees are better able to function informally, yet such distinctions as full- and part-time classifications demand clarification. Job-sharing is a relatively new status of employment and necessarily carries special terms. There is some tendency for academic libraries to link librarian positions to promotion and tenure decisions rather than to emphasize a system of relative classifications or ranks. Therefore, the sections on Personnel Classification and Evaluation and Promotion need to be used together.

Working conditions are rather static lines in personnel policies, except for the advent of "flex-time." Examples of such innovation are reprinted in this compilation.

The section on benefits is not lengthy but serves to show a variety of ways in which librarians are further compensated by their institutions. Some detail is omitted. Where a vacation or holiday is concerned, that benefit may be considered in the section on absences. The major change occurring in the administration of leaves from an institution is probably the growing availability of paternity leaves, examples of which are reprinted.

Terminations come about because of resignation, layoff, dismissal, retirement, or death. These conditions are reprinted in detail in the final section of partial selections. Collective bargaining is a force where absences and terminations in particular are concerned, and reprints of agreements are included in these two sections.

The need for a written and organic personnel manual in libraries has not changed. Issues of personnel management do change, and they changed rapidly in the 1960s and 1970s. It is essential that libraries respond to these conditions in the form of a written and comprehensive personnel policy.

Survey

The questionnaire being reported on in this section was developed after the examination of many personnel policies. Its questions were designed to determine whether libraries in fact have personnel policies, written or understood, and the areas of personnel relations addressed.

Questionnaires were sent to over 1300 public libraries and to over 1000 academic libraries. Public librarians returned approximately 510 useable questionnaires, and academic librarians, 416. Approximately 50 questionnaires were returned a few weeks after the data were compiled. The original mailing, sent to a smaller group of libraries to request copies of their policies, announced that a questionnaire survey would follow and invited these librarians' participation. Confidentiality was assured.

The questionnaire, nearly two legal pages in length, consisted of over 35 questions or statements asking for a response. Librarians were incredibly generous in their willingness to answer the questions. Many wrote personal letters of enthusiastic support as well as lengthy amplifications of the actual practice at their institutions. The compiler was concerned that some responders might feel that there were ulterior motives for questions about collective bargaining, affirmative action procedures, and other volatile issues. But if librarians felt threatened or saw a proverbial red flag, they exercised their reserve simply by not identifying their library in the optional blanks provided.

What was sought, however, was not to embarrass institutions, but rather to get a reading about the state and variation of personnel practices across libraries in this country. *It should be emphasized that the analysis of the questionnaire responses which follows intends to reflect trends in personnel practice rather than scientific documen-*

tation on the state of the art. Broad representation was sought both in size and geographical situation of libraries.

Size and type of library are especially important determinants of personnel policy. The first line on page one of the questionnaire asked the type of library. The bottom of the second page asked for the name, address, and city (these lines were marked *optional*), total budget, number of population served, and staff professional and non-professional full-time employees (FTEs).

Academic institutions returning the questionnaire were divided into two categories: four-year colleges and universities. Public libraries were divided into three categories: libraries serving fewer than 20,000 people; libraries serving 20,000 to 99,999 people; and libraries serving 100,000 or more. The maximum number of respondents to any one question for each of the five groups is as follows:

1. Public libraries serving a population less than 20,000—   54
2. Public libraries serving a population of 20,000 to 99,999—   259
3. Public libraries serving a population of 100,000 or more—   197
4. Academic libraries: four-year colleges—   178
5. Academic libraries: universities—   238

It should be noted that since not all libraries responded to every question, there will be some discrepancy between these totals and the numbers shown in the tables in the following section.

STATUS OF PERSONNEL POLICY

The questions below were asked in an effort to determine if a written personnel policy for the library existed, if personnel practices were simply tacitly understood, if the written policy was that of a larger administrative unit than the library, and if the policy was ever revised.

- Does the library have a written personnel policy or component statements that function as such?
- Does the policy serve both professional and nonprofessional staff?
- Is the library's personnel policy (written or understood) that of the library, city, county, school, state, or other body? Specify.
- If the personnel policy is not designed by the library but by a larger jurisdiction, does it define librarians' rights and conditions of employment specifically? Or do librarians fall into a general category of employees?

- If you have a written personnel policy, how often is it reviewed? By whom (title)? Who wrote (or is writing) the personnel policy (indicate title or position)?
- When was the policy written (date)?

Responses to these questions were not tabulated individually. Rather, the relationship of the questions to their answers was analyzed for each questionnaire to determine the status of that library's personnel policy. Table 1 shows the responses to the broad question: Does the library have a written personnel policy which defines librarians' rights and their conditions of employment, and is that policy an active policy, current and subject to revision?

TABLE 1

	Yes	*No*
Public libraries serving population of less than 20,000	38	16
Public libraries serving population of 20,000 to 99,999	187	72
Public libraries serving population of 100,000 and up	142	55
Academic libraries: four-year colleges	94	84
Academic libraries: universities	136	102

Because the assignments of librarians are different from those of other employees in counties, municipalities, universities (regardless of faculty status), etc., a general policy for the Village of Auburn, the University of East Orange, or the City of Corning, for example, will only pay lip-service to library personnel needs *unless* policies and practices of librarians as a class of employees are specified.

A few librarians commented that they were in the process of writing the first personnel policy their institution had ever had. Policies which are currently being written are included in the "yes" category in Table 1.

STAFF MEETINGS

Does the library have staff meetings?

TABLE 2

	Yes	No
Public libraries serving population of less than 20,000	43	13
Public libraries serving population of 20,000 to 99,999	246	13
Public libraries serving population of 100,000 and up	190	7
Academic libraries: four-year colleges	160	13
Academic libraries: universities	228	10

How often?

TABLE 3

	Weekly, Biweekly	Monthly	1–9 Annually	Infrequently, Irregularly
Public libraries serving population of less than 20,000	11	12	7	13
Public libraries serving population of 20,000 to 99,999	49	103	45	49
Public libraries serving population of 100,000 and up	28	79	46	37
Academic libraries: four-year colleges	54	48	21	42
Academic libraries: universities	36	93	61	38

PERFORMANCE EVALUATIONS

Are library employees given performance evaluations?

TABLE 4

	Yes	No
Public libraries serving population of less than 20,000	34	29
Public libraries serving population of 20,000 to 99,999	196	58
Public libraries serving population of 100,000 and up	180	17
Academic libraries: four-year colleges	143	35
Academic libraries: universities	217	21

How are these evaluations used?

TABLE 5

	Reappointments, Promotions	Tenure	Demotion	Self-Improvement	Salary Raises	Dismissal
Public libraries serving population of less than 20,000	9	0	2	23	22	13
Public libraries serving population of 20,000 to 99,999	50	32	46	153	155	100
Public libraries serving population of 100,000 and up	79	44	82	136	129	130
Academic libraries: four-year colleges	98	62	9	98	96	70
Academic libraries: universities	170	147	49	191	188	156

How often are performance evaluations conducted?

TABLE 6

	3–6 Months	*Annually*	*2–5 Years*	*Irregularly, Infrequently*
Public libraries serving population of less than 20,000	3	22	2	
Public libraries serving population of 20,000 to 99,999	23	154	4	15
Public libraries serving population of 100,000 and up	17	145	2	9
Academic libraries: four-year colleges	5	124	7	11
Academic libraries: universities	8	190	7	8

Some librarians responded that probationary evaluations occur after the first six months of an individual's employment. After the probationary period, evaluations may be conducted annually, every 2 years, etc. Occasionally the probationary evaluation scheme is more complicated: every six months for the first two years of employment. Others said "as requested" or "as needed" but offered no further explanation. Some academics reported "at the appropriate time for reappointment or tenure" or "annually until tenure," implying that evaluation does not occur after tenure is obtained; others said "annually until tenure, then every five years."

Who conducts performance evaluations?

TABLE 7

	Supervisors	Supervisors and Peers	Peers	Supervisors and Subordinates	Peers and Subordinates	Supervisors, Peers, and Subordinates	Self and Others
Public libraries serving population of less than 20,000	22	1			1		3
Public libraries serving population of 20,000 to 99,999	187	2		3		3	6
Public libraries serving population of 100,000 and up	171	6					3
Academic libraries: four-year colleges	111	23	11			14	
Academic libraries: universities	135	39		4	1	14	6

The blanks offered for answering who conducts evaluations were "supervisors," "peers," "subordinates," and "other." People checked one or more of them. Some respondents noted "Library personnel committee" under "other."

PROMOTIONS

Are promotions given at administrative initiative?

TABLE 8

	Yes	No
Public libraries serving population of less than 20,000	22	4
Public libraries serving population of 20,000 to 99,999	184	38
Public libraries serving population of 100,000 and up	122	40
Academic libraries: four-year colleges	113	26
Academic libraries: universities	146	62

Or at employee initiative in applying for positions?

TABLE 9

	Yes	*No*
Public libraries serving population of less than 20,000	18	9
Public libraries serving population of 20,000 to 99,999	163	59
Public libraries serving population of 100,000 and up	147	22
Academic libraries: four-year colleges	96	46
Academic libraries: universities	160	48

These questions may appear a bit ambiguous or obscure in intent, but they were included to get a sense of employees' opportunities to be promoted from within. Obviously there will be fewer vacancies in some situations than in others, and likewise libraries without position classification schemes are less likely to have promotional opportunities available. However, the responses seem to indicate that both administrators and employees exercise promotional initiative.

If performance reviews or evaluations are used for reappointments and/or promotions, how do the following characteristics rank in importance? Rate from 1 (high) to 5.

TABLE 10

	Job Performance	*Service to the Institution*	*Service to Community*	*Professional Activities and Development*	*Publications and Research*
Public libraries serving population of less than 20,000	1	2	4	3	5
Public libraries serving population of 20,000 to 99,999	1	2	3	4	5
Public libraries serving population of 100,000 and up	1	2	3	4	5
Academic libraries: four-year colleges	1	2	4	3	5
Academic libraries: universities	1	2	5	3	4

One might have expected that small public libraries would have put greater emphasis on service to the community than on professional activities. If a larger number of libraries serving under 10,000 people had been polled (by far the majority here are in the 10,000–20,000 population category), the ranking might have placed service to the community higher. Universities clearly are the category placing greater emphasis on publications and research, with least interest in service to the community. Of course, those institutions which do not have a process of performance evaluation generally did not respond to this question. Other characteristics of one's employment which were sometimes added to the list by respondents were years of service, time in grade, attitude, compatibility with staff and patrons, and internal politics.

POSITION CLASSIFICATION

Does the library have a position classification plan with salary rankings that provides the basis for compensation?

TABLE 11

	Yes	No
Public libraries serving population of less than 20,000	37	20
Public libraries serving population of 20,000 to 99,999	220	33
Public libraries serving population of 100,000 and up	189	8
Academic libraries: four-year colleges	96	81
Academic libraries: universities	141	97

Some responses to this question were "yes, city has one" or "no, but city has one." The former was counted as a "yes" because one might infer that even though the plan is that of the city, it adequately deals with librarians. Correspondingly the "no, but city has one" category of response was counted as a "no" because it would appear that librarians do not feel enfranchised by the city plan even when they are city employees. Similar allowances were made for college and university responses. The data for colleges and universities show that over half of them have position classification plans. However, it was difficult to find comprehensive position classification plans for colleges and universities for the section of this book which reprints them. It seems that frequently professional librarian classes are not in a classification system, but rather, classification schemes are a component of the evaluation for reappointment and tenure system.

LAYOFF

Does the library have specific criteria or a plan for eliminating positions in the event of budget or service cutbacks?

TABLE 12

	Yes	No
Public libraries serving population of less than 20,000	6	50
Public libraries serving population of 20,000 to 99,999	71	180
Public libraries serving population of 100,000 and up	80	111
Academic libraries: four-year colleges	39	138
Academic libraries: universities	65	168

RETIREMENT

What is the retirement age?

TABLE 13

	65 or Younger	67, 68	70	70+	65, with Annual Extension to 70	None
Public libraries serving population of less than 20,000	10		16	3	4	20
Public libraries serving population of 20,000 to 99,999	68	5	104	1	8	65
Public libraries serving population of 100,000 and up	45	2	108	3	7	32
Academic libraries: four-year colleges	78		59	29	12	
Academic libraries: universities	85	10	94		11	35

Responses to this question are affected by the new federal legislation which was only beginning to receive attention when the questionnaire was written. Rather than reflecting a strictly mandatory retirement age, the answers more likely suggest a range of ages at which retirement is allowed and/or encouraged.

GRIEVANCE

Does the library have a formal grievance procedure?

TABLE 14

	Yes	No
Public libraries serving population of less than 20,000	34	22
Public libraries serving population of 20,000 to 99,999	193	53
Public libraries serving population of 100,000 and up	175	17
Academic libraries: four-year colleges	98	73
Academic libraries: universities	168	48

BENEFITS

Which of the following benefits does the library offer?

TABLE 15

	Sick Leave	Paid Vacation	Paid Holidays	Health Insurance	Life Insurance	Maternity Leave	Paternity Leave	Retirement	Leave without Pay
Public libraries serving population of less than 20,000	53	55	54	46	30	43	34	54	52
Public libraries serving population of 20,000 to 99,999	250	251	250	242	192	174	25	242	218
Public libraries serving population of 100,000 and up	197	197	197	190	161	170	36	193	193
Academic libraries: four-year colleges	173	172	175	173	149	121	24	168	156
Academic libraries: universities	233	229	230	232	204	201	29	233	225

This list does not include all benefits offered. Others were added by respondents: bereavement time, snow days, personal business days, dental care, longevity pay, and tuition reimbursement. Academics frequently add sabbaticals, faculty development funds, and tuition remission plans.

Are these benefits available to all full-time employees? Prorated to part-time employees? Prorated to permanent part-time employees? These questions were tabulated to produce the following configuration of information.

In addition to providing these benefits to full-time employees, the benefits are also prorated to part-time employees according to the following counts:

TABLE 16

Made a Response in the Blanks Which Asked Whether or Not Permanent Part-Time and Temporary Part-Time Employees are Provided Benefits; and Therefore, Presumably Those Institutions with Such Category of Employees		*Provide Most Benefits to Permanent Part-Time Employees*		*Provide Most Benefits to Temporary Part-Time Employees*	
		Yes	*No*	*Yes*	*No*
Public libraries serving population of less than 20,000	n = 45	32	8	13	12
Public libraries serving population of 20,000 to 99,999	n = 214	71	23	19	43
Public libraries serving population of 100,000 and up	n = 163	126	20	66	32
Academic libraries: four-year colleges	n = 98	72	16	44	23
Academic libraries: universities	n = 170	140	20	86	33

This question has implications in the area of affirmative action and particularly women's rights because, overwhelmingly, part-time jobs are held by women. Institutions providing part-time employment which fail to provide prorated fringe benefits such as health insurance, vacation, sick leave, and retirement plans are then subject to charges of abuse and exploitation.

STAFF DEVELOPMENT

Are professional employees given time off to attend conferences, meetings, and workshops?

TABLE 17

	Always	Sometimes	Never
Public libraries serving population of less than 20,000	37	18	0
Public libraries serving population of 20,000 to 99,999	125	126	0
Public libraries serving population of 100,000 and up	77	120	0
Academic libraries: four-year colleges	106	73	0
Academic libraries: universities	138	97	0

Are expenses (registration, travel, etc.) for meetings paid? Are there special conditions regarding eligibility for these benefits (specify)?

TABLE 18

	In Full	In Part	No
Public libraries serving population of less than 20,000	34	19	1
Public libraries serving population of 20,000 to 99,999	144	97	10
Public libraries serving population of 100,000 and up	61	128	8
Academic libraries: four-year colleges	58	113	9
Academic libraries: universities	43	190	2

Answers to these questions do not intend to provide precise information as to the exact state of professional travel and subsequent financial support; the questions were constructed to allow for a better picture of the availability of opportunity than would have been gained by questions answered simply yes or no.

Comments under "special conditions" indicate that individuals with special responsibilities such as an officer, delegate, leader, or those who have an official part in a program are always given time off to attend these meetings. One would mentally insert "within reason," of course. Beyond these priorities, employees' requests to attend meetings are considered in light of relevancy to their positions, membership held in the organization, and in some cases, seniority. Some respondents comment on rotating the opportunities.

Insofar as payment of expenses for attending meetings, it seems that there is a tendency for expenses to be paid in full by the institution

when an individual has official program or representational responsibility; when the employee elects to attend a conference or workshop,
it is more likely that partial reimbursement is offered. Another
situation described and which can be inferred from the answers
checked is that some institutions provide annually to each employee
a flat allotment for travel, regardless of the occasion, while other
institutions may provide funds for all of one or more trips according
to the demands being made on funds. Some state laws govern those
institutions' policies on travel and conference funds. Some states set
maximum allowable expenditures for professional meetings, while
others restrict the use of money according to in-state and out-of-state
gatherings. Travel and conference budgets may be among the first
items to be affected by retrenchment. Finally, some respondents
report that employees who attend meetings are required to report to
the staff about their experience. Some librarians answered that there
are *no* special conditions governing time off for meetings or the
financial support available for attending them.

Are nonprofessional employees eligible for similar continuing education benefits?

TABLE 19

	Yes	No
Public libraries serving population of less than 20,000	44	8
Public libraries serving population of 20,000 to 99,999	220	20
Public libraries serving population of 100,000 and up	184	13
Academic libraries: four-year colleges	110	67
Academic libraries: universities	191	44

Examples of opportunities available to nonprofessional employees
and activities in which they are eligible to participate were often
noted: local workshops, time off for courses, free tuition, meetings
which improve their job performance, etc. Priorities here inevitably
differ from those for professional employees, but some opportunities
for nonprofessional staff development are clearly available.

Is further education (or degrees) necessary for advancement? Recommended for advancement?

TABLE 20

	Recommended for Advancement	Necessary for Advancement
Public libraries serving population of less than 20,000	33	24
Public libraries serving population of 20,000 to 99,999	80	118
Public libraries serving population of 100,000 and up	70	137
Academic libraries: four-year colleges	46	90
Academic libraries: universities	60	150

Many variations are likely among libraries, in part because of the differences in availability of opportunities for advancement and certainly the qualifications desired for various positions. The answers indicate a tendency toward encouraging some level of advanced or further education.

Does the library have a staff development policy?

TABLE 21

	Yes	No
Public libraries serving population of less than 20,000	8	50
Public libraries serving population of 20,000 to 99,999	34	193
Public libraries serving population of 100,000 and up	87	110
Academic libraries: four-year colleges	21	147
Academic libraries: universities	45	175

TENURE

Are professional employees eligible for tenure?

TABLE 22

	Yes	No
Public libraries serving population of less than 20,000	5	43
Public libraries serving population of 20,000 to 99,999	60	167
Public libraries serving population of 100,000 and up	60	118
Academic libraries: four-year colleges	91	78
Academic libraries: universities	150	77

Public librarians frequently comment that tenure is known as "permanent employment" in their institutions. In some cases "permanent employment" is assumed after the successful completion of a six-month probationary period; in others, a more formal process exists. Some academic institutions provide tenure to librarians on approximately the same basis as to teaching faculty members; others have a system of "de facto" tenure.

SABBATICALS

Are sabbaticals available to professional employees?

TABLE 23

	Yes	No
Public libraries serving population of less than 20,000	5	45
Public libraries serving population of 20,000 to 99,999	35	193
Public libraries serving population of 100,000 and up	35	153
Academic libraries: four-year colleges	100	69
Academic libraries: universities	130	89

COLLECTIVE BARGAINING

Are employees represented by a collective bargaining agency?

TABLE 24

	Yes	No
Public libraries serving population of less than 20,000	3	53
Public libraries serving population of 20,000 to 99,999	77	174
Public libraries serving population of 100,000 and up	77	120
Academic libraries: four-year colleges	45	133
Academic libraries: universities	65	170

Does the agency represent professional employees? Nonprofessional employees? Both? Are they required to join?

TABLE 25

	Professionals		Nonprofessionals	
	Repre-sented	Required to Join	Repre-sented	Required to Join
Public libraries serving population of less than 20,000	3	1	3	1
Public libraries serving population of 20,000 to 99,999	67	14	75	17
Public libraries serving population of 100,000 and up	62	10	76	17
Academic libraries: four-year colleges	41	12	34	18
Academic libraries: universities	46	8	41	6

AFFIRMATIVE ACTION

Does the library have an affirmative action policy?

TABLE 26

	Yes	*No*
Public libraries serving population of less than 20,000	17	30
Public libraries serving population of 20,000 to 99,999	155	87
Public libraries serving population of 100,000 and up	150	39
Academic libraries four-year colleges	133	47
Academic libraries: universities	212	22

Libraries reporting that their city or college has an affirmative action policy which the library follows are counted in the "yes" category.

List of
Library Policies

REPRINTED IN FULL

Columbia University Libraries, New York NY 10027. *Handbook for Librarians, 1979.*

Lower Merion Library Association, Ardmore, PA 19003. *Personnel Guide.*

St. Joseph Public Library, St. Joseph, MO 64501. *Staff Manual.*

Salt Lake City Public Library, Salt Lake City, UT 84111. *Personnel Code* (Patterned after the Dayton & Montgomery County (Ohio) Public Library).

PARTIALLY REPRINTED

Atlantic City Free Public Library, Atlantic City, NJ 08401. *Work Week, Breaks, Overtime*

Augsburg College, George Sverdrup Library, Minneapolis, MN 55454. "Promotion in Rank and Tenure of Librarians; Article 1, By-Laws to the Constitution," *Augsburg College Faculty Handbook*, revised January 1975, p. 9.7.1.

Boise State University, Boise, ID 83703. *Longevity Statement.*

California State University and Colleges, Long Beach, CA 90840. *New Personnel Plan for Librarians; Guidelines for Campus Development of Evaluation Criteria*. Developed by Office of Faculty and Staff Affairs, Office of the Chancellor.

California State College, Stanislaus, Turlock, CA 95380. *Standards of Conduct*.

Central North Carolina Library, Burlington, NC 27215. *The Personnel System; The Position Classification Plan; The Salary Plan Organization Chart; Probation . . . Personnel Evaluations; Vacation— Education Leave; Maternity/Paternity Leave of Absence*.

Champaign Public Library and Information Center, Champaign, IL 61820. *Methods of Determining Rates of Compensation; Classification and Pay Plan; Fringe Benefits; Leaves of Absences; Statutory Benefits; Medical Coverage; Holidays; Vacations*.

Cherry Hill Free Public Library, Cherry Hill, NJ 08034. *Staff Development Policy*.

Crystal Lake Public Library, Crystal Lake, IL 60014. *Probationary Periods; Evaluation; Grievances*, Policy Committee, Crystal Lake Public Library Board.

Earlham College, Richmond, IN 47374. *Review of Librarians*.

Eastern Michigan University, Ypsilanti, MI 48197. *Professional Responsibilities; Layoff and Recall*, agreement between EMU and the Eastern Michigan University Chapter of the American Association of University Professors, 1978.

El Paso Public Library, El Paso, TX 79901. *Employment—Recruitment*.

Ela Area Public Library, Lake Zurich, IL 60047. *Scope*.

Georgia College, Ina Dillard Russell Library, Milledgeville, Ga 31061. *Employment Procedures for Faculty Positions*.

Georgia State University, William Russell Pullen Library, Atlanta, GA 30303. *Meetings of Professional and Scholarly Organizations; Faculty Research Assistance*.

Indiana Universities Libraries, Bloomington, IN 47405. *Criteria for Promotion and Tenure* (rev. 1978); *Staff Development/Continuing Education Activities* (1976 ed.); *Guidelines for Librarians' Promotion and Tenure Dossiers* (rev. 1978).

Jefferson-Madison Regional Library, Charlottesville, VA 22901. *Relationship with the Community Statement; Working Conditions.*

Minnesota Valley Regional Library, Mankato, MN 56001. *Dismissal, Resignation, Retirement; Hours of Work; Benefits and Insurance.*

Montgomery County-Norristown Public Library, Norristown, PA 19401. *Meetings, Conferences, and Educational Courses; Staff Meetings; Conduct.*

Mt. Carmel Public Library, Mt. Carmel, IL 62863. *Professional Meetings.*

Mt. Lebanon Public Library, Mt. Lebanon, PA 15228. *Appointment Statement; Professional Meetings; Education and In-Service Training.*

Natrona County Public Library, Casper, Wyoming 82601. *Natrona County Personnel Policy: Separation and Suspension; Handling of Complaints or Appeals.*

Paramus Public Library, Paramus, NJ 07652. *Staff Positions; Salaries and Classifications; Performance Reviews; Working Conditions; Professional Conduct; Holidays and Emergency Closings; Vacations; Sick Leave; Personal Leave; Emergency Leave; Terminal Leave; Leave Without Pay; Benefits.*

Pikes Peak Regional Library District, Colorado Springs, CO 80901. *Recruitment; Reappointment Statements; Termination; Death.*

River Bend Library System, Coal Valley, IL 61240. *Appointment.*

Rockford Public Library, Rockford, IL 61101. *Communications; Standards of Service; Staff Lounge; Code of Ethics for Staff Members.* Staff Committee, Ms. Alma Bridge, Chairperson.

St. John's University, Alcuin Library, Collegeville, MN 56321. *Continuing Education through Conferences and Conventions Statement; Termination of Administrative Appointments; Faculty and Administration Fringe Benefits.*

Maude Shunk Library, Menomonee Falls, WI 53051. *Organization Chart.*

Skokie Public Library, Skokie, IL 60077. *Affirmative Action Statement; Statement on Recruitment; Statement on Selection and Appointment.*

Sonoma County Library, Santa Rosa, CA. *Philosophy of Library Service; Affirmative Action Plan; Appointment Procedure for Librarian III; Probationary Period; Administration Policy— Transfers.*

Southern Illinois University at Carbondale, Morris Library, Carbondale, IL 62901. *Library Affairs; Library Orientation; Association Meetings, Conferences, Workshops, and Seminars; Other Travel; Research and Publishing.*

Spokane Public Library, Spokane, WA 99201. *Affirmative Action Program; Professional Conduct; Professional Organizations.*

Tacoma Public Library, Tacoma, WA 98402. *Grievance Procedures.*

Toledo-Lucas County Public Library, Toledo, OH 43624. *Recruiting Statement; Appointments Statement; Salary Scale and Position Classification; Staff Development; Employment Benefits; Time Regulations; Dismissal; Suspension; Resignation; Retirement; Probation; Promotion; Transfer; Grievance Procedure; Conduct.*

Union Theological Seminary in New York City, New York, NY 10027. *Classification for Librarians; Benefits; Personnel Policy for Full-Time Professional Librarians.*

University of Missouri-St. Louis Libraries, St. Louis, MO. Reprinted with permission from the *Policy Manual* of the University of Missouri-St Louis Libraries: *Permanent Part-Time Employment Policy; Grievance Procedures; Academic and Non-Regular Vacation and Leave Policy; Guidelines and Procedures for Recruitment and Hiring of Permanent Academic Staff Members.*

University of New Mexico, Albuquerque, NM 87131. *Personnel Policies and Practices Manual.*

University of Pittsburgh Libraries, Pittsburgh, PA 15260. *Appointment Statement.*

University of Portland, Portland, OR. *Affirmative Action Statement.*

The University of Tennessee, Knoxville, TN 37916. *Equal Employment Opportunity and Affirmative Action Statement; Workweek; Work Schedules; Overtime and Compensation; Training; Travel.*

Viking Library System, Fergus Falls, MN 56537. *Application and Appointment; Staff Development; Hours of Work; Separations; Organizational Chart.*

West Georgia College Library, Carrollton, GA 30118. *Organization Chart; Flextime Policy.*

Western Illinois University Library, Macomb, IL 61455. *Professional and Community Service Statement from Library Personnel Committee.*

Western Michigan University, Kalamazoo, MI 49008. *Sabbatical Leave Policy*, agreement between Western Michigan University and the Western Michigan University American Association of University Professors Chapter.

Western Michigan University Libraries, Kalamazoo, MI 49008. *Sabbatical Leave Policy Statement.*

Whittier College, The Wardman Library, Whittier, CA 90608. *Statement on Equal Opportunity.*

Winnetka Public Library District, Winnetka, IL 60093. *Selection of Staff; Hours of Work.*

Worthington Public Library, Worthington, OH 43085. *Employee Relations; Professional Activities; Working Conditions; Vacations.*

Complete
Library
Personnel
Policies

Academic Library Personnel Policies

COLUMBIA UNIVERSITY LIBRARIES
(New York, New York)

*Handbook for Librarians
(June 1978, June 1979)*

INTRODUCTION

This handbook provides information on the administration and organization of the Columbia University Libraries and outlines the principal personnel policies and practices affecting the professional library staff. Although it should be of most interest to new members of the staff, the handbook is also intended to provide all staff members with explanations and interpretations of current policies, practices, and procedures.

The information in this handbook is, in many instances, general and not intended as a definitive summary of all professional personnel policies and practices. Of necessity, there will be variations within the library system in the implementation of certain policies (scheduling vacations, for example) because of service or other departmental priorities. Therefore, members of the professional staff are advised to contact the Library Personnel Office if they have questions concerning the specific implications of a particular policy or practice.

A number of staff members provided the staff of the Library Personnel Office with valuable assistance in updating the handbook. The Representative Committee of Librarians was particularly helpful in suggesting items for inclusion in the handbook, and the Professional Review Committee was instrumental in rewriting the sections on the system of professional ranks.

Signed by the University Librarian

CONTENTS

Leave
  Sick Leave
  Maternity Leave of Absence
  Paternity Leave of Absence
  Jury Duty
  Death in the Family
  Leave Without Pay

BENEFITS

Tuition Exemption
  Graduate Courses
  Auditing Courses
  Spouses
  Children
  After Retirement
Scholarships for Children
  Tuition Scholarship Program for Private Schools
  College Tuition Scholarship Program
Life Insurance
Major Medical Insurance
Blue Cross and Blue Shield
Total Disability Benefits Plan
Retirement
  University Policy
  Retirement Plan for Officers–TIAA/CREF
Social Security
New York State Disability
Worker's Compensation
Unemployment Insurance

MISCELLANEOUS (this chapter omitted)

University Publications
  A Guide for Newcomers to Columbia University
  Columbia University Calendar
  Columbia University Directory
  MEMO
  Columbia Spectator
Library Publications
  Columbia Library Columns
  Columbia Librarian
  University Librarian's Newsletter
  Guides to the Columbia University Libraries
Useful Publications About New York City

University Facilities and Services
  Dining Halls
  Check Cashing
  Health Services
  The Marcellus Hartley Dodge Physical Fitness Center
  University Bookstore
  Faculty House
University Apartments

APPENDIXES

A   Organization Chart
B   University Statutes (omitted)
C   List of Staff by Professional Rank (omitted)
D   Grievance Procedure
E   Positions by Current Title
F   Affirmative Action Program
G   Leave and Travel Policy
H   Guidelines for Performance Appraisals
I   Performance Appraisal Form
J   Mailing Lists (omitted)

THE COLUMBIA UNIVERSITY LIBRARIES

The Libraries in the University

The University Libraries are charged with supplying the collections, the reference and bibliographic services, and facilities for library use for the support of the instructional and research programs of the University. While the needs generated by current programs are of first concern, the resources of the Libraries must necessarily reflect the past and anticipate the future. The supportive nature of library service, however, should be viewed in the context of Columbia's distinctive collections, which often generate activities that involve staff, directly and indirectly, in both research and instruction. In addition, the nature of many of the collections has implications involving a commitment to the scholarly community at large. As a result, Columbia has long acknowledged an obligation to share resources, while actively participating in regional and national efforts aimed at resolving some of the major problems facing all large research libraries.

Through the years, the administrative organization of the Columbia Libraries has been adjusted to meet changing demands and the requirements of a more complex university. The organization of the Libraries was modified in 1973-74 as the result of recommendations and suggestions that were forthcoming from a management study. The primary objective of this study, which was part of a program of the Association of Research Libraries and the American Council of Education, was to devise a plan for the development of library programs that would be responsive to the changing academic requirements of individual users and suitable for meeting long-term library needs. The focus of the study was not principally cost reductions; rather, it was to secure maximum benefits from library resources—funds, staff, collections, and space.

Organizations, however, are means to ends, and are meaningless without the people who make them function. The organization of the Columbia Libraries is intended to enhance the collective capability to respond effectively to academic requirements. It recognizes the importance of a balanced receptivity to the ideas of those who can and should contribute to meeting objectives and priorities; it seeks to assign and clarify individual responsibilities for the fundamental elements that together constitute research library operations; and perhaps more importantly, it encourages prompt and direct response by individual staff members to immediate needs of users without losing sight of the historical perspective that has shaped, and must continue to shape, the collections, procedures, and service capabilities that have made Columbia's libraries distinctive.

The University Libraries include more than 35 reader service units created and maintained to provide the resources and services required by students and factulty. The several technical and administrative departments provide various services in support of these units. The staff includes some 130 librarians and other professionals, almost 300 supporting, technical, secretarial, and supervisory staff members, and a part-time staff equivalent of some 96 full-time employees. More than 600,000 square feet of assignable space are devoted to library purposes.

Library collections as of June 30, 1977, included some 4.7 million cataloged volumes, 1.7 million units of microform, 9 million manuscript items in 850 separate collections, and important collections of maps, phonorecords, pamphlet material, and certain uncataloged but organized special groups of books. More than 57,000 serial titles are maintained on a continuing basis.

The Libraries are normally used by 13,000–15,000 individuals each week day during the academic year. Of these users, about 25 percent are undergraduates, 50 percent graduate and professional school students, 11 percent faculty and staff, and 14 percent students and faculty from affiliated institutions or individuals with no formal Columbia ties. These users borrow about 1.3 million items each year.

Perhaps twice as many volumes, as well as hundreds of thousands of manuscript items, are used within the Libraries, but much of this use is unrecorded.

Total annual operating expenditures exceeded 8.4 million in 1976-77, with 85-90 percent of this sum coming from the University's general income, and the balance from specific endowments, gifts and contracts. As is typical of large, decentralized, general research libraries, something less than one-third of all expenditures is for materials for the collections, while the remaining two-thirds is for staff and supplies and equipment. Viewing the budget programmatically, recent investigation indicates that one-third of all expenditures support instructional programs, while the remaining two-thirds support research activity.

Most of the principal elements within the Libraries and the University that help to form Library objectives and priorities are reflected in the organization chart of the Libraries, Appendix A. Although these elements vary in their impact on library service, each is an essential factor in the continuing process of adjusting activities and monitoring results.

Library Components Influencing Objectives and Priorities

Within the Libraries, four components share responsibility for advising the University Librarian on library objectives and priorities: the Professional Advisory Committee, the Professional Review Committee, the Representative Committee of Librarians, and the Library Operations Committee.

The Professional Advisory Committee (PAC). The role of the Professional Advisory Committee (PAC) is to provide comprehensive professional advice and counsel, often based on specific studies, to the University Librarian and the Planning Office.

The Professional Advisory Committee comprises ten members and a chairperson appointed by the University Librarian for terms of one to three years. The Representative Committee of Librarians is asked to make recommendations for these appointments to the University Librarian. The Assistant University Librarian for Planning is an ex officio member of the Committee. Because the Committee represents a cross-section of the professional staff, its work supplements that of the Library Operations Committee.

The Professional Advisory Committee or its representatives, usually the chairperson or the Assistant University Librarian for Planning, meet with the University Librarian and submit recommendations in the form of task force reports. Minutes of meetings are maintained in the Planning Office for examination by interested staff members.

The Professional Review Committee (PRC). The role of the Professional Review Committee is to provide the University Librarian with recommendations concerning promotion in rank of professional staff members and to consult with the Assistant University Librarian for Personnel on evaluation procedures. PRC also advises the University Librarian on professional ranks for new appointees to the staff.

The five members of the Professional Review Committee including the chairperson are appointed for staggered terms of three years by the University Librarian. The Representative Committee of Librarians is asked to make recommendations for these appointments to the University Librarian.

The Representative Committee of Librarians (RCL). The Representative Committee of Librarians is comprised of seven staff members elected to two-year terms by the professional staff. The slate of nominees is provided by a committee headed by the two Library Senators and by petition. It is primarily responsible for communicating the views of the professional staff to the University Librarian and for advising the University Librarian on matters affecting the role and functioning of the Libraries and the librarians within the University. As such, the Committee also represents the librarians to the University Administration through the Office of the University Librarian and serves as a channel for communicating the views of the professional staff to the University Senate through the Library Senators.

The Library Operations Committee (LOC). The role of the Library Operations Committee, which is comprised of the principal administrative officers of the Libraries, is unique since, as a group, it has responsibility for policy implementation in specific administrative divisions. Members of LOC are the Assistant University Librarian for Planning, the Directors (Resources, Services, and Support), the Division Chiefs (Bibliographic Control, Humanistic and Historical, Sciences, Social Sciences), the Heads of Acquisitions and Preservation, and the Librarians of the Distinctive Collections (Avery, East Asian, Health Sciences, Law, Rare Books and Manuscripts).

University Influences on Library Objectives and Priorities

Departments of Instruction. Almost all departments of instruction have committees or representatives working in an advisory capacity with the appropriate library units on subjects of primary interest to their departments. Many of these committees include both students and faculty in their membership. The committees are significant because they are a direct and readily available link between major user groups and specific libraries. Moreover, they are in a position to assess library operations and objectives in the context of current academic activities and goals.

The University Senate. The University Senate, which was established in May 1969 to succeed the University Council, is involved in the process of setting University objectives and priorities. There are 101 members of the Senate, 9 are appointed or ex officio members of the University administration and 92 are elected for two year terms to represent various components of the University. The Libraries are represented by two Senators elected from and by those who hold full-time Trustee or Presidential appointments in the Libraries.

One of the 13 Standing Committees of the Senate . . . is the Committee on Libraries, which has 13 members apportioned as follows: 4 Tenured Faculty, 1 Non-Tenured Faculty, 3 Students, 1 Administration, 3 Library Staff, 1 Research Staff. The stated purpose of the Committee is to "review and recommend University policies relating to the University Libraries so as to advance the role of the libraries in the effectuation of the University's educational purposes." The Senate Library Committee also provides the University Librarian with a means for obtaining advice and action on matters requiring University-wide support for implementation.

The library staff is also represented on five other standing committees of the Senate, including Education, External Relations and Research Policy, Honors and Prizes, Physical Development of the University, and Rules of University Conduct.

Office of the Executive Vice-President for Academic Affairs and Provost. The third link between the Libraries and the University as a whole is the Executive Vice-President for Academic Affairs. While the Executive Vice-President is the central administrative officer for the Libraries, it is in his capacity as chief academic officer of the University that he has a critical and central role in setting objectives and priorities, simply because his office is the focal point linking long-range academic planning with long-range library planning.

Extra-Institutional Relationships
The primary influences on the development of programs and resources of the Libraries come from within the University. Relationships with other institutions and agencies, however, have affected and will continue to affect the Libraries. Some examples of these are: participation in cooperative library activities, interlibrary loan agreements, service obligations assumed in conjunction with state or federal

programs, contracts with commercial firms to increase the availability of bibliographic information, and projects supported by outside funding agencies. Although many extra-institutional relationships generate additional service obligations, they also provide needed services to Columbia and, in addition, serve as links with other academic communities. Such relationships, moreover, can offer a variety of advantages for participating institutions by revealing opportunities for cooperative efforts that may eventually be used to supplement local resources, thereby making possible certain local activities which would otherwise not be economically feasible.

In addition to agreements directly entered into by the Libraries, proposals for outside funding to improve the University's instructional or research capacity often have some impact on library resources, requiring additional facilities or redirecting current resources. Efforts by faculty, staff, administration and students to develop external relations in ways that will generate support for the University's key activities are, however, seen as helpful and in fact essential. Fundamental to these efforts and external relationships of the Libraries is the principle that they contribute to the University's and the Libraries' service goals without compromising academic values and standards.

Shared Resources Program

The Research Libraries Group (RLG) . . . .
Center for Research Libraries (CRL) . . . .
The New York Metropolitan Reference and Research Library Agency (METRO) . . . .

The Friends of the Columbia Libraries
The Friends of the Columbia Libraries is an organization of interested persons within and outside of the University who promote interest in the role of a research library in education and who contribute funds or books to the Libraries . . . .

The Administrative Organization of the Libraries

The administrative organization of the Libraries is constructed around four fundamental segments of library activity which together encompass the full range of operating responsibilities: operations and staff planning and review, development of bibliographic resources and records, services to the academic community, and resources and materials processing. (See organization chart, Appendix A.)

Office of the Vice President and University Librarian

This office has responsibility for operations planning and review, a function that includes (a) accumulating and evaluating information affecting basic library objectives and priorities; (b) establishing and implementing, with the principal library officers, policies designed to accomplish established objectives; (c) providing resources in terms of budgeted funds, personnel, appropriate space, and effective procedures required to carry on the library program; and (d) assessing, on a continuing basis, the effectiveness of library performance in the accomplishment of University objectives. The Library Personnel Office and the Planning Office, comprising Systems and Financial Services, are attached to the Office of the Vice President and University Librarian.

Library Resources Group

This administrative component includes units and individuals responsible for the content of the collections and for most primary bibliographic control activities. Some individual members of the professional staff of this group, notably those with extensive subject or linguistic skills, provide specialized reference or instructional services for students and faculty members.

Library Services Group

This administrative unit is responsible for the delivery of library services through a physically decentralized group of subject-oriented collections, thus providing local flexibility within an administratively centralized organization. These services include general and specialized bibliographic, reference, and instructional programs, orientation activities, photocopy and microform reading facilities, and access to shared resources through interlibrary loan and consortium agreements. Staff members of this group share book selection and preservation responsibilities in specialized areas with the Resources and Support Groups.

Library Technical Support Group

This unit is responsible for the business and processing functions required to support all aspects of library operations. The underlying principle here is to consolidate the many activities which sustain the library as an enterprise. Here are found the acquisitions processing units, supplies maintenance, bibliographic searching, systems input preparation and quality control, collection preservation activities, and reprographic activities.

Distinctive Collections

In addition to these four broad functional areas, library service to the academic community is provided by several components which offer collections of unique depth and nationally significant excellence. These have been designated Distinctive Collections, and include the Avery Architectural and Fine Arts, East Asian, Health Sciences, Law, and Rare Book and Manuscript Libraries.

THE PROFESSIONAL STAFF ORGANIZATION

Introduction

The professional members of the staff of the University Libraries are responsible for daily library operations and for the general character and quality of the collections, bibliographic systems and service programs. A statement establishing the authority and the responsibilities of the University Librarian and Officers of the Libraries is provided in the *University Statutes* (Appendix B), and the administrative plan established to carry out those responsibilities is described in detail in *The Administrative Organization of the Libraries of Columbia University* (revised 1975).

The *Statutes* chapter underscores the relationship between the University Libraries and the academic programs of the University and reaffirms the traditional Columbia view that Officers of the Libraries, a distinctive group within the University, are allied with several faculties in accomplishing instructional and research objectives. Librarians are expected to continue study and research in their field and to advance themselves professionally. This perception of research librarianship at Columbia has served as the cornerstone of our professional staff structure.

The general outline of professional staff organization at Columbia includes two parallel elements, (a) a system of position categories and (b) a system of professional ranks. With the exception of a few senior officers, each professional staff member holds a *position* that is classified into one of five categories on the basis of the degree of administrative or policy-making responsibility involved. Initial assignment to a specific position and any subsequent reassignments are handled administratively. In addition to a position assignment, each professional staff member holds a title denoting professional *rank*, which is independent of the position and which reflects the level of professional achievement of the individual, largely as perceived by peers, that is, librarians within the Columbia system and other professional colleagues. A new appointee to the staff is assigned an initial rank and promotion review date by the Assistant University Librarian for Personnel after consultation with the Professional Review Committee. Subsequent promotion is based on the peer evaluation system described below [in "The System of Professional Ranks"].

Reflecting these two systems and dependent on them, salary guidelines have been established to assure appropriate salary levels and equity of remuneration. In brief, an individual's salary at any point in time is governed by three factors: (a) the individual's professional performance, (b) the character of the position held and administrative responsibilities assumed, and (c) length of service. Implicitly, merit is the dominant factor: the initial provisional appointment is a search for distinction; promotion in rank reflects merit largely as seen by peers; and promotion to positions of greater responsibility reflects a judgment by library management of both performance and potential.

The formulation of the system of position categories and the establishment of the system of professional ranks provided the impetus for a number of important procedural changes designed to assure the continuing development of a distinctive professional staff.

1. The provisional nature of the initial appointment to the professional staff has been formalized, as has the process of performance review, both during the provisional period and immediately prior to consideration for promotion to the permanent staff.

2. Periodic supervisory appraisals and peer review process to assess professional performance and to provide a basis for determining further promotion in rank have been established.

3. Individual positions have been carefully classified, with special attention given to the description of levels of administrative responsibility and to the identification of positions that affect, in substantial ways, general library directions and overall library performance.

An important goal of the Columbia program is to upgrade the profession of academic and research librarianship by raising the sights of individual members, by encouraging higher standards of performance, and by identifying ways for Columbia's librarians to contribute even more effectively than they now do to the academic purposes of the University. In the long run, the quality of recruits to the profession, the nature of professional education, personal satisfaction, and financial rewards will all be influenced by Columbia's professional staff program.

The Presidential appointment is and continues to be the appropriate form of appointment to the professional staff, and is used for all but the rank of Librarian IV, for which a Trustee appointment is used.

The System of Professional Ranks

The original impetus for the development of the system of professional ranks and peer review came from the Representative Committee of Librarians (RCL), which submitted two documents to the University Librarian: "A Recommended System of Professional Levels," September 17, 1970, and "Draft Proposal for Peer Evaluation," October 29, 1971. The Staff Development Committee (SDC), which was established as part of the general reorganization of the Libraries in July 1972, was given the task of developing these proposals during the following two years.

During the course of its work, SDC examined the tenure review procedures for the Columbia faculty, and obtained documents from other major research libraries which had or were in the process of developing similar systems. Both of these sources of information were useful to the Committee in clarifying its own thinking, insuring that the promotional review process for professional librarians met the rigorous standards of the University, and clarifying the similarities and distinctions between the tenure system for Officers of Instruction and the emerging promotional system for Officers of the Libraries.

The entire professional staff was involved in shaping the system of rank and peer review as it now stands. The two RCL documents were distributed for study and comment by the professional staff, and SDC conducted a series of meetings to review with the staff the materials it was developing which outline the philosophy and procedures of the review process (these now appear as Section II of this HANDBOOK, and the PROFESSIONAL REVIEW COMMITTEE MANUAL). On the recommendation of the University Librarian, the system was authorized by the Executive Vice President for Academic Affairs and Provost, and implemented in December, 1974, when staff members were first assigned a rank and given a promotion review date.

The Staff Development Committee was reconstituted as the Professional Review Committee (PRC) in July 1975, and charged with carrying forward the system of ranks and peer review. Modifications and improvements based on experience with the system and suggestions from the staff through RCL continue to be made. Among these have been the institution of summary statements to provide candidates with the reasons for promotional decisions, the inclusion of professional supervisees among those who may be contacted for additional documentation, and increased access to information about the process and the Committee's activities through expanded and updated statements in this HANDBOOK and availability of the PRC Manual and other documents for study by the staff.

Two frequently-asked questions are:

If this is a peer review process, why is PRC not an elected committee?

The Professional Review Committee is analagous to and modeled on the Ad Hoc Committees appointed by the Provost to advise on the faculty tenure recommendations to be made to the President and Trustees. Under the University Statutes, only the University Librarian has the authority to recommend to the President and Trustees, through the Provost, the promotion in rank of Officers of the Libraries. The University Librarian delegates to the Professional Review Committee the responsibility for conducting a peer review and reporting to him/her the results of that review with a recommendation for action.

The term "peer" denotes "one that is of the same or equal standing (as in law, rank, quality, age, ability) with another" (Webster's Third). "Peer review" therefore implies professional evaluation by colleagues from among one's own ranks. The peers involved in reviewing each candidate are not just the members of the Professional Review Committee, but all those professional colleagues, both within and outside the Libraries, who contribute their thoughtful impressions to the Committee, which is responsbible for assembling and synthesizing this information.

Since the Professional Review Committee can only be advisory to the University Librarian, the "Draft Proposal for Peer Evaluation" developed by RCL envisioned from the start a Committee appointed by the University Librarian. Committee members must have a broad view of the Libraries and the profession and be in a position to devote a substantial amount of time to the committee's work (weekly meetings plus much homework). When the system was implemented, a procedure was established by which RCL provides the University Librarian with a slate of nominees for PRC when vacancies on the Committee occur. The Librarian retains the authority to supplement this list to insure a balanced committee familiar with the widest possible range of Library and professional activities.

Why are candidates not told who is asked to write about them, nor allowed to see those letters?

The original RCL document provided: "All relevant documents . . . will be kept in strictest confidence. Likewise, all Committee discussions and results will be confidential." The models from which this recommendation derives are those of the tenure review procedure for the Columbia faculty and of similar systems at a number of other major research libraries. Confidentiality is an integral aspect of the faculty review process at Columbia, as it is in most colleges and universities, and is intended to protect the privacy of candidates, while encouraging a rigorous and impartial review in recognizing and rewarding distinction. Documents from other libraries with similar systems also indicate that confidentiality is essential to obtain an accurate view of a candidate's strengths and weaknesses, and to encourage individuals to be frank in their letters. At the time our system was developed, most librarians on the staff agreed that it was essential for the documentation assembled by the Committee to be held in confidence.

To protect the candidate, PRC procedures require that there be evidence of professional contact between the candidate and anyone asked to write a confidential letter, and that the Committee, if it asks any, must ask more than one co-worker or subordinate for letters. Each candidate is invited to submit names, and the Committee selects additional names, with the total number of letters solicited being related to the range of the candidate's professional activities both within and outside the Libraries, and normally increasing for those being considered for promotion to the higher ranks. These procedures are designed to insure that the Committee does not receive a one-sided picture of the job performance and professional activities of a candidate, and that no single letter can determine the outcome of an individual's promotion review.

The documents assembled for the review are accessible only to the PRC, the University Librarian, and the Assistant University Librarian for Personnel. When the review is completed they are placed in a special locked file for a three-year period and are then destroyed. The only records from the whole promotion review process which are placed in an individual's permanent personnel file, and are therefore accessible to his/her supervisor(s), are the letter from the University Librarian communicating the decision and the summary statement explaining the reasons.

It is interesting to note that under the Columbia faculty tenure review system the candidate does not know who is appointed by the Provost to serve on his/her ad hoc committee, what evaluation his/her dean or department director may have submitted, or who is asked to be a witness or to write a letter (see pp. 23-24, THE FACULTY HANDBOOK OF COLUMBIA UNIVERSITY, 1975, for a general description of tenure procedures; copies may be obtained from the Assistant University Librarian for Personnel). The Libraries promotional system is more open: PRC is a standing committee whose members are known; the supervisory performance appraisal is given to the staff member who is encouraged to respond in writing if s/he wishes. In addition, it has always been understood that, while PRC carefully protects the confidentiality of all letters submitted as part of the review process, the writers of those letters are free to share them with the candidate should they wish to do so.

The original RCL proposal, and the system of ranks and peer review which resulted from it, were meant to benefit both the members of the professional staff and the Libraries. For the librarian, the plan establishes a mechanism to acknowledge professional growth and accomplishment. The system of ranks provides for recognition of individual merit, quality of performance, and professional and scholarly contributions. Further, it allows each librarian to receive appropriate financial compensation and significant professional advancement without necessarily assuming management responsibility. The evaluation and review procedures for promotion in rank help assure that each librarian will be appraised fairly on the basis of criteria listed in this document. These criteria provide guidelines for uniform assessment throughout the system and facilitate recognition of achievement.

The system is based on the premises that librarianship is a field in which a variety of skills and talents are valued and that the quality of library operations is governed by distinctive professional performance. The system of ranks and the related performance review process encourage individual professional development in the context of library and university objectives, and thus promote the development of an effective professional staff of the highest quality to provide excellent library service to the University.

Professional Ranks

Members of the professional staff of the University Libraries, with the exception of the University Librarian, hold one of four ranks. Initial determination of rank and subsequent promotion are largely governed by a review process conducted by the Professional Review Committee. While PRC recommendations are advisory to the University Librarian and ultimately to the University administration, the work and judgment of the Committee are fundamental to the ranking process. Committee procedures have been carefully established to assure comprehensive and fair reviews while maintaining confidentiality. General descriptions of each of the four professional ranks follow.

Librarian I. This rank designates the beginning level of librarianship.

The title Librarian I is assigned to individuals who have completed the required professional and/or other graduate training, but have little or no pertinent experience in research or academic librarianship. A Librarian I receives a Presidential Appointment which is renewed annually. Individuals must be promoted from this provisional rank by the end of the third year or be subject to termination.

Librarian II. This is the initial career rank, and individuals promoted to Librarian II are those who have adequately displayed professional skills and perceptions as well as an affinity for academic and research librarianship. It generally indicates that the individual has demonstrated the ability to master the skills and techniques of librarianship and has the potential for further development and accomplishment.

The title Librarian II is used for individuals who have fully demonstrated professional competence either as Librarian I at Columbia or as a librarian elsewhere. A Librarian II receives a continuing Presidential Appointment. Normally, a minimum of three years experience at this level will be required before consideration for promotion to the next rank.

Librarian III. This is the principal professional rank, which it is assumed a majority of staff members will attain. It generally indicates that the individual has mastered the skills and techniques of librarianship, has demonstrated a high level of professional performance, and has made meaningful professional contributions.

The Title Librarian III recognizes individuals with substantial and successful experience as a Librarian II at Columbia or as a professional staff member elsewhere. A Librarian III receives a continuing Presidential Appointment. Normally, a minimum of five years experience at this level will be required before consideration for further promotion.

Librarian IV. This highest professional rank is reserved for individuals who have made distinctive contributions over a significant period of time to the University Libraries and to the profession. Promotion to Librarian IV is exceptional rather than usual.

The title Librarian IV acknowledges sustained professional accomplishment and outstanding performance as a Librarian III at Columbia or as a professional staff member elsewhere. A Librarian IV receives a Trustee Appointment.

Criteria

The general criteria for promotion in rank are quality of performance in the area of the candidate's responsibility, as well as the quality of service on library committees and task forces, library instructional activities, professional activity outside the library, research and academic achievement, and participation in University affairs. The criteria are not of equal significance and the degree of importance given to any one of them may vary from one candidate to another. It is the intent of the system to foster the professional development of the individual through external activities and the pursuit of advanced degrees in conjunction with, but not at the expense of, fulfillment of responsibilities to the Columbia Libraries. Although talents, inclinations and specialities of individuals and demands of positions may vary, high quality job performance is one criterion which must be met for any promotion. Advancement in rank is not automatic upon cumulation of years of experience, but is based on appraisal of the performance of each librarian. In promotion from ranks I to II and II to III, job performance is typically the single most important factor. In promotion from ranks III to IV other factors in addition to job performance are given increasing weight. The specific criteria listed below indicate the basic factors considered by the Professional Review Committee in making recommendations for promotions in rank. They apply to all levels of ranks although expectations of growth and accomplishment increase at each level.

Job Performance. The candidate is expected to demonstrate competence in his/her assigned areas of responsibility, such as collection or systems development, bibliographic organization, management, reference, reader service, or some combination thereof. The supervisory evaluation is a key element in the determination of the quality of performance. Among the factors to be considered are: consistency of performance, ability to innovate, initiative, ability to work effectively with others, responsibility, ability to organize work, ability to relate job functions to the more general goals of the library and University, response to criticism, dependability, accuracy, oral and written skills, judgment, professional attitude, adaptability, and leadership.

Library Committees and Instructional Assignments. The quality and extent of contributions made to the solution of library problems through service on internal committees, task forces, and the instructional program will merit consideration for promotion, even though such service may be unrelated to the individual's primary area of responsibility. Among the factors to be considered are: fulfillment of basic obligations of attendance and participation, working relations with other members, membership, chairmanship of subcommittees, timely completion and quality of committee assignments.

Professional Activities, Continuing Education, Research, Publications and Teaching. Meaningful participation in professional activities on local, state, regional, and national levels will be considered in promotion. Examples of such participation include offices held, committee assignments, papers presented, awards received, and leadership of seminars and workshops. The candidate is expected to continue study and research in fields relevant to librarianship. Involvement in continuing education activities, such as formal courses, seminars and workshops, as well as advanced degrees obtained or in progress will be considered in promotion. Professional contributions such as books, articles, book reviews, editorships, bibliographies, handbooks, teaching appointments and lectures will also be considered.

University Service. Consideration will be given to relevant University service, such as participation in the work of Senate Committees, departmental and ad hoc committees, and other University organizations.

Function of the Professional Review Committee

Guided by the criteria for promotion in rank, the Professional Review Committee reviews the performance, professional competence, and contributions of librarians being considered for promotion in rank based on the documentation described below. The Committee is responsible for recommending action to the University Librarian when members of the professional staff are under consideration for promotion in rank. In addition, the Committee advises on the appropriate rank and promotion review date for individuals appointed from outside the library system.

Composition, Term, and Eligibility of the Professional Review Committee

The Professional Review Committee is an administrative committee appointed by the University Librarian in consultation with the Representative Committee of Librarians. The Professional Review Committee is composed of five members of the professional staff, including the chairperson, also appointed by the University Librarian, all holding the rank of Librarian II or higher. There must be at least one member of the Committee who is a Librarian IV. The term of office is three (3) years, and the terms will be staggered with no more than two (2) new appointments being made in one year (except replacements for unexpired terms). No one may serve two (2) terms in succession.

Documentation for Promotion in Rank

Names of candidates submitted to the Committee for consideration will be accompanied by the following documentation:

Brief Education/Employment History. Prepared by the Office of the Assistant University Librarian for Personnel, and completed/verified by the candidate.

Performance Appraisal Form. Completed by the supervisors; signed by the candidate who may add written comments; and submitted to the Committee by the Office of the Assistant University Librarian for Personnel.

Current Position Description. Updated as necessary by the candidate and supervisors; forwarded to the Committee by the Office of the Assistant University Librarian for Personnel.

Summary of Professional Activities during the Review Period. Prepared by the candidate, signed by the supervisors, and forwarded to the Committee by the Office of the Assistant University Librarian for Personnel.

Additional Documentation Form. The candidate may submit a list of no more than five individuals (except, up to eight for candidates being considered for promotion to Librarian IV) from inside or outside the Libraries who may be asked for additional information concerning the candidate's professional capabilities and accomplishments. The list may include librarians, faculty members or other colleagues who have had sufficient contact with the candidate during the review period to be able to evaluate his/her professional skills and performance.

Other. The Professional Review Committee may request additional information from inside and outside the Libraries in order to complete documentation needed to make a recommendation.

Procedures for Promotional Consideration (see also PRC MANUAL)
   The process is routinely initiated by the Library Personnel Office as follows:

Promotion from Librarian I. Promotion review is mandatory for librarians at this rank and is based on the anniversary date of appointment. At least four months prior to the anniversary date, the Library Personnel Office initiates requests for documents required for the review process.

Promotion from Librarian II and III. At the beginning of each fiscal year, the Library Personnel Office sends eligibility notices to those scheduled for review during the coming fiscal year to determine if they wish to be reviewed. If the staff member wishes to be reviewed, the request for the required documents is initiated. Staff members who decline review become eligible again three full years from the time they decline review.

The Professional Review Committee assembles and reviews the documentation for each candidate and submits a written recommendation to the University Librarian synthesizing that documentation in relation to the promotional criteria.

The decision of the University Librarian and the reasons supporting it are communicated in writing to the candidate with copies to his/her supervisor(s). The summary statement briefly synthesizes the contents of the documentation, highlighting strengths and weaknesses in performance in as much detail as possible while maintaining the confidentiality of the original documents.

The review process from Librarian I to II is completed prior to the third anniversary date of appointment. The review process for promotion from Librarian II to III and III to IV is normally completed within the fiscal year in which it begins.

Determination of Review and Promotion Dates

Librarian I. Normally persons with up to three years of professional experience.

Review for promotion to Librarian II normally begins four months prior to the end of the third year of appointment at Columbia. (For persons with at least one year of previous relevant experience, review for promotion to Librarian II begins four months prior to the end of the second year of appointment at Columbia.)

Promotion to Librarian II, if granted, is announced immediately and becomes effective July 1 following completion of the third year (unless anniversary date is between 7/1 and 9/30, in which case promotion is retroactive to the previous July 1).

If promotion from Librarian I to Librarian II is denied, the individual's appointment will not be renewed.

Librarian II. Normally persons with more than three years of professional experience.

Review for promotion to Librarian III normally begins after three years as Librarian II (after at least six years of professional experience).

Promotion to Librarian III, if granted, is effective July 1 following the fiscal year in which the review occurred (normally after at least seven years of professional experience).

If a staff member is denied promotion to Librarian III, the next automatic review will begin three years after the denial of promotion. The staff member may request consideration for promotion prior to the end of this three-year period by stating his/her case in writing to the Assistant University Librarian for Personnel.

Librarian III. Normally persons with more than seven years of professional experience.

Review for promotion to Librarian IV normally begins after five years as Librarian III (after at least twelve years of professional experience).

Promotion to Librarian IV, if granted, is effective July 1 following the fiscal year in which the review occurred (normally after at least thirteen years of professional experience).

If a staff member is denied promotion to Librarian IV, the next automatic review will begin three years after the denial of promotion. The staff member may request consideration for promotion prior to the end of this period by stating his/her case in writing to the Assistant University Librarian for Personnel.

Early Promotion. Consideration for early promotion may be initiated, normally by a supervisor, in recognition of superior performance and rapid professional development. If a staff member is denied early promotion, the next automatic review will begin three years after the denial of promotion. The staff member may request consideration for promotion prior to the end of this period by stating his/her case in writing to the Assistant University Librarian for Personnel.

New Appointees. The review date for a librarian appointed from outside of Columbia will be determined at the time of hire, primarily based on the nature and length of previous professional service. A librarian appointed to a position from outside of Columbia is normally required to have a minimum of two years on the staff before becoming eligible for promotion review.

Variation for candidates from the Law Library
The Professional Review Committee's recommendation is made to the Dean of the School of Law, who, along with the Vice President and University Librarian and the Assistant University Librarian for Personnel, has access to the documentation.

Appeals
If a staff member wishes to appeal the decision regarding promotion in rank, the appeal should be submitted to the Assistant University Librarian for Personnel within ten (10) working days following the receipt of notification. (See Appendix D., paragraph C.2.,ff.)

The System of Professional Position Categories

The classification scheme described herein consists of five Position Categories. Positions not included in the classification are those designated as University Librarian, the Directors of Resources, Services and Support, and the Law and Health Sciences Librarians. (See Appendix E for a list of positions by current title.)

A "position-grading" system was used to determine appropriate position categories. This process involved analyzing each position in relation to other positions and classifying it in terms of level of responsibility. Factors taken into consideration in this process were: complexity of the skills required for the position; nature and extent of relationships with students, faculty, the general public, and academic and administrative components of the University; responsibility for developing and implementing policies, programs and services; and supervisory or administrative responsibilities (including composition of staff). In essence, the analysis of these factors indicates that there is an ascending level of position categories governed by the extent of administrative duties and/or policy-making responsibilities.

The classification scheme views the function of a position as constant although the manner and the effectiveness with which the function is accomplished varies, depending on a number of factors including the training, background, and experience of the incumbent. Because this is a classification of positions, not of people, the concept of a "beginning" professional position, i.e., one budgeted at the current beginning professional salary and usually filled by a recent library school graduate with little or no previous professional experience, is not reflected in the scheme. Theoretically, a "beginning librarian" could be appointed to a position in any category. Realistically, however, such appointments would be unlikely for positions requiring substantial administrative, technical, or program responsibilities.

Position Categories

The following paragraphs describe the general functional characteristics of each position category. The nature and degree of the direction or supervision received in each category cannot be generalized. Direction will vary, depending on the experience of the individual at Columbia and elsewhere and on the priorities of the unit and the library system.

Position Category I. Positions in this category are responsible for performing duties requiring the utilization of the fully realized professional skills and techniques of the trained and experienced librarian. They involve complex technical, bibliographical, or administrative skills. These positions may have supervisory responsibility for supporting staff and for a relatively small number of professional librarians. Administrative responsibility for relatively small units may be involved. These positions may participate in the development of policies, programs and services and have responsibility for their implementation.

Position Category II.   Positions in this category are responsible for administrative, bibliographical, or technical functions of a broader scope than those in Position Category I or for performing an unusual amount of original bibliographical research. These positions may have supervisory responsibility for a medium to large unit, or share such responsibility for a relatively large number of professionals with a senior officer. Responsibility for the development and implementation of policies, programs and services is generally more extensive in this category.

Position Category III.   Positions in this category are responsible for service, technical, bibliographical, or administrative functions which have substantial implications for library operations and performance, including responsibility for the development and implementation of policies, programs, and services.

Position Category IV.   Positions in this category are responsible for service, technical, bibliographical, or administrative functions which have more substantial implications for library operations and performance than those in Position Category III. These positions are heavily involved in the development and implementation of policies, programs, and services.

Position Category V.   Positions in this category are responsible for major administrative components of the library system or for formulating and executing system-wide policies, programs, and services, with appropriate consultation.

Qualifications for Appointments

Normally, the basic educational requirement for appointment to a professional librarian position is a graduate degree in librarianship from an accredited library school. Under exceptional circumstances, academic specialization in another subject area relevant to the needs of Columbia may be substituted for the library degree. It is impractical to state specific qualifications for the five Position Categories because of the variety of functions found within any one category. Therefore, prior to posting and advertising an opening, the qualifications for a specific position will be determined in accordance with equal opportunity requirements.

Procedure for Applying for Position Vacancies

The Assistant University Librarian for Personnel is required to review the duties and responsibilities of a position with the appropriate administrative officers to determine if any changes have occurred which might affect the classification of the position.

The University's Affirmative Action Program requires that recruitment normally include both internal and external searches. The internal search requires the posting of the vacancy throughout the library system (see Appendix F, Non-Discrimination Policy).

Internal Applicants. Staff members interested in a posted vacancy should contact the Assistant University Librarian for Personnel during the period indicated in the posting. This should be done in writing since the application and interview processes are considered confidential. Generally, a brief memorandum stating the specific position being applied for should be sent to the Assistant University Librarian. If, however, an applicant has special qualifications relevant to the job requirements, and these may not be apparent from records on file in the Library Personnel Office, the memorandum should include a statement of these qualifications. The Assistant University Librarian contacts all applicants and arranges formal interviews for those who qualify for the position. Staff members are not required to inform their supervisors of their application for a position until they are notified that they will be scheduled for formal interviews.

External Applicants. The external search varies, depending upon the nature of the position and qualifications required. External sources of recruitment include but are not limited to the following publications or agencies: the "librarian openings" section of the Sunday *New York Times* book review; the placement offices of various accredited library schools, primarily on the Eastern Seaboard and in the Mid-West; and the "Jobline" of the New York State Library Association. The "Job Roster" of the Social Responsibilities Round Table of the Task Force on Women, a component of the American Library Association, is used when an extensive search is made for candidates for senior level positions.

Appointment to the Staff. After interviews within the libraries and consultation, when appropriate, with academic or administrative components of the University, the Assistant University Librarian for Personnel submits a recommendation to the University Librarian, who is responsible for submitting nominations for appointment or promotion to the Executive Vice President for Academic Affairs and Provost.

In accordance with the Affirmative Action Program, the Libraries may inform a proposed candidate of his or her nomination but the candidate is also informed that no offer can be made until the proposed appointment has been reviewed by the Executive Vice President for Academic Affairs and Provost. The purpose of this review is to ascertain that the procedural requirements of the University's Affirmative Action Program have been followed. An Affirmative Action Advisory Committee has been appointed to assist the Executive Vice President in this review.

Non-University Professional Activities

The University exercises no set control upon an officer's outside activities as consultant, writer, or specialist. But this freedom puts upon the individual an obligation to keep these activities within such bounds that the discharge of his primary responsibility to the University is not impaired.

Teaching in the University

On occasion, individual librarians are invited to teach in one or another school of the University. Normally, full-time members of the professional staff above the beginning level or grade will be able to accept such an assignment on a continuing basis only if it is made an integral part of the individual's University duties. Ideally, such assignments would be held to one course per year, but it is possible that a one course per term assignment as a maximum might on occasion be worked out. The individual would receive one salary from the University, with the library budget covering the bulk of the salary cost and the school or department budget the balance. The actual proportions would be worked out by the Libraries and the concerned school or department and governed by the number of courses, hours, etc. Any such continuing arrangement would require the approval of the appropriate Division Head and the University Librarian.

Under exceptional circumstances and to meet specific short term needs, alternate arrangements might be made, but such action would not modify the general policy noted above.

Staff Development

Orientation

Orientation programs are scheduled for new staff members to provide them with information on the history, resources, organization, programs, and objectives of the University Libraries. They include structured combinations of lectures, audio-visual presentations, and discussions. The programs include presentations by the chairpersons of the standing committees and the Library Senators.

Job Training

The operations of a research library are complex and require varying degrees of on-the-job training, depending on the nature and complexity of the assignment. All supervising librarians are involved in near continuous on-the-job training for new or recently appointed staff members. The amount of time new staff members spend in on-the-job training varies in relationship to the nature of the assignment.

Professional Conferences

Travel funds are available for members of the professional staff who wish to attend professional conferences. Because of the number of professional association programs and conferences held each year and the variation in expenses because of location, full or partial financial assistance is determined after review of requests and in the context of available funds and library priorities. At the beginning of each fiscal year, staff members are asked to submit requests for leave and travel assistance through the appropriate administrative channels. (See Appendix G for policies and procedures concerning requests for leave and travel assistance.)

To encourage participation of beginning librarians in professional activities, funds are generally made available to help cover travel and limited per diem expenses for one or more professional staff members to attend a major professional conference. The Representative Committee of Librarians is asked to make recommendations after reviewing applications from interested staff members with less than five years of service and who have not previously attended such a conference.

Workshops and Seminars

From time to time, in-house workshops and seminars are held to improve intralibrary communications, to improve the staff's understanding of library programs and objectives, and to develop skills necessary for the performance of various work functions.

The professional staff is encouraged to participate in staff development activities sponsored by professional organizations and other agencies. Staff members may be asked to attend specific workshops, seminars, or institutes at the expense of the Libraries. Whenever possible, funds are made available to individuals who initiate requests for assistance to participate in such activities. These requests should be made through the appropriate administrative channels.

Research Leaves

The Libraries provide professional librarians with paid leave in order to provide periods of time for concentrated research or investigation of substantive topics of professional significance. Requests for professional leave should be submitted through the appropriate channels to the Assistant University Librarian for Personnel and should include a thorough description of projected work, a request for a specific period of leave time (normally not to exceed four months) and evidence of administrative approval verifying that such leave will not have an unacceptable effect on library services and operations. Prior to final decision by the University Librarian, proposals will be assessed in terms of their potential for enhancing professional performance by appropriate library and University groups or individuals. Because it is the intent of this program to enable individuals to capitalize on and enhance professional competence, it is noted that paid leaves will not be granted for the purpose of attending graduate school and that formal reports or publications will normally be required as evidence of project completion.

Normally, those requesting leave should have been full-time members of the professional staff for five years prior to the date of any proposed leave. Acceptance of a research leave implies intent to return to full-time status at the end of the leave period.

Because the research leave program has budgetary implications, requests should be submitted a year prior to the proposed date. The number of individuals on leave during any year will necessarily be controlled by operating and financial realities. Normally an aggregate of no more than 24 months of leave time for the total professional staff will be approved in any given year.

Participation in Decision-Making

Various efforts are made to provide staff members with opportunities to participate in the establishment of library policies and objectives. Staff input in the decision-making process is obtained formally through the Professional Advisory Committee, the Professional Review Committee, various ad hoc and standing committees and task forces and through meetings and discussions at the unit level, as well as informally through the Representative Committee of Librarians.

Tuition Exemption

The University's tuition exemption program for members of the professional staff is described in [the section on "Benefits—Tuition Exemption"] of this handbook.

Performance Appraisals

The schedule of performance appraisals outlined below has been established to insure that members of the professional staff obtain an assessment of their accomplishments and developmental needs on a regular basis. Prior to conducting an appraisal, supervisors are advised to review the "Guidelines for Performance Appraisals," Appendix H.

Periodic Performance Appraisals

Six-Month Review. During the first month of employment, it is assumed that a new staff member or one promoted or transferred to a new position will meet with his immediate supervisor to discuss job responsibilities and performance objectives. At the end of six months, the supervisor is required to schedule a meeting with the staff member to discuss progress to date and to review performance objectives. The Library Personnel Office sends a notice to supervisors informing them of the need to schedule a six-month review. Although a written summary of this meeting is not required, one copy of the notice is returned to the Library Personnel Office to verify that the meeting took place.

Annual Reviews. The "Performance Appraisal" form, Appendix I, is used to conduct annual reviews. The schedule outlined below is based on anniversary date of appointment, promotion, or transfer and applies to those appointed to the staff commencing with fiscal year 1977-1978. Schedules for those appointed prior to 1977-78 are based on a combination of length of service and date of last appraisal.

Annually for the first two years in a position.
Biannually for the fourth through tenth years in a position.
After the tenth year, appraisals are scheduled every third year.
Exception: If a staff member is under consideration for promotion in rank, an annual review will not be scheduled.

Appraisals for Consideration for Promotion in Rank

The "Performance Appraisal" form, Appendix I, is used to conduct reviews for librarians under consideration for promotion in rank. As indicated in [the section on "System of Professional Ranks"], a promotional review for a staff member at the rank of Librarian I is mandatory at the end of the third year of appointment. A staff member at the rank of Librarian II or III may request that a promotional review not take place as scheduled. Consideration for early advancement may be initiated sooner, normally by a supervisor, in recognition of superior performance and rapid professional development. The schedule for those under consideration for promotion in rank is as follows:

Librarian I: four months prior to the end of the third year of appointment.
Librarian II: at the end of the third year as Librarian II.
Librarian III: at the end of the fifth year as Librarian III.

Summary of Performance Appraisals:

At the end of	New appointee or new position	Review for consideration for promotion in rank
(6 months)	x (informal)	
1st year	x	
2nd year		
2 years, 8 months		Librarian I (review for promotion to rank II)
4th year	x	
5th year		
6th year	x	
7th year		Librarian II (review for promotion to rank III)
8th year	x	
9th year		
10th year	x	
11th year		
12th year		Librarian III (review for promotion to rank IV)
13th year	x (every 3rd year)	

Flexible Scheduling

A uniform application of flexible scheduling is difficult to formulate or implement because the nature of obligations and operations of individual units within the library system varies widely. However, librarians should feel at liberty to discuss work schedules with appropriate supervisors. The needs of the unit are of primary consideration, but working within necessary parameters, development of a mutually acceptable schedule should usually be possible. This kind of input and opportunity for self-determination on the part of individuals will further enhance a sense of personal responsibility relative to job performance and do much to create a more pleasant and productive working atmosphere.

Separation from Service

Resignation

Generally, members of the professional staff are obliged to submit written notification of resignation to their supervising librarian at least 30 days in advance. A substantially longer period of notification is expected from those having signficant administrative or supervisory responsibilities.

Program Reduction

In the event of financial exigency or discontinuance or curtailment of an activity, it may be necessary to terminate a staff position. In such a case, every effort will be made to relocate the staff member within the Libraries. Should no other suitable position be available in the library system, however, the staff member will be given written notice of termination, one to six months in advance, depending on the length of his service.

Release

A release is a form of termination employed at the convenience of the University, normally without prejudice. An individual might be "released," for example, because he is judged not well suited to his position even though attempting to perform to the best of his ability. Any individual who is released generally receives 30 days notice with necessary time off to seek other employment. This type of termination generally applies to individuals in lower level positions with less than three years of service.

Termination for Cause

If it becomes necessary to terminate an individual's appointment for cause or for reasons of inadequate performance, such action will be taken only after the individual has been sent a written statement of the reasons for the termination. The individual may wish to contest such action by requesting a hearing before a committee constituted within the University for the purpose. The University Librarian will give full consideration to the findings and recommendations of the committee in reaching a final decision.

VACATION, HOLIDAYS AND OTHER LEAVE

Vacation

Members of the professional staff holding Presidential or Trustee appointments are eligible for a vacation of one month (23 working days) each fiscal year (July 1 through June 30). New staff members hired after July 1 receive prorated vacation for that portion of the fiscal year worked from their date of hire (1 11/12 day per completed month of service up to 23 days). Those with 20 years of service as of the beginning of the fiscal year in which the vacation accrues are eligible for 28 working days of vacation (2⅓ days per month). Appointed staff may not receive pay in lieu of unused vacation, except upon resignation.

University policy is that carry-over of vacation from one fiscal year to another is not usually possible. However, staff members who wish to request an exception to this policy should discuss their requests with the appropriate administrative officers in their units prior to submitting requests in writing to the Library Personnel Office. Valid requests for such exceptions will only be approved if they do not interfere with the needs and priorities of the unit. The maximum number of vacation days which may be carried over from one fiscal year to another is ten (10) days. Pay in lieu of vacation carried over is not possible.

Vacation schedules are sent by the Library Personnel Office to the Group Directors and Heads of the Distinctive Collections in the spring of each year. The schedules indicate the projected vacation allowance for each staff member through June 30.

Vacations are generally scheduled following the completion of the spring semester in May, but not later than June 30 following the year of accrual. Of necessity, there will be some variations in scheduling vacations because of service or other unit priorities. Generally, it is not possible for staff to schedule vacation during peak or rush periods of the fall and spring semesters. Staff in service units, for example, should schedule the bulk of their vacations during January, May, June, July, and August; however, approval may be given to schedule a maximum of one week of vacation when school is in session. Staff members in Resources, Support, and the Distinctive Collections should review unit priorities with the appropriate supervisors so that vacations do not coincide with peak or rush periods.

University Holidays

The University currently observes the following ten holidays each year:

New Year's Day	Thanksgiving Day and the
Memorial Day	following Friday
Independence Day	Christmas Day and 2 days
Labor Day	selected by the University during
Election Day	the Christmas/New Year season

Since the Libraries may remain open on certain holidays, depending on the academic calendar, professional staff assigned to reader service units may be scheduled to work on a University holiday (generally, Election Day and the Friday following Thanksgiving). Those who work on these days are entitled to compensatory time off at a later date. Compensatory time has to be used within the year in which it is earned, i.e., within the 12-month period following the holiday. Carry-over from one year to another, or payment in lieu of time off, is not permissible. A memorandum is distributed by the Library Personnel Office prior to each holiday outlining library schedules and the status of the holiday for each category of staff.

Floating Holidays

In addition to the holidays mentioned above, three additional days, termed Floating Holidays, are observed as paid leave time. Floating Holidays replace the H-Day concept which observed Martin Luther King's Birthday, George Washington's Birthday, and Good Friday as earned holidays even though the University remains open on these days. Floating Holidays accrue each fiscal year and are earned at the rate of one paid leave day for each four-month period worked. They are pro-rated for those in their first year of service who are appointed after July 1. Floating Holidays may be used to observe the former "H" days, religious holidays or for any other purpose. Earned Floating Holidays may not accumulate, and payment in lieu of Floating Holidays upon resignation is permissible. Normally, Floating Holidays are to be taken as whole or half days.

Religious Holidays

Staff members who wish to be absent from work in observance of a religious holiday may charge the absence to vacation or a Floating Holiday.

Leave

Sick Leave

Professional staff members are entitled to paid sick leave upon appointment. There is no specific annual allotment of paid sick leave for professional staff. In instances of prolonged illness, individual consideration is given for paid leave based on the staff member's length of service.

Maternity Leave of Absence

A professional librarian who has completed six months of employment and who is required to cease work because of pregnancy is entitled to a maternity leave of absence without pay, not to exceed twelve months. Active employment may continue during pregnancy at the staff member's discretion; however, the University reserves the right to require an authorization from the staff member's attending physician. If a staff member's position cannot be left vacant or filled on a temporary basis during the anticipated absence, a replacement may be found. Staff members, upon return to active status, shall be re-employed in the same position or in a position of equivalent rank and salary, for which they qualify. Requests for maternity leaves of absence should be submitted to the immediate supervisor in writing and then forwarded, through the appropriate administrative offices, to the Library Personnel Office. The effect of the leave on benefits is as follows:

Vacation. The leave is taken into account in prorating the amount of vacation earned during the fiscal year in which the leave is taken.

Major Medical Insurance and Life Insurance. If the leave exceeds one month, staff members have the option to pre-pay their Major Medical and/or contributory life insurance premiums.

Blue Cross and Blue Shield Insurance. The University does not continue to provide non-contributory coverage of Blue Cross-Blue Shield after the commencement of a leave. Staff members have the option, however, of continuing coverage by pre-payment at group rates which include Blue Cross Prescription Cards.

TIAA-CREF. The University does not contribute to TIAA-CREF during the leave period. Those staff members who wish to continue their contribution have to contact TIAA directly.

Tuition Exemption. During the period of a leave of absence, staff members are not eligible for tuition exemption benefits.

Promotion in Rank. During the period of a leave, a staff member does not accrue time for consideration for promotion in rank. Upon returning from the leave, an adjustment is made in the length of service record for the purpose of determining eligibility for promotion in rank.

University Seniority. Staff members are credited with University seniority for an unpaid leave of absence up to six months. For benefits purposes, University seniority is adjusted for any portion of a leave in excess of six months.

NOTE: The University Personnel Office, Benefits Administration, 313 Dodge, contacts staff members directly with details concerning the status of their various University benefits as soon as they are made aware of the impending leave of absence by the Library Personnel Office. Staff members are required to contact the Library Personnel Office approximately one month before the expiration of their leave to verify the anticipated return date.

Paternity Leave of Absence

A male employee who elects to cease work in order to care for his infant child is entitled to a paternity leave of absence without pay not to exceed six months. This policy pertains only in the case of an infant child whose age does not exceed one year at the time of the staff member's scheduled return from paternity leave of absence.

If a staff member's position cannot be left vacant or filled on a temporary basis during the anticipated absence, a replacement may be found. Staff members, upon return to active status, shall be re-employed in the same position or in a position of equivalent rank and salary, for which they qualify.

The effect of a paternity leave on benefits is the same as it is for a woman on maternity leave (see above).

Jury Duty

Staff members who are required to be absent for jury duty receive full pay for such absences. Those released from jury duty during the course of the day are expected to report to work.

Death in the Family

A maximum of three days leave with pay is granted in the event of a death in the immediate family. The immediate family, for purposes of this policy, includes a spouse, parent, grandparent, child, sister, brother, mother-in-law or father-in-law.

Leave of Absence for Personal Reasons

A member of the professional staff who has completed one year of service may be granted a leave of absence for personal reasons without pay, not to exceed six months. Such leaves require the appropriate administrative approvals. Typical reasons for granting such leaves include but are not limited to illness in the family, education, or compelling personal needs. The University requires a written substantiation of the conditions prompting the need for the leave.

If a staff member's position cannot be left vacant or filled on a temporary basis during the anticipated absence, a replacement may be found. Staff members, upon return to active status, shall be re-employed in the same position or in a position of equivalent rank and salary, for which they qualify.

BENEFITS

Tuition Exemption

The various components of the University's tuition exemption program outlined below apply to full-time officers of the Libraries on Presidential or Trustee appointment with salary from the Columbia Corporation. Tuition exemption does not apply to fee basis courses in which the instructor is paid on the basis of the number of students registered for the course, courses given in the short-term Winter Session or the Continuing Education Program. Staff members who wish to enroll in job-related courses not covered by tuition exemption are eligible for full or partial reimbursement of fees under the Libraries program for professional and continuing education activities (see Appendix G).

Members of the professional staff may take one daytime course per semester without formally scheduling make-up time, provided they have consulted with the appropriate supervisors to verify that their professional obligations are being met and that service will not be hampered. This arrangement is normally possible only when the course is not given during evening hours and when the individual is either matriculating for a graduate degree at Columbia or elsewhere or auditing a graduate course or enrolled in an undergraduate foreign language course relative to his work assignment.

Prior to each semester, a summary of tuition exemption policies and procedures is distributed by the Library Personnel Office, which is responsible for processing permits.

Graduate Degree Candidates
Tuition exemption is granted to officers who have been accepted as candidates for a graduate degree or statutory certificate at the University or its affiliates. Since a number of graduate divisions require full-time residency for degree candidates, it is necessary to consult with the appropriate school to determine its current policy.

Non-Degree Candidates
An officer may be granted tuition exemption for one course per semester regardless of point value. The course must be given by one of the schools of the Columbia Corporation. Courses given by Teachers College or Barnard are not exempt under this program. To be eligible for this benefit, an officer must have been admitted as a non-matriculated (special) student by one of the schools of the University.

Auditing Courses

Auditing privileges in Graduate School courses for officers not registered in regular programs are limited to categories of courses specified by each Committee on Instruction, and each course opened to such auditors must have the approval of the instructor, the department, and the Committee on Instruction. Permission to audit is not normally given for seminars or colloquia or for courses beyond the introductory graduate level.

Spouses

Husbands and wives of full-time officers holding a Trustee or Presidential appointment are granted tuition exemption for courses given by the Columbia Corporation, provided they have been admitted as degree candidates or non-matriculated students in one of the schools of the University. (Courses given by Teachers College or Barnard are not exempt under this program even if they are cross-listed in Columbia bulletins.) There is no limitation to the number of courses or points that may be taken, except as specified by the student's advisor . . . .

Children

Children of full-time officers holding a Trustee or Presidential appointment are granted tuition exemption for courses taken in the schools of the Columbia Corporation, Barnard, and Teachers College, provided that the student is a candidate for a degree or statutory certificate. If a child is a candidate in good standing at another institution or needs special preparation to enter a graduate program at Columbia University or elsewhere, he or she may be granted tuition exemption benefits when registered at Columbia as a non-matriculated student. There is no limitation on the number of courses or points that may be taken under this program except as specified by the student's advisor; however, tuition exemption coverage at Barnard is limited to eight semesters . . . .

If the officer dies while in service, the son or daughter may complete the degree program with tuition exemption benefits. If the officer was employed by the University for at least ten years of full-time service, had met the eligibility requirements at death, and dies while in service, the son or daughter will be eligible for the benefits of this program if he or she chooses to enter any of the above named schools in the future.

Retired Officers

Retired officers who met the eligibility requirements at the time of their retirements are eligible for the benefits described above.

Scholarships for Children

Tuition Scholarships for Private Schools

The University provides scholarship aid, based on need, to those officers having financial problems resulting from the tuition fees of private schools in one of the five boroughs of New York City. To be considered for such assistance, the parent:

1. Must hold a full-time Presidential or Trustee appointment with salary from the Columbia Corporation;
2. Must have the family residence in one of the five boroughs of New York City (the school also must be located in one of the five boroughs);
3. Must have a child in grades Kindergarten—eighth grade (assistance is not available for children in nursery school or grades 9–12) . . . .

College Tuition Scholarships

Sons and daughters enrolled at other accredited undergraduate institutions in a four-year course leading to a bachelor's degree or in a combined plan, or in a non-terminal program of a junior college that anticipates transfer to a four-year college may receive as a scholarship one-half the tuition, excluding all fees, for a period of eight semesters or the equivalent, provided the officer holds a full-time Presidential or Trustee appointment with salary from the Columbia Corporation above as specified. Further information on eligibility for this benefit can be obtained from the Library Personnel Office.

NOTE: The following benefits are administered by the Office of University Personnel, which sends new appointees a benefits packet consisting of "A Summary of Your Columbia University Benefits Program" and applications for participation in the various programs.

Life Insurance

Contributory group life insurance coverage is required of all full-time Presidential and Trustee appointees. Basic coverage is effective on the date of appointment. Staff members are insured in the amount of their base annual salary. The cost to the staff member, by salary deduction, is 33¢ per month per $1,000 of insurance. If a staff member waits more than 120 days after becoming eligible to elect the optional insurance, he or she must provide proof of insurability. Staff members may name anyone as their beneficiaries. The beneficiary designation can be changed at any time by contacting the University Personnel Office . . . .

Major Medical Insurance

Membership is required immediately upon appointment; family coverage is optional. (Eligible dependents are spouse and unmarried children from birth to age 19 or to age 23 if a full-time student and dependent on you for support.) Each insured employee as well as each insured dependent is covered initially for a benefit amount of $250,000, except that, for covered expenses for mental or nervous disorders, the maximum benefit amount is $50,000. Major Medical insurance protection is continued during retirement for eligible employees and their spouses at a reduced rate. The rates are $3.92 per month, by salary deduction, for an individual contract and $10.71 per month for a family contract.

Blue Cross and Blue Shield

This plan, the cost of which is entirely paid by the University, covers all regular full-time Presidential and Trustee appointees receiving full salary from the University. Family membership includes the staff member, his or her spouse, all unmarried children under 19 years of age and unmarried dependent children between the age of 19 and 23 who are enrolled on a full-time basis in an accredited institution of higher education. Family membership also includes unmarried mentally or physically handicapped children over the age of 19 who became so incapacitated before reaching age 19 and are incapable of self-support. Also included is a Prescription Drug Program which enables staff members to have prescriptions filled by participating pharmacies at a cost of only $1.00 per prescription. (Reimbursement is also possible for prescriptions filled by non-participating pharmacies.)

A Blue Cross and Blue Shield Identification Card and a Prescription Drug Program Identification Card are forwarded to staff members by the University Personnel Office as soon as the application forms have been completed and returned to that office for processing. The "Summary of Your Columbia University Benefits Program" folder contains a separate booklet giving more detailed information about these plans as well as information on how to proceed with benefit claims.

Total Disability Benefits Plan

Total disability under this program is the "inability of the employee, by reason of sickness or bodily injury to engage in any occupation for which the employee is reasonably fitted by education, training, or experience."

All regular full-time officers of the University who are under age 64 are eligible for optional participation in this plan on the first day of the month coinciding with or next following the completion of one year of continuous full-time employment. Staff members who apply more than 31 days after they become eligible must furnish evidence of insurability before the insurance can take effect. The cost of this insurance is paid entirely by the staff member but at inexpensive group rates that have been contracted between the University and TIAA. TIAA administers the plan under a group contract. The amount of monthly premium, through salary deduction, is $4.87 per $1,000 of the monthly base salary. Benefits begin on the first day of the month following twelve consecutive months of total disability and continue during the disability until a staff member reaches age 65 (when a staff member may begin receiving retirement income), or until death, whichever is earlier. The plan provides two types of benefit: one to provide a staff member with monthly income during disability, and the other to protect a staff member's retirement income . . . .

Retirement

University Policy
The statutory age of retirement for a member of the professional staff is 68. Retirement takes effect on June 30 of the fiscal year in which the 68th birthday occurs. However, an individual or the Libraries may request, for a variety of reasons, that retirement begin at any time after age 65. Retirement prior to age 65 is also possible.

Retirement Plan for Officers of Columbia University—TIAA and CREF
The University's Retirement Plan, in compliance with the Employee Retirement Income Security Act of 1974 (ERISA) for regular, full-time Presidential and Trustee appointees, is provided by contracts with the Teachers Insurance and Annuity Association of America (TIAA-CREF). The TIAA-CREF system permits staff members a choice in investing their monthly annuity premium into CREF, in common stocks, and/or into TIAA, in fixed dollar obligations. The CREF retirement income fluctuates with the investment experience in CREF common stocks. The TIAA retirement income does not vary except for dividends, thereby providing a solid base of income during retirement. The purpose of the TIAA-CREF system is to provide a combined income that is more responsive to changes in the cost of living than a fixed-dollar annuity alone and less volatile than a variable annuity alone.

Full-time officers of the University become participants in the retirement plan on the first day of the month coincident with or next following the date of their appointment with contributions made by the University on behalf of the employee.

The University's Retirement Plan has been designed to integrate with Social Security. The actual percentage contributed by the Uni-

versity for each staff member is based on the staff member's total
base salary and is figured in two segments: one, a percentage of that
part of a staff member's base salary which is subject to Social Security
taxes (see below, Social Security, for the prevailing Social Security
wage base); the other a percentage of the remaining base salary in
excess of the Social Security base. The actual percentage of base
salary contributed by the University, below and above the prevailing
wage base, depends on age and length of service. In combination, the
two plans—the University's Retirement Plan and Social Security—
provide retirement income based on total base salary.

Staff members have a choice with respect to how the contributions
(both University and voluntary) are invested. This is done initially
on the application form forwarded to the staff member by the University Personnel Office shortly after employment begins. Thereafter,
changes in investment can be made by contacting the University
Personnel Office . . . .

Approximately twenty-two percent of the base salary, inclusive of
the University contribution, may be contributed to the plans. Staff
members interested in making additional voluntary contributions
should contact the Controller's Office directly to find out the exact
maximum dollar amount they may contribute. These contributions
can be included into the regular TIAA-CREF contracts or into a
Supplementary Retirement Annuity. An important feature of the
Supplementary Retirement plan is that it can be surrendered for its
cash value at any time. Such contributions are also tax deferred at
the time of deduction.

Staff members are given the opportunity to indicate whether or not
they wish to make voluntary contributions each year. Forms for this
purpose are sent directly to each staff member before the start of each
calendar year. Each staff member receives an annual statement from
TIAA-CREF keeping them updated on the growing value of their
contracts . . . .

Social Security

The Social Security Act includes income insurance (for retirement
disability, survivors) and health care insurance ("medicare" for people
65 and over, as well as for those who have received disability benefits
for 24 consecutive months or more).

Social Security taxes, through payroll deductions, are required of
all persons employed by the University, including non-citizens. Staff
members and the University pay equal Social Security taxes up to a
certain limit each year. This limit, known as the Social Security wage
base, changes from time to time. The rate of the Social Security tax
also increases periodically . . . . If you are earning more than the Social

Security wage base, only that part of your salary up to the wage base is covered under Social Security . . . .

New York State Disability

Professional librarians are not covered by New York State Disability Laws and, therefore, not subject to deductions for such coverage. If your monthly check indicates that you are being deducted, contact the Library Personnel Office.

Worker's Compensation

Professional librarians are covered by the provisions of the New York State Worker's Compensation Law. Benefits are provided under this law for job-related illnesses or accidents. Staff members may receive benefits of two-thirds their weekly salary up to a maximum of $95 or $125 depending upon the severity of the illness or accident. The law provides that weekly benefits begin after the seventh calendar day of absence. Should the period of disability extend beyond 14 days, the first week's absence is also covered. The law also provides for payment of certain medical expenses and certain other expenses caused by the illness or accident.

The continuation of regular University salary following a staff member's absence because of a job-related illness or injury is based on a graduating scale depending on length of service.

In order that all job-related illnesses or accidents are reported promptly to the Worker's Compensation Board, as required by New York State Law, the supervisor must send a report of the illness or accident to the Library Personnel Office as soon as the illness is diagnosed or the accident occurs. (Copies of the "report of accident" form can be obtained from the Library Personnel Office.) The Library Personnel Office forwards the information to the University Personnel Office for processing. Follow-up on claims should be directed to the University Personnel Office . . . .

New York State Unemployment

Professional librarians are covered by the New York State Unemployment Laws.

MISCELLANEOUS

This chapter includes a list and description of University publications and Library publications. It describes basic University facilities and services such as dining rooms, check cashing, health services, athletic and recreational opportunities, bookstores, and housing.

APPENDIX A: ORGANIZATION CHART

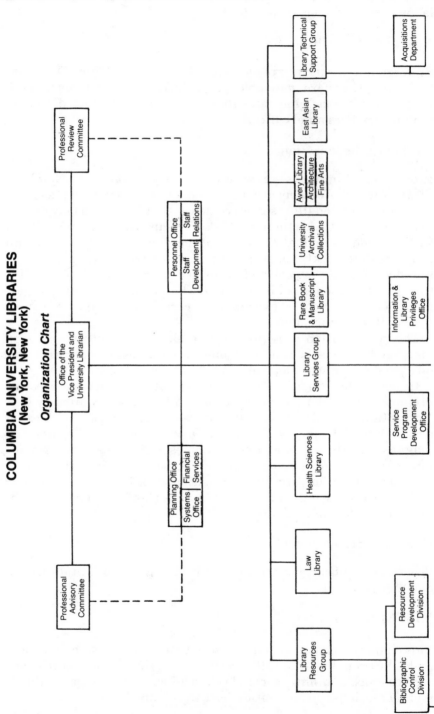

COLUMBIA UNIVERSITY LIBRARIES
(New York, New York)

Organization Chart

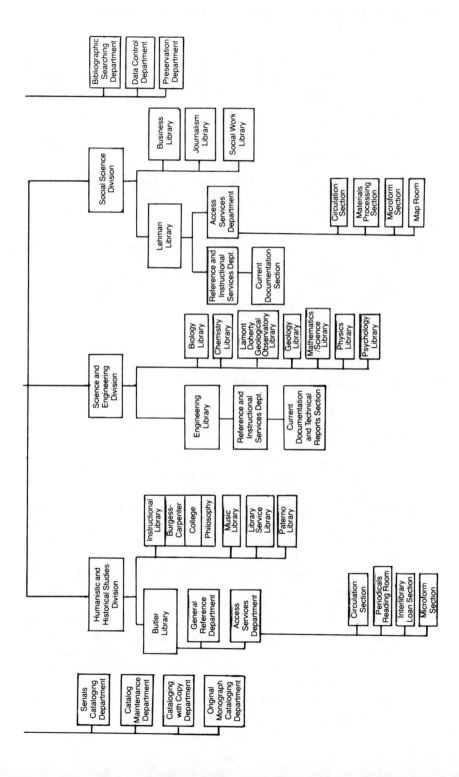

APPENDIX D: GRIEVANCE PROCEDURE FOR PROFESSIONAL LIBRARIANS

This procedure is based on the Grievance Procedure for Officers of Administration, Research, and the Libraries (Policy No. 602, July 1, 1976). It has been modified to reflect the administrative structure of the University Libraries.

A. *Covers:* Librarians on Presidential and Trustee Appointment and regular part-time librarians.

   Excludes: Part-time librarians and appointed staff not included in the System of Professional Position Categories.

B. *Grievable Issues:*
   1. Disciplinary actions and discharges for cause where the validity or appropriateness of the cause is in question.
   2. Application of announced personnel policy and/or procedure in individual cases where violation, misinterpretation, or discrimination is charged.

   Not Grievable:
   1. Terminations related to reductions in force where due notice or severance pay is provided under University policy.
   2. The content of published personnel policy and procedure.

C. *Steps in the Formal Grievance Procedure* (The appellant may choose to be represented at any step by a member of the professional staff of the Libraries):
   1. The appellant shall first discuss the matter with the immediate supervisor. The supervisor is expected to render a decision within five (5) working days.
   2. If there is no resolution at Step 1, the appellant can, within five (5) working days, next present the matter in writing to the Assistant University Librarian for Personnel, who serves as the designee of the Vice President and University Librarian at this step of the appeal procedure. The Assistant University Librarian is expected to render a decision in writing within five (5) working days.
   3. If there is no resolution of the grievance at Step 2, the appellant can, within five (5) working days of the decision at Step 2, write to the Vice President for Personnel Management requesting a formal hearing. During a period of five (5) working days following the receipt of this request, the Vice President for Personnel Management or his or her designee will attempt to mediate a solution.

4. If there is no resolution of the problem at Step 3, a grievance committee consisting of three members shall be established to hear the grievance. Members of this committee shall be officers of the University and shall be selected as follows:
   a. One member designated by the Vice President for Personnel Management in consultation with the Vice President and University Librarian.
   b. One member designated by the grievant.
   c. One member, who serves as Commitee Chairperson, will be selected by the first two members from a standing panel of seven. This panel, composed of appointed officers of the University, is appointed annually by the President on nomination by the Executive Committee of the University Senate.
5. The report of the grievance committee will be directed to the Executive Vice President for Administration in cases involving Officers of Administration or to the Executive Vice President for Academic Affairs in cases involving Officers of the Libraries or Research. The appropriate Executive Vice President will then reach a decision based upon the report of the grievance committee. This decision will be final and binding on all parties. The decision will be communicated in writing, together with a copy of the report of the grievance committee, to the grievant and the appropriate department head within fifteen (15) working days of the receipt of the report.
6. Conduct of the Hearing
   a. Attendance at meetings of the grievance committee is limited to persons determined by the committee to have direct connection with the appeal.
   b. The committee will have available to it relevant records and can call appropriate witnesses that it deems necessary to complete its deliberations.

APPENDIX E: THE SYSTEM OF PROFESSIONAL POSITION CATEGORIES

The system of professional position categories is described [above in] the *Handbook for Librarians*. This listing, which is up-dated periodically, identifies each position by current title.

Position Category I

Acquisitions Librarian. Chinese Section, East Asian Library; *Assistant Librarians*, Access Services, East Asian Library (College; School of Social Work); *Bibliographers*, (Africa, Asia, Avery, Latin America, Middle East, Serials Acquisitions, Slavic and East Central Europe); *Bibliographer and Cataloger, Japanese Section, East Asian Library; Catalogers* (Cataloging With Copy, Documents Service Center, East Asian Library, Health Sciences, Law, Music, Original Monographs); *Curator (Columbiana and Russian Archives), Heads* (Access Services, Lehman; Gifts and Exchange; Health Sciences Acquisitions; Interlibrary Loan, Korean Section, East Asian Library; Reprography); *Librarians* (Biological Sciences; Chemistry; Geoscience; International Law; Media Services, Health Sciences; Psychology); *Library Services Coordinator*, Health Sciences; *Reference Librarians* (Avery-Fine Arts, Business, Engineering; Health Sciences, Humanistic and Historical Center, Law, Lehman, Rare Books and Manuscripts); *Reference Librarian and Bibliographer* (Fine Arts; Japanese Section, East Asian Library); *Reference Librarian/Indexer*, Avery-Fine Arts.

Position Category II

Assistant Head, Reference, Humanistic and Historical Center; Assistant Librarians (Manuscripts, Rare Books); *Assistant to the Director, Library Technical Support Group; Assistant to the Head, Original Cataloging; Bibliographers* (Documents Service Center, General Library, Legal Bibliographer); *Heads* (Access Services, East Asian Library; Bibliographic Searching; Book Acquisitions; Catalog Maintenance, Bibliographic Control Division; Health Sciences Cataloging; Law Cataloging); *Librarians* (Engineering, Journalism, Legal Research, Mathematics-Physics); *Library Programmer Analyst; Rare Book Cataloger.*

Position Category III

Heads (Access and Support Services, Health Sciences; Cataloging With Copy; Chinese Section, East Asian Library; Health Sciences Reference; Japanese Section, East Asian Library; Preservation; Resources and Technical Services, Law; Serials Acquisitions; Serials Cataloging); *Librarians* (Lehman, Music, School of Library Service, Social Work); *Systems Planning Coordinator.*

Position Category IV

Assistant Law Librarian; Heads (Access Services, Humanistic and Historical Center; Acquisitions Department, Support; Original Cataloging; Reference, Humanisitic and Historical Center); *Librarians* (Burgess-Carpenter and College, Business).

Position Category V

Assistant University Librarians (Personnel, Planning); *Chiefs* (Bibliographic Control Division, Humanistic and Historical Center (Butler Librarian), Science and Engineering Division, Social Science Division); *Librarians* (Avery, East Asian, Rare Book and Manuscript).

Exempt Positions

Directors (Resources, Services, Support); *Librarians* (Health Sciences, Law); *University Librarian.*

APPENDIX F: NONDISCRIMINATION AND AFFIRMATIVE ACTION

The University will recruit, hire, promote and compensate without regard to race, color, creed, national origin, disability, sex or age, except where sex, age or disability is a bona fide occupational disqualification. In order to maintain its commitment to this policy, and to provide equal employment opportunities (in compliance with Executive Order 11246 and the Civil Rights Act of 1964 as amended), the University has instituted an Affirmative Action Program.

NOTES:

1. Copies of the Affirmative Action Program are on file at the reference desks in Butler Library, the Health Sciences Library, and the Lamont Geoscience Library.
2. All solicitations or advertisements for University employees will include the statement "an equal opportunity employer" to inform all qualified applicants that they will receive consideration for employment without regard to race, color, religion, age, sex, or national origin. All such advertisements should be placed through the Library Personnel Office.

APPENDIX G: LEAVE AND TRAVEL POLICY FOR PROFESSIONAL AND CONTINUING EDUCATION ACTIVITIES

This policy applies to full-time professional staff members on Presidential and Trustee Appointment and reflects recommendations made in 1974 by the Representative Committee of Librarians and the Professional Review Committee.

Policy

The philosophy underlying the participation of staff in professional activities and continuing education programs is as follows:

1. It is the policy of the University Libraries to foster participation in important and productive professional activities and to encourage maintenance and further development of established specialized subject competence and distinctive professional expertise. The objectives sought through the implementation of this policy include the improvement of library performance by the extension of staff capabilities and the professional development of those who, individually and collectively, determine the quality of the University Libraries.
2. There should be reasonable flexibility in all library divisions in setting staff schedules to accommodate professional and educational needs. At the same time, these educational and professional activities must not jeopardize library services or performance standards.
3. It is assumed that each individual will exercise critical and continuing judgment as to what is truly important and productive among an almost infinite variety of possible professional activities.
4. The amount of time needed for a single course, a special program or lecture, or a professional meeting will normally be worked out with the appropriate administrative officer in light of each individual's professional obligations to the University Libraries and the rights of other staff members.

The following should be considered when requests are made for short-term leaves and for full or partial reimbursement of directly related expenses. The sequence of these factors is not intended to indicate an order of importance, nor should the factors be considered all inclusive.

1. The extent of the individual's program or committee responsibilities;
2. The relevance of the activity to the individual's professional development;
3. The relevance of the activity to the University Libraries;
4. The quality or value of the activity.

Short-Term Leaves

Definition
Short-term leaves are leaves with pay for periods of time ranging from a few hours up to one week, in the case of certain professional association conferences. Generally, such leaves will involve less than half a day.

Purpose
Short-term leaves are for the purpose of participation in institutes, seminars, continuing education programs, and similar professional activities which have direct relevance to an individual staff member's functional assignment or which provide opportunity for professional development.

Procedure (Submit on Form A3)

Requests for short-term leaves only. Such requests are to be submitted by the staff member through the appropriate administrative channels to the Librarians of the Distinctive Collections (Avery, East Asian, Law, Health Sciences, Rare Books and Manuscripts); the Directors of Resources, Services or Support; or the Assistant University Librarians (Personnel, Planning), who are authorized to approve requests for short-term leaves. Requests which include application for financial assistance or reimbursement for transportation, registration, or other fees should be submitted through the appropriate administrative channels at least *two weeks* in advance and promptly forwarded to the Assistant University Librarian for Personnnel.

NOTE: Staff members with committee and other on-going commitments with professional associations should see the procedures for submitting such requests.

Reimbursement
When feasible, full or partial reimbursement may be authorized by the Assistant University Librarian for Personnel in accordance with the guidelines [found in the previous section, "The Administrative Organization of the Libraries."]. The record of prior financial assistance received by the individual will be taken into consideration.

Record of Leave
Short-term leaves are to be reported on the "Quarterly Report of Vacation and Leave."

Report of Activity

Staff members may be asked to present an oral or written report on their professional activities, and they are encouraged to share informally their experiences and insights with other members of the staff.

Other Leaves

Requests for leaves for educational or professional activities which exceed one week should be referred to the Assistant University Librarian for Personnel through the appropriate administrative channels well in advance of the time period involved.

Funds for Travel and Related Expenses (Submit on Form A3)

Since funds for travel and related expenses are limited, priorities governing their allocation are necessary. The Assistant University Librarian for Personnel is authorized to review applications and approve expenditures for this purpose.

Official Business

Individuals conducting official business for the University Libraries receive full coverage for travel and living expenses within established limits. Activities included in this category are those directly related to functional responsibilities, such as recruitment and site visits, participation in institutes, specialized conferences, or meetings which are central to current library activities.

Designated Representatives

Individuals in this category are those designated as formal representatives of the Libraries at an institute, workshop, conference, or meeting which is concerned with matters or issues significant to the operations or interests of the University Libraries.

Procedure. Librarians of the Distinctive Collections; Directors of Resources, Services, and Support; and the Assistant University Librarians should submit the request to the Assistant University Librarian for Personnel at least *two weeks in advance* (three weeks, if a travel advance is requested).

Professional Association Conferences

Because of the number and variety of professional association programs and conferences held each year and the variation in expenses because of location, full or partial financial assistance will only be provided after review of requests and in the context of available funds and library priorities. As with financial assistance for continuing education activities, previous financial assistance received by individuals will also be taken into consideration. *At the beginning of each fiscal year, the Librarians of the Distinctive Collections; the Directors of Resources, Services, and Support; and the Assistant University Librarians will be asked to survey staff in their units who have definite plans to attend professional association conferences and meetings because of committee or other on-going commitments.*

Support of Beginning Professionals

To encourage participation of beginning librarians in professional activities, funds to cover travel and limited per diem expenses for one or more professional staff members to attend a major professional conference will be made available when possible. The Representative Committee of Librarians will be asked to make recommendations after reviewing applications from interested staff members with less than five years of service and who have not previously attended such a conference.

Record of Leave

Leave time is to be reported on the "Quarterly Report of Vacation and Leave."

Report of Activity

Staff members may be asked to present an oral or written report on their professional activities, and they are encouraged to share informally their experiences and insights with other members of the staff.

University Travel Policy Booklet

Instructions governing travel and procedures for completing a travel voucher are explained in the booklet "University Travel Policy."...

APPENDIX G: APPLICATION FOR PROFESSIONAL LEAVE AND/
OR TRAVEL

I. NAME & UNIT _____

   LEAVE TIME REQUESTED: _____

   PURPOSE OF REQUEST: _____

   SIGNATURE: _____ DATE: _____

II. IF FINANCIAL REIMBURSEMENT REQUESTED, PROVIDE
    ESTIMATE:

III. ADMINISTRATIVE RECOMMENDATIONS

   Name: _____ Initials & Date: _____
   RECOMMENDATION:

   Name: _____ Initials & Date: _____
   RECOMMENDATION:

   Name: _____ Initials & Date: _____
   RECOMMENDATION:

IV. FORWARD COMPLETED APPLICATION TO:
    Assistant University Librarian for Personnel
    317 Butler Library

INSTRUCTIONS

Prior to completing this application, see "Leave and Travel Policy for Professional and Continuing Educational Activities," Appendix H of the "Professional Staff Handbook."

SECTION I:

- Completed by the applicant.
- Under "Purpose of Request," please be specific. Indicate nature of activity, involvement (e.g., committee member or chairman, speaker, panel member, etc.), and relevance of activity. See "Leave and Travel Policy."

SECTION II.

- Completed by the applicant.
- If financial reimbursement is involved, estimate the total costs for various expenses (e.g., registration fees, travel, hotel accommodations) and the amount of reimbursement or assistance requested.

SECTION III.

- The appropriate administrative officers are to review the request and to specify the reasons for their recommendation.
- If the applicant is being sent on official business (e.g., recruitment, site visit, interinstitutional activity) *or* recommended as a representative of the Libraries at an institute or workshop, the officer making the recommendation should so specify.
- If the application is for a short-term leave only and *does not* include a request for financial reimbursement, the authorizing officer (Librarians of the Distinctive Collections; Directors of Resources, Services, or Support; Assistant University Librarians) should inform the applicant of the disposition of the request and forward the application to the Assistant University Librarian for Personnel.

SECTION IV.

- All applications are to be forwarded to the Assistant University Librarian for Personnel.
- The Assistant University Librarian for Personnel will inform the applicant and the appropriate officers in writing of the disposition of all applications involving other than short-term leave requests.

APPENDIX H: GUIDELINES FOR PERFORMANCE APPRAISALS
(Appointed and SCATS Staff)

The purpose of this document is to provide supervisory and administrative staff with general guidelines for conducting performance appraisals for appointed and SCATS staff. Appraisals are done for different reasons, and the supervisor must consider the purpose before beginning an appraisal. For example, if the appraisal is being done for an individual who is completing the probationary period, it would be appropriate to emphasize progress made in mastering the basic elements and techniques of the position and to provide relevant information on developmental needs and potential. On the other hand, if the appraisal is being done for an individual who is under consideration for promotion to Rank III or IV, such information would not be appropriate since the criteria for these ranks require "significant achievement at the career level" and "distinctive contributions" respectively. Other types of information would be needed if the appraisal is a periodic review for a staff member who is under consideration for a higher level position or whose work performance requires corrective action.

In preparing the enclosed appraisal, it is important that you give careful consideration to all significant aspects of the individual's work performance during the period covered by the review. The general guidelines which follow will not apply to all types of appraisals; however, they should be reviewed and adapted accordingly.

Performance Appraisal Objectives

Significant objectives to be realized in the performance appraisal process are:
1. Improved performance and development of the staff member.
2. Precise and comprehensive input from the supervisor which will provide realistic information on accomplishments and developmental needs. It is important to remember that appraisals done for those under consideration for promotion in rank should emphasize quality of performance to date, in addition to noting developmental needs or potential if appropriate.

Procedural Guidelines

The four key steps in the appraisal process are the preliminary assessment; the review with your immediate supervisor; the appraisal interview; and the follow-through. A description of each step and suggestions to assist in the process follow:

Preliminary Assessment
Remember that an appraisal is most likely to be sound if it is based on relevant, accurate, and complete information. Prior to writing the appraisal, give careful consideration to the following:

1. What kind of performance should be expected of a staff member in the position? It is understood that these expectations or requirements had been previously covered in performance objectives meetings or other goal setting discussions.
2. The staff member's strengths and weaknesses in accomplishing the objectives of the position.
3. Steps that can be taken to meet the developmental needs of the staff member.
4. The staff member's potential.

Review With Your Immediate Supervisor
This step is necessary for several reasons:

1. You as a supervisor or manager are responsible for meeting your objectives and those of your staff.
2. The review process provides your supervisor with information which is needed to relate the accomplishments of your unit with those of other units.
3. Your supervisor may be able to assist you in formulating the appraisal.

The Appraisal Interview
Because of the importance of this aspect of the review process, the following steps should be taken:

1. Several days in advance, arrange the date and time for the interview with the staff member, and give a copy of the appraisal to the staff member.
2. The physical arrangement should be properly arranged so that it is private and sufficient time is available.
3. Indicate to the staff member that an open and frank discussion should be a mutual objective.
4. Begin by discussing some strengths—be specific and use examples.

5. When weaknesses are discussed, emphasize that one of the purposes of the appraisal is to help the staff member to help himself. Again, be specific and use examples.
6. Encourage self-examination on the part of the staff member.
7. When reviewing areas in which the staff member needs development, direct the discussion to major areas which are critical to job performance.
8. Inquire about problems or obstacles that the staff member feels are impeding progress and job satisfaction—mutual understanding of the problem may help to resolve it.
9. Be a good listener.
10. Ask the staff member if you can do anything (e.g., behavior, attitude) to help on the job (this may provide you with feedback which can lead to constructive change).
11. At the conclusion of the interview, be sure that the staff member understands the key items discussed by reviewing briefly the areas covered.
12. After the interview, tell the staff member to consider both the written appraisal and the interview and encourage him to add his comments to the appraisal form. Allow him several days or a week to do so.

The Follow-Through

It is your responsibility to review the staff member's progress and to encourage as well as facilitate actions to build on strengths and to improve on weaknesses or resolve problems covered in the appraisal.

Guidelines for Assessing Job Performance

Overall Performance

Remember that a balanced appraisal is what is needed and that specificity is critical. Identify the top priorities of the job and give specific examples to demonstrate accomplishments and developmental needs. Bear in mind the length of time that the staff member has been in the job and base your comments on what is reasonable to expect in view of length of service. Review the factors listed on the appraisal form and consider the following, which are not to be viewed as all inclusive and will not apply to all appraisals:

1. *Acceptance of Responsibility.* Is the staff member willing to assume responsibility and to perform with a minimum of supervision?
2. *Adaptability.* Does the staff member adjust to unusual and/or new situations? Consider the individual's willingness to ac-

cept assignments outside the routine, to exercise good judgment, and to maintain priorities in stress situations.

3. *Adherence to Procedures and Policies.* Consider whether the
   staff member functions within the structure provided to achieve
   unit objectives or does he consistently circumvent established
   procedures and policies?

4. *Extent and Application of Subject and/or Technical Skills.*
   Are the skills of the staff member developed sufficiently to
   meet the performance requirements? If not, suggest ways to
   improve skills. If they are developed sufficiently, consider the
   staff member's efficiency in applying the skills and work techniques to achieve maximal performance requirements.

5. *Human Relations.* Is the staff member effective in working
   with supervisors, subordinates, fellow employees, the public?
   For example, consider the staff member's effect on others as a
   result of disposition, tact, enthusiasm, initiative, creativity,
   receptivity to new ideas, and cooperation.

6. *Initiative.* Does the staff member examine current methods
   and procedures and initiate actions to make constructive change?
   Consider also whether the staff member takes the intiative to
   resolve interdepartmental problems or to determine why such
   problems exist.

7. *Judgment.* Does the staff member use common sense and logic
   in approaching problems? Consider the staff member's approach
   to major and minor problems and the resolution of problems
   interfering with an orderly performance of duties.

8. *Quality of Work Performance.* Does the staff member plan and
   schedule assignments to achieve efficiency, completeness, and
   accuracy? Consider whether the staff member is aware of quality standards and if he works toward achieving them.

9. *Quantity of Work.* Is the staff member industrious and does he
   apply himself? Consider whether the staff member plans and
   organizes his work to achieve desired objectives.

10. *Reliability.* Does the staff member consistently fulfill job
    requirements and meet deadlines? Consider whether the staff
    member plans and organizes his work to achieve desired objec-
    tives.

11. *Resourcefulness.* Consider the staff member's ability to deal
    skillfully and efficiently with new situations, assignments, or
    problems.

Performance of Supervisory Responsibilities
In addition to the factors listed above, consider the staff member's
strengths and weakness as a supervisor. Again, remember that spe-

cific examples are essential. The key question to consider is the staff member's success in accomplishing unit objectives through the effective utilization of personnel under his supervision. The following standard areas of accountability should be considered in appraising a supervisor:

1. *Communication.* Does the staff member communicate relevant information effectively to personnel under his supervision, to the appropriate department and unit heads, and to senior officers?
2. *Cost Effectiveness.* Does the staff member take action to decrease costs by eliminating unessential materials and equipment or duplicative systems and procedures? Does the staff member take constructive action to deal properly with unproductive or inefficient staff? Does he make proper utilization of exceptional staff members?
3. *Delegation.* Does the staff member make appropriate distinctions in the delegation of assignments and responsibilities?
4. *Follow-Through.* Does the staff member follow-through on work assigned in his unit to insure that priorities are being met and that work is done correctly?
5. *Organization of Work.* Does the staff member organize his own and the work of those in his unit to achieve maximum efficiency and productivity?
6. *Planning Abilities.* Does the staff member plan effectively to meet current and future objectives for the unit?
7. *Problem-Solving.* Does the staff member respond constructively to problem situations and take appropriate actions to resolve them?
8. *Time Management.* Does the staff member make the best use of his own time and insure that those under his supervision are also giving appropriate time to priorities?
9. *Training.* Does the staff member provide appropriate orientation and training for those in his unit? Consider methodology and follow-up.

REMEMBER: A sound appraisal is based on relevant, accurate and sufficiently complete information.

APPENDIX I: PERFORMANCE APPRAISAL FORM

COLUMBIA UNIVERSITY LIBRARIES
Library Personnel Office
C O N F I D E N T I A L

TO: _____

SUBJECT: Request for Performance Appraisal

Please complete the enclosed performance appraisal and return it under CONFIDENTIAL cover to: PERSONNEL RECORDS, Library Personnel Office, 315 Butler Library

Staff member to be appraised: _____

Return to the Library Personnel Office by: _____

Instructions for Completing Appraisal Form (A74)

This form is to be used in appraising appointed staff and those in positions covered by the Classification Scheme for Supervisory, Confidential, and Technical ("SCATS") Positions. This form is <u>not</u> to be used for review of "performance objectives."

REASON FOR APPRAISAL.   Completed by the Library Personnel Office

- PERIODIC REVIEW. An appraisal may be requested if the staff member has not had a recent performance appraisal.

- END OF PROBATION. Appointed staff are to be appraised after completing six months in a position; staff in "SCATS" positions, after eight weeks. This applies to new staff members and to those assuming new positions.

- CONSIDERATION FOR PROMOTION IN RANK. Such appraisals apply only to professional librarians included in the system of ranks. Supervisors are required to do an appraisal when a staff member is under consideration for promotion in rank, regardless of when the most recent appraisal was completed.

- TERMINATION. Such appraisals are required for reference purposes and, like other appraisals, are discussed by the supervisor with the staff member. Such appraisals are generally not required when a staff member retires.

I.   NAME OF STAFF MEMBER BEING APPRAISED. Completed by the Library Personnel Office.

II.   SUPERVISOR. Completed by the Library Personnel Office.

III.   PREVIOUS SUPERVISOR. Completed by the Library Personnel Office.

IV.   RESPONSIBILITIES AND PRIMARY TASKS PERFORMED BY THE STAFF MEMBER. To be completed by the supervisor.

V.   EFFECTIVENESS OF WORK PERFORMANCE OF STAFF MEMBER. To be completed and signed by the supervisor. The "factors" listed on the bottom of the page are suggested for consideration. All will not apply in individual cases; others may be more appropriate.

VI.   THE SUPERVISOR IS TO FORWARD THE APPRAISAL UNDER CONFIDENTIAL COVER TO THE APPROPRIATE OFFICERS OF THE UNIT (i.e., Department Head, Division Chief, Group Director, and/or Librarian of a Distinctive Collection, up to but not including the University Librarian, prior to discussion with the staff member. The senior officers are to review and sign the form and may comment in the space provided.)

VII.   SIGNATURE AND COMMENTS, IF ANY, OF STAFF MEMBER. After the supervisor has discussed the appraisal with the staff member, the staff member is required to sign the appraisal to indicate that he/she has been informed of the nature of the appraisal. The staff member may comment on the appraisal in the space provided.

VIII.   The completed form is to be forwarded under confidential cover to the Library Personnel Office via the senior officers.

COLUMBIA UNIVERSITY LIBRARIES

PERFORMANCE APPRAISAL

PROFESSIONAL AND "SCATS" STAFF

CONFIDENTIAL

CHECK REASON FOR APPRAISAL:

☐ Periodic Review

☐ End of Probation

☐ Consideration for Promotion in Rank (Librarians only)

☐ Termination

<u>PLEASE SEE INSTRUCTIONS PRIOR TO COMPLETING</u>

I. NAME: _____

POSITION TITLE & UNIT_____

POSITION CATEGORY OR GRADE:_____ EFFECTIVE DATE:_____

RANK (Librarians only):_____ EFFECTIVE DATE:_____

II. SUPERVISOR:

NAME: _____

POSITION TITLE & UNIT_____

LENGTH OF TIME ASSIGNED TO SUPERVISOR_____

III. PREVIOUS SUPERVISOR (Complete only if assigned to current supervisor for less than 6 months):

NAME: _____

POSITION TITLE & UNIT:_____

DATE OF LAST APPRAISAL:_____ REASON FOR LAST APPRAISAL:_____

IV. BRIEFLY DESCRIBE THE STAFF MEMBER'S RESPONSIBILITIES AND SPECIFY THE PRIMARY TASKS PERFORMED (Refer to current position description on file in your office. <u>Or</u> See enclosed position description):

V. HOW EFFECTIVELY HAS THE STAFF MEMBER FULFILLED THE RESPONSIBILITIES OF THE POSITION? PLEASE CONSIDER THE FACTORS LISTED BELOW IN APPRAISING THE STRENGTHS AND WEAKNESSES OF THE STAFF MEMBER.

SIGNATURE OF SUPERVISOR:_____DATE_____

Some factors for consideration in answering V

Adaptability	Human Relations	Organization and Planning
Attitude	Initiative	Professional Skills
Extent and application	Judgment	Reliability
of subject and/or	Leadership	Resourcefulness
technical skills	Oral and Written Skills	Supervisory Abilities

VI. REVIEWED BY (Section V is to be reviewed by the appraiser's senior officers, up to but not including the University Librarian, prior to the discussion with the staff member):

Name:_____Initials & Date:_____

COMMENTS, IF ANY:

Name:_____Initials & Date:_____

COMMENTS, IF ANY:

Name:_____Initials & Date:_____

COMMENTS, IF ANY:

Name:_____Initials & Date:_____

COMMENTS, IF ANY:

VII. SIGNATURE AND COMMENTS, IF ANY, OF STAFF MEMBER BEING APPRAISED:

VIII. FORWARD UNDER CONFIDENTIAL COVER, TO: Personnel Records
(via the senior officers, up to but not including   Library Personnel Office
the University Librarian)   315 Butler Library

Initials & Date: _____ _____   Initials & Date: _____ _____

Initials & Date: _____ _____   Initials & Date: _____ _____

Public Libraries Personnel Policies

SALT LAKE CITY PUBLIC LIBRARY
(Salt Lake City, Utah)

Personnel Code
(2nd edition, 1978)

CONTENTS

INTRODUCTION

This is the second edition, revised, of the Salt Lake City Public Library
Personnel Code. Each section of this edition has been reviewed and revised in accordance with federal and state legislation, court decisions and legal opinions. The Affirmative Action Policy adopted by the Library Board of Directors, June 15, 1977, is an appendix to these regulations. This policy is the Personnel Code of the Board of Directors of the Salt Lake City Public Library.

The Personnel Code will be reviewed every three years following Board approval of the second edition.

Additional members will be elected to the committee by the staff at large through open nomination. One of these will represent the extension agencies. Employees should make all recommendations, or observations, on the effectiveness of the code, in writing, to the committee member(s) of their choice.

Submitted by the Committee

Approved by the Board of Directors of the Salt Lake City Public Library.

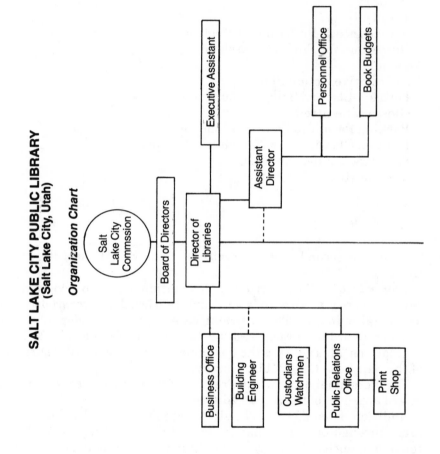

SALT LAKE CITY PUBLIC LIBRARY
(Salt Lake City, Utah)

Organization Chart

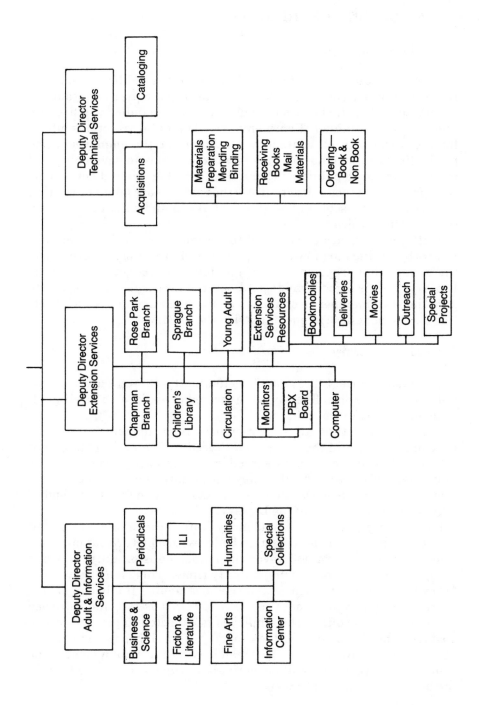

RESPONSIBILITY OF THE STAFF

Toward the Community

The primary duty of the Library is to serve the public. All patrons regardless of sex, race, creed, or age are to be given the same standard of service. All contacts with the public are to be handled in a friendly and courteous manner. Every employee is a public relations officer for the library. In all contacts with the public the employee *is* the public library. Each has an important role to play in developing and maintaining good public relations. Staff members should not become so engrossed in mechanical routines that patrons are ignored. Visiting with friends or discussing personal affairs should not occur while on duty at a public desk.

Staff members are encouraged to become involved in community affairs by taking part in workshops, discussion groups, lectures, book talks, and other programs which benefit both the community and the Library. This is a good way to publicize the Library's services, and to give the staff members a chance to utilize a particular area of expertise for the benefit of agencies outside the library.

Toward the Library

All members of the Library staff including the Director are accountable to someone else. Everyone is expected to work in an intelligent, efficient, and courteous manner.

It is required that all staff members read and understand the Personnel Code and the Policy and Procedure Manual. A statement attesting to this fact must be signed by the employee and filed in the Personnel Office within thirty days after date of employment. This Code must be returned to the Business Office when the staff member leaves the employment of the Library.

For security reasons and to identify staff to the public, every staff member is issued an identification badge with a picture but no name. These are to be worn whenever the employee is on duty, or when using non-public areas during off-duty times. This is in effect at the Main Library, the branches, and the bookmobile. If a badge is lost, there will be a replacement fee of $2.00. If it is lost and returned through the post office, the employee is expected to pay the return postage. The ID badges are the property of the Library and must be returned to the Business Office when leaving the employment of the Library. The ID badge will be worn above the waist, on the front of the body, and in a visible position.

Toward Co-workers

Supervisors toward Staff. One of the main responsibilities of the supervisor is to help new staff members learn the work, to become acquainted with the library building and personnel, and to know library policies and procedures. Supervisors should compliment a staff member when a job is well done. If a suggestion for improvement or reprimand is necessary, it should be discussed courteously and, if possible, privately in a nonpublic area.

Staff toward Supervisors. Staff members are responsible for doing the work assigned by the immediate supervisor, accurately, efficiently, and as pleasantly as possible. If there is a question or complaint about the work assignment, the employee should feel free to discuss it privately with the immediate supervisor. If that is not possible, the employee may talk to the Deputy Director in charge of the service, Director of Personnel, or Director. If no solution can be reached, the employee can follow the Grievance Procedure as outlined in this code.

The Director welcomes inquiries and suggestions from staff members concerning the Library's administration and general procedures. These should be discussed first with the staff member's immediate supervisor who, whether approving or not, will refer them to the Director.

Staff toward Staff. It is important that cooperation exist not only between individuals but between departments as well. All staff members should be considerate, courteous, and helpful toward each other, especially when it may be necessary to work at a task which is not specifically a part of the employee's particular job description.

Staff toward Volunteers. Although volunteers are not employees of the Library, they are an essential part of such programs as BOND (Books on Delivery) and others. Their exemplary devotion and support of library service deserves the respect and cooperation of all staff members.

Staff Meetings

Various staff meetings are held regularly.

1. A staff Agency Head meeting is held monthly, at 9 a.m. on the second Tuesday of the month. This is an informational and problem identifying session. Minutes are written and distributed to all staff members.

2. Administrative meetings are held each Thursday at 9 a.m. This is an administrative planning session to identify and solve problems.

3. A "coffee hour" with the Director is held on an irregular basis. Seven staff members from various agencies in the system are invited for an informal meeting.

4. The Adult Services department heads meet with the Deputy Director for that service on the first Tuesday of the month at 9 a.m. to discuss department problems, services, and budgeting,

5. A branch, Children's and Young Adult meeting is held monthly on the last Tuesday at 9 a.m. This is a system wide session to coordinate and plan programs, services, and to review children's and young adult books.

6. Area department meetings are also held, some on a regular basis and some on call by the agency head.

7. Library Employees' Organization Executive Board meets once each month. There is an annual meeting for the entire Library Employees' Organization membership.

Professional Attitudes and Conduct

It will, at all times, be the policy of the Salt Lake City Public Library to practice equal employment opportunity to all persons without regard to race, creed, religion, color, sex, national origin, age in the case of individuals below the age of 65, and when they do not interfere with job performance, physical or mental handicap, or individual life style.

Conversation. Conversations with either public or co-workers should be kept to a minimum and should never interfere with service to patrons. Loud conversations are disturbing to everyone.

Equipment. All staff members should take care of Library equipment, furnishings and property. At the end of the day, public and private desks should be tidied, work materials put away, and typewriters covered. All work areas should be maintained in a neat, orderly condition.

Fees and Honorariums. Fees and honorariums for talks, lectures, workshops, etc., conducted by staff members are permitted if done on the staff member's own time. No fee may be received by the staff member if the lecture, workshop, etc., is performed on Library time, or is sponsored by the Library, or is conducted in the name of the Library.

Gifts. The library is a public institution and its services are equally available to all. Members of the staff may not accept valuable gifts or money from patrons. Staff members are permitted to accept candy and other inexpensive items.

Grooming. The community image of the library is, at least in part, projected by the wearing apparel and appearance of staff members. It is, therefore, very important that all employees be well-groomed and properly dressed. It is assumed that an employee hired by the library will show good common sense and a maturity of self expression. Clothing should be selected that is neither distracting to other staff members and patrons, nor unbefitting that of a professional library employee. Clothing should be fresh and neat. Careful personal hygiene is essential. Hair, regardless of length, should be clean. Within these concepts there is plenty of room for the expression of individual taste and the exercise of individual choice of apparel suited to a particular library position.

Gum Chewing and Eating in Public. Neither gum chewing nor eating, while on duty, is permitted. Food and beverages are not to be consumed outside the staff room, unless specific permission is given by the Director.

Punctuality. All staff members should be in the library and ready for work on time. This means arriving at the building ahead of schedule. Staff members going off duty from public desks should explain clearly and completely the work left to the staff member replacing them. If a staff member is to be absent from the duty area for longer than five minutes, the immediate supervisor or co-workers should be notified.

Reading. The patron has a right to expect the staff to be familiar with the book collection and to keep informed about new titles. Staff reading while on duty at a service desk is limited to professional periodicals, book reviews, and other materials required for general job assignments. However, the individual staff member remains responsible for giving priority to patrons.

Salesmen and Canvassers. Salesmen, solicitors, and persons circulating petitions should be asked to see staff members outside the library unless library matters are involved or the project has been approved by the Board of Directors. Proselytizing, selling merchandise, tickets, or chances of any kind in public areas, whether by staff members or others, is prohibited, unless it is approved by the Library Administration.

Smoking. Smoking by staff members is permitted only in the staff room, on the patio, and in private offices. It is not allowed in workrooms, in the public or staff rest rooms, or in the women's quiet area.

Telephone Calls. Personal telephone calls are discouraged except in emergencies. All personal telephone calls should be kept as brief as possible and made from a phone in a nonpublic area.

Welfare and Social Activities. Nonstaff related social activities must be arranged and held on staff member's own time. No staff member is obligated to contribute time or money to such activities. See also the Library Employees' Organization Handbook for staff related welfare and social activities.

PROVISIONS FOR STAFF CONVENIENCE

Borrowing Privileges

All circulating materials including records and art prints are available to the staff. All materials must be checked out with library card when removed from shelves. Any staff member removing materials from the library without authorization will be subject to immediate dismissal. Although staff members are not charged overdue fines, they are expected to return materials on time. If the materials are not returned by the time the bill notification is generated by the computer (usually six weeks after the material is due), that staff member's borrowing privileges will be suspended until the overdue materials are returned. Materials in the Technical Services area are not to be removed or handled for browsing or for any purpose.

Personal Orders

Staff members may purchase books and other materials through the Library special account at library prices, which are generally at a considerable saving. Leased McNaughton books may also be purchased by staff after their use by the Library. Personal books may be rebound through Library facilities. See Procedure Manual for information on ordering materials. Consult Acquisitions Department regarding binding.

Hospital and Medical Insurance

All employees are covered by Workmen's Compensation, a protection in case of injury or illness as the result of a service connected accident or condition. Group insurance, which includes life, hospitalization, and medical plans, is available to employees working a forty hour week. The basic payment for the program is made by the Library. Employees working less than the forty hour week are not eligible for the group insurance program. Coverage will be granted upon application after 30 days of beginning employment. All changes in marital status and dependents must be reported to the Business Office for adjustment. Employees on leave without pay may make arrangements to pay the premiums in advance at the Business Office.

Savings Plans

All employees of the Library are eligible to join the Salt Lake City Employees Credit Union and may authorize deductions from paychecks into a savings plan. There are many advantages to membership in the Credit Union. Please contact the Credit Union office directly at 1360 South Main.

Employees may also participate in the United States Savings Bond program. Inquire in the Business Office for details.

Nonpublic Areas

A staff room located on the third floor of the Main Library is maintained by the Library Employees' Organization for the use of Library personnel. This is a "staff only" facility and no guests are allowed except those visiting the Library in an official capacity. A lounge, kitchen facilities, and vending machines are provided. Staff members using the facilities are responsible for cleaning up after themselves.

Except for guests visiting the Library in an official capacity or having prior approval, no friends or relative of staff members may enter or exit the building through staff doors or use the staff elevator unless they are accompanied by a staff member. Family or friends who call for staff members must wait in public areas.

These rules also apply to staff room facilities at branch libraries.

At the Main Library the basement doors, both the outside door and the inside door to the first basement level, will be locked at 6 p.m., Monday through Saturday and locked at 1:30 p.m. on Sunday.

Miscellaneous Information

Accidents. See Procedure and Policy manual for policy on reporting accidents. Report immediately any personal injury or accident to department supervisor and/or the Librarian in Charge who must file a written report at the Business Office within 24 hours.

Discount Admissions. Members may obtain discount theatre tickets from the Credit Union office.

Evacuation of the Building. If evacuation of buildings becomes necessary, procedures have been posted in each department and branch and spelled out in the Procedure Manual.

First Aid. A basic first aid kit is available at each service desk. More complete kits are located in the Business Office, at the Information Desk, and at the Branches. Oral medication, including aspirin, must not be dispensed to patrons. A wheelchair is available from the custodian at the Main Library.

Lockers. Employees at the Main Library will be provided with a locker for personal belongings. Keys may be obtained upon payment of a $2.00 deposit to the Business Office. If a key is lost, the deposit is forfeited and an additional deposit will be required for a replacement key. The Library assumes no responsibility for belongings not safely locked.

Name and Address Records. An employee's local address and telephone number, along with name and address of next of kin, must be sent to the Personnel Office. Any changes are to be reported to the office immediately. Staff members' names, addresses, and telephone numbers are to be given to other staff members only when a library connected reason can be given, and they are not to be released to any other person or entities except as required by law, i.e., I.R.S., court order, etc. Names of Library Administrators (the Director, the Assistant Director, the Deputy Directors) and the names of the Library Board members may be released to patrons if requested since these names are a matter of public record. However, only the name (not the married name), title, and phone number, if requested, should be given.

Parking. Limited parking in the City Complex lot is available on a first come, first served basis. The Library is allotted a given number of parking stickers by the City. Employees may apply for a parking permit in the Business Office at which time the regulations governing parking and care of the parking permit will be explained. Normally, Library Aide I, non-supervisory branch personnel, temporary and substitute staff are not eligible for parking permits . . .

Personnel Files. Although personnel files belong to the Library, and since they contain information of a private nature, they will be available for perusal only to the employee, his/her supervisors, or the personnel office. These files may not be removed from the Personnel Office.

Problem Patrons. All incidents involving problem patrons, i.e., indecent exposure, abusive drunkenness, abusive language, mental disturbances, etc., should be reported immediately to the Director or Librarian in Charge, followed by a written report. See Policy and Procedure Manual.

Staff Bulletin Boards. Staff members should consult bulletin boards in departments and branches for announcements.

Library Employees' Organization

The Library Employees' Organization is comprised of all staff members, and exists for the social, professional, and economic betterment of the staff. New employees will be contacted by a member of the Organization with an invitation to become active members.

POSITIONS

Recruitment

The Board of Directors approved the Affirmative Action Plan, which is appended to the Personnel Code, on June 15, 1977. Recruitment in the Library is conducted in accordance with this policy.

The Personnel Office is in charge of recruitment of new staff members and handles applications for promotions and transfers within the system. Prospective employees must complete an application form which is retained by this office. When a position opens for which applicants are qualified, an appointment for an interview is scheduled with the Personnel Director who in turn will schedule an interview with the Agency Head and/or Deputy Director of the area where the vacancy exists. Applicants for the positions of Agency Head and/or Deputy Director will also be interviewed by the Director of the Library.

Appointments

Appointments of all salaried personnel are made by the Board of Directors upon recommendation of the director, and are in accordance with the Affirmative Action Plan. A salaried employee regularly works halftime or more in any classification other than Library Aide I at an annual salary approved by the Board of Directors. Except for specialized positions, a staff member classified in the professional group must have received a master's degree from an ALA accredited library school. A staff member classified in the paraprofessional group must have a baccalaureate degree from an accredited college or university or any equivalent combination of experience and training which provides the required knowledge, skills, and abilities. Proof for such experience is the responsibility of the applicant and the decision is that of the administration.

New employees hired at the paraprofessional level or above will furnish the Personnel Office with a certified transcript of academic credentials showing the receipt of a baccalaureate and/or advanced degree. This transcript must be mailed from the Registrar's Office of the university granting the degree. If it is not received within one month of the date of employment and there is no satisfactory explanation of the delay, the employee will be subject to termination or placement on a lower pay scale. When the proper documentation is received, the employee will return to the original pay scale but no retroactive pay will be issued. This policy also applies to promotion of present staff.

Appointment of members of immediate families of the Board of Directors and administrative officers (Agency Heads or above) even for hourly employment, is made only after this relationship is brought to the attention of the Board.

If any members of the same immediate family are appointed, they will be placed in different agencies.

For temporary positions, preference is given to persons with qualifications which would entitle them to consideration for permanent positions. Staff members who resign are eligible for reappointment at a future time when a suitable opening for which they qualify is available, providing that the former employees' evaluation ratings were satisfactory during the period of the first appointment.

Hourly employees are generally assigned to areas where the work to be done does not require a full-time staff member. Both students and nonstudents may be used to fill these positions. Substitutes and temporary staff are considered to be hourly employees even though their work week may exceed 20 hours.

Job Classification, Pay Plan, and Job Descriptions

All positions have been analyzed, classified and placed on a salary scale so that those requiring similar duties and responsibilities are grouped together. Positions are reviewed periodically to account for change in duties and to remove inequities. A request for review of any position may be made once a year to the Personnel Office by the incumbent or supervisor. Vacant positions are reviewed before being posted for application. A summary of the Classification and Pay Plan is appended. For a more detailed analysis, see the Personnel Office. Periodically, an outside consulting firm is engaged to review the Classification and Pay Plan.

Probationary Period

Each new staff member shall be considered to be on probation for six months. If the administration wishes to terminate the employee for reasons of unsuitability during the initial period, it may be done without the right of appeal. A review of the employee's work performance is made halfway through the probationary period as well as at the end. This performance evaluation is discussed with the employee by the immediate supervisor. Upon promotion, an employee enters a new probationary period. Probation time may be extended if deemed necessary by supervisors but may not exceed an additional three months. For vacation and sick leave purposes, time worked during a probationary period will be counted toward vacation and sick leave eligibility.

Tenure

After completion of the probationary period, the employment (but not the assignment) of the staff member, except for temporary positions, is considered to be continuous and permanent as long as performance evaluation interviews are satisfactory. If a tenured employee ceases to meet the required standards of the position, the supervisor, in a staff counseling interview, made in writing and documented, will call the employee's attention to this fact so that work performance will be improved. If improvement does not occur, the supervisor shall recommend to the Deputy Director, if applicable, to the Personnel Director, and to the Director that the employee be warned, reprimanded, transferred, demoted, or dismissed. The employee will receive a written copy of all charges, and may appeal the supervisor's recommendation to the Director. The Director's action could then be appealed to the Grievance Committee, and to the Board of Directors.

Complaints

Staff Complaints. When a staff member has a legitimate complaint against another member of the staff, all parties involved should meet and attempt to reach a workable solution. If a solution cannot be reached, or if the employee cannot discuss the problem with the other party, the documented complaint may be taken directly to the immediate supervisor, the Deputy Director, the Personnel Director, and/or the Director. If there is still no satisfactory solution, the matter may be taken through the Grievance Procedure.

Patron Complaints Against Staff. When a patron has a legitimate complaint against a staff member, the complaint should be discussed privately and as soon as possible by the employee named and the direct supervisor. If the complaint is received by anyone other than the direct supervisor, the direct supervisor should be informed immediately by the staff member to whom the complaint was made. If the complaint has come to the Director, the Director may be the one to speak to the staff member, but not before informing the accused employee's supervisor. If the employee feels that the charge is unfair, and the supervisor does not agree, the matter may be taken through the established channels. (See Staff Complaints paragraph above.)

Grievance Procedure

The Grievance Procedure is to be used only after the complaint has been discussed through regular channels of communication and still has not been satisfactorily resolved. It is designed to deal with serious problems and should not be undertaken lightly.

A written and documented statement of the charge must be sent to the Chairperson of the Personnel Relations Committee of the Library Employees' Organization and the person or persons against whom the charge is made. Within five (5) working days the Personnnel Relations Committee will hold a meeting of all parties involved to determine the validity of the case. Within three (3) working days the Personnel Relations Committee must send to the Director, the Personnel Director, the President of the Library Employees' Organization and all parties involved a written report of the meeting including the written charges and the recommendation of the Committee. If so recommended, the Director and the President of the Library Employees' Organization within five (5) working days must create a five (5) member committee composed of persons from various levels of the staff to hear the case. The Director and the President of the Library Employees' Organization will jointly select a chairperson and then each will appoint two members. Within five (5) working days after appointment the committee will meet with the parties involved. The two sides may be represented by themselves or by persons of their choice, including legal counsel. The committee will attempt to help the opposing parties reach a workable solution and, failing such, will recommend a course of action to the Director. A written report of the meeting must be sent to the Director, the Personnel Director, the President of the Library Employees' Organization and all parties involved. The Director will send a written reply of the recommendations to all appropriate persons after complying with the obligation to seek Board approval with legal counsel if necessary. The Director will periodically monitor the implementation of the recommendation. If either party disagrees with the Director's decision, a final appeal, including full documentation, can be made to the Board of Directors.

CHANGES IN POSITION

Transfers

Transfers are changes in assignment in which the salary rate and job level remain the same. Transfers are made for the good of the service and the development of the staff member's potential. Whenever possible, the needs and desires of the employee are taken into consideration. An employee may request, in writing, a transfer through the Personnel Office.

Promotions

Notices of vacancies are posted on the Staff Room Bulletin Board in all Branches. Staff members who wish to be considered for the position may apply, in writing, at the Personnel Office. For purposes of informing the staff, a notice will also be posted if the duties of a position are realigned, reassigned, or if the position is abolished. In seeking the best candidate the Personnel Office may consider outside applications along with those from within the system. All action will be taken in accordance with the appended Affirmative Action Plan.

Employees who obtain higher degrees are not automatically guaranteed a promotion.

Resignations

An employee who intends to resign informs the immediate supervisor as soon as possible and then submits a written resignation to the Personnel Director. Four weeks notice before the last working day is the minimum required for all professional positions, and two weeks for all other positions. A staff member in an important administrative position should give a longer notice when possible. However, in all cases, it would be appreciated by the Personnel Office if notice of resignation is given as soon as the employee is certain of the time. Upon submission of a letter of resignation, an exit interview must be scheduled with the immediate supervisor.

Dismissals

Employees are dismissed or suspended by the Board upon recommendation of the Director. A tenured employee may be dismissed for incompetence, constant documented rudeness to patrons and/or staff, noncompliance with Library policies and procedures, frequent unexplained absences from duty, or conduct which is criminal, infamous or dishonest in the eyes of the law. Employees are subject to immediate dismissal for removing materials from the Library without proper authorization; for the falsification of time sheets; or for the misrepresentation of information on applications. The Director will notify the employee of the dismissal charges by registered letter. The employee may make written reply to the charges and may request that the Director arrange a hearing before the Board of Directors. This hearing shall be held at least ten (10) working days and not more than thirty (30) working days after the written charges are sent by registered letter to the employee. The viewpoint of the staff member may be presented and a representative of the Library Employees' Organization, legal counsel, or another interested party may be asked to speak on the accused employee's behalf.

Retrenchment

In the unlikely event that retrenchment becomes necessary because of a change in library services, or a major budget upheaval, the services of some staff members may need to be terminated. WHENEVER POSSIBLE, THIS WILL BE ACCOMPLISHED THROUGH NORMAL ATTRITION. Any staff reduction will take into consideration job performance and seniority, and will be in reasonable conformity with the Equal Opportunity Employment principles.

Reductions will be made, with consideration of specific skills and specialties, in the following order:

1. Those who have passed the retirement age of sixty-five (65) but have continued employment.
2. Temporary and probationary employees.
3. Those with the shortest period of employment.

Staff members in agencies affected by termination of service or reorganization will have the opportunity to ask for reassignment to other positions of the same or lower levels for which they are qualified.

Since the Director is responsible for all staff performance, total library service within the system, and the maintenance of Equal Opportunity Employment practices, the Director thereby reserves the right to make such reassignment. This reassignment will be made with respect to the qualifications of the staff member, the effects of the reassignment within the system, and will also be made in consultation with Deputy Directors and/or Agency Heads. As long a notice as possible will be given if the release of staff members becomes necessary.

Retirement

Retirement benefits are provided through the Utah State Retirement System which covers all state employees and those of covered political subdivisions such as cities, towns, counties. Membership in this system is compulsory for full-time employees and for those working 20 hours or more who are not full-time students. Members who reduce their work hours are still covered by the program.

Both employee and employer are required to contribute to the system. Benefits and contributions may change from time to time. On

July 1, 1978, the contribution for the employee was 9.20% of his/her salary. Of this amount the Library pays 5% for the employee, leaving only 4.20% to be withheld from the employee's pay check. In addition to this amount, the Library also pays a matching amount for the total contribution for the employee. Each year a statement of the employee's account is prepared by the system.

Upon resignation an employee may apply for a refund for the employee contribution only. This includes the 5% contribution paid by the Library under the "employer-pay" plan, plus accrued interest. Funds may be left in the system and withdrawn at a later date in a lump sum. Refunds take several weeks to process.

Normal retirement age under the system is sixty-five (65), and all staff members reaching that age by December 31st will retire by June 30th of the following year. Annual extensions until the age of seventy (70) may be requested and approved by the Board of Directors with the recommendation of the Director. The Personnel Director will discuss retirement benefits with employees six (6) months prior to retirement.

STAFF DEVELOPMENT

In-Service Training

An in-service training program, under the supervision of the Personnel Office, consists of an orientation program for new employees and ongoing training programs for current staff. These programs are designed to encourage continuous development, increased efficiency, and individual job satisfaction.

The Orientation Program is planned regularly by the Personnel Office with assistance from Deputy Directors and Agency Heads. It is designed to give new employees an overall view of the Library: its history, organization and management, the services of various agencies, explanation of personnel policies, and other basic information.

Ongoing training programs for all staff members may be scheduled for various reasons:

1) to implement a new service to patrons; 2) to demonstrate the use of new equipment; 3) to teach new policies and procedures; 4) to provide "refresher courses" and workshops; 5) to build skills and knowledge in all aspects of library service. Staff members are encouraged to make recommendations for in-service training programs based on staff needs.

The in-service training programs supplement, but do not replace, departmental training. Supervisors are responsible for the continued development of their staff members. They are expected to see that each one is thoroughly familiar with the assigned duties of the position, trained in efficient performance and informed of new plans and policies. Supervisors are expected to give each individual an opportunity to assume responsibility, to find means of self-development and to make use of special interests, knowledge, and abilities. The supervisor should seek constantly for those staff members who are best qualified for promotion, and should assign duties which will aid in the development of characteristics and abilities needed for advancement.

Staff members are encouraged to visit other agencies in the system and other libraries to develop further their professional knowledge. When possible, supervisors should cooperate in scheduling employees to work for a short time in each others' agencies. Staff participation in committees, conferences, and department staff meetings is an excellent method of in-service training and guarantees the benefit of cooperative thinking in library planning and policy formation.

Performance Appraisal (Staff Counseling Interviews)
(This is a committee recommendation for future study and Board action.)

The Personnel Committee recommends that the Library consider adoption of a system of performance appraisal based on written performance standards and job descriptions. Both supervisors and employees would be involved in the writing of these standards, and evaluation interviews would take place after both had agreed upon evaluation criteria. We also recommend that this performance appraisal system be tied in with a system of merit raises.

The goal of these performance appraisals is to develop both the library and the employee; therefore, the emphasis at all times is on the job, not the person. We agree that this system is much superior to the usual checklist evaluations, which measure personality and are extremely subjective.

Until action is taken on this recommendation the current Classification and Pay Plan remains in effect. See Appendix.

Formal Education

The primary purpose for employment with the Salt Lake City Public Library is to fulfill a service as needed by the library. Employees are expected to place responsibilities to job before class schedules and requirements.

It is to the Library's advantage to have a well-educated staff. The administration encourages employees to develop their abilities by both informal and formal methods. Although the library cannot give released time for formal courses leading to a degree, supervisors, whenever possible, will try to arrange schedules so that staff members desiring to continue their education may be able to do so, especially if it is pertinent to their job. Already earned compensatory time may be used to offset hours used for classes. Service to the public must not be curtailed solely to allow a staff member to take classes, nor may schedules of employees not in school be changed without their consent to permit a co-worker to attend classes. This means that because some departments have larger staffs than others, it may be easier for those departments to comply with employee requests. Any change in the eight (8) hour workday to accommodate class schedules must be approved by the immediate supervisor, the Deputy Director, and the Director.

Released time for library-approved and job-related seminars, workshops and specific courses of study must be requested in writing and may be allowed at the discretion of the Director upon recommendation by the immediate supervisor.

Full-time staff enrolled in a formal educational program may reduce their work schedules up to four (4) hours per week for the period of a full quarter or semester and take a cut in their pay scale, without losing fringe benefits. Any requests for such a reduction must be made in writing to the Personnel Office and resubmitted for each additional quarter or semester.

The Library periodically offers, as budgets permit, funds to aid staff members to attend continuing education programs directly related to library issues or to the position. The Library Administration is charged with evaluating all applications. Further information is available from the Personnel Office.

Professional Affiliations

Membership for staff members in the associations of the profession is urged, but is not mandatory. These professional associations represent the purpose of all libraries, namely the improvement and extension of library service for all. They promote libraries as major educational institutions; establish standards of library service; assist librarians, libraries, and directors; publish articles, booklists, bulletins, etc., for the profession.

1. *American Library Association* . . . . is the national organization of the profession. Members receive the monthly publication. If re-

quested, the Library will pay basic dues for all Branch Heads, Department Heads, Deputy Directors, Assistant Director and Director.

2. *Utah Library Association* is the state association . . . .

3. *Salt Lake City Public Library Employees' Organization* is comprised of all staff members and exists for the social, professional, and economic betterment of the staff. Dues for active members are determined at the last Executive Board meeting of each year.

SALARIES AND HOURS

Salaries

Salaries of employees are reviewed annually in accordance with the job classifications and pay plan.

Each position in the Salt Lake City Public Library system has been classified in an attempt to relate each position to others in the system and to assign each a specific salary range. When new employees begin work, they will be told their position classification.

If the budget permits, salaries will be adjusted for cost of living increases at the beginning of the fiscal year (July 1st). These increases will be across the board for all employees. Pending the adoption of the Performance Appraisal Committee's report, other salary increases will be based on a system of performance appraisal tied in with merit raises, and will be given in January after an annual review.

The annual rate is based on 260 working days. The hourly rate may be determined by dividing the annual rate by 2080 hours.

Payment

All members of the staff are paid by check on the 5th and 20th of each month. Paychecks are available in the Business Office after 8:30 a.m. on these days. If the 5th or the 20th of the month falls on a Saturday, paychecks will be released on the preceding Friday. If payday falls on a Sunday, the checks will be held until the following Monday. In the case of the payday falling on a Sunday when the following Monday is a legal holiday, paychecks will be released on the preceding Friday *if at all possible* . . . .

Deductions

Regular deductions on each payroll are made for federal and state taxes, and social security (F.I.C.A.). Salaried employees' portions of the pension fund will also be deducted. Upon authorization by the employee, deductions are also made monthly for insurance coverage, the Credit Union, and the United States Savings Bonds program. Deductions for United Way are made as authorized by staff members.

Time Sheets

In order to insure that an employee receives due conpensation, each member of the staff keeps a daily record of the time worked on a staff time sheet provided at each agency in which the person works. This record shows the time the employee begins and stops work, as well as for salaried employees' overtime, undertime, vacation and sick time, making a complete record of the working time of each person. At the completion of the pay period the staff member totals and signs the time sheet attesting to the accuracy of the entries. Entries must also be approved and signed by the supervisor of the agency or the person in charge certifying the hours worked and their mathematical accuracy. The time sheets are then forwarded before 9 a.m. to the Business Office by an authorized person in each agency on the first day of the next time sheet period (usually the 1st and the 16th day of the month). The Business Office will make payment in accordance with the time sheet as submitted and certified. Discrepancies in time sheets may result in deductions which cannot be corrected until the supervisor certifies a correction or overpayment causing later deductions which cannot be corrected until the supervisor certifies a correction or overpayment causing later deductions which may inconvenience the employee. It is, therefore, important that all staff members and supervisors make every effort to insure the accuracy of the time sheets as submitted.

Any deliberate misrepresentation on the time sheet will result in the dismissal of the responsible person.

Overtime and Undertime

Salaried staff members are not usually paid for overtime because of budgetary limitations. However, salaried part time staff will be paid for Sunday time and any authorized overtime. If staff members are required to work overtime to cover a schedule, the time should be certified on the time sheet as compensatory time due. Certifiable overtime includes time spent at book talks, staff meetings, etc. No staff member may certify his/her own overtime or carry it over for more than two pay periods. When a supervisor certifies overtime for an employee, the purpose must be noted under "Remarks" on the time sheet. Overtime will be certified for compensatory time only when it is necessary for the operation of the library and not for the convenience of the staff member. No time credit will be given for work done at home. Overtime cannot be carried over into another calendar year, without the written approval of the Director.

Compensatory time should be taken as soon as possible. The days for a holiday should be taken in the two week period preceding or following the holiday if possible. The compensatory time for a Sunday should follow the Sunday worked within the pay period. Sunday compensatory time is reimbursed at time and a half. However, if the Sunday occurs toward the end of a pay period, it may be carried over to the next pay period. If Agency Heads find it difficult to arrange such released time, they should suggest some alternative and receive permission from the Director or the Assistant Director before proceeding with it.

Compensatory days are not cumulative as an area needs substitutes for long periods of leave. If an employee is ill on a day scheduled as a compensatory day, there is no further time due. It is inadvisable to schedule more than one compensatory day in conjunction with a holiday or annual leave. Agency Heads may schedule such time if it benefits the Library or if there are extenuating circumstances. These exceptions should be kept to a minimum.

Undertime may be carried forward but must be made up within the next two time sheet periods in 30 minute periods or more at the discretion of the supervisor, or deductions will be made. Previously accumulated overtime or vacation time may be used to cover undertime.

Hours of Work

The official work week for the Library is from Sunday through Saturday.

Each regular full-time salaried staff member usually works a five day, forty hour week. Custodians work the forty hours in different shifts.

The Main Library is open to the public from 9 a.m. to 9 p.m., Monday through Friday; 9 a.m. to 6 p.m., Saturday; and 1 p.m. to 5 p.m., Sunday. From May through September the Library is closed Sunday.

Rose Park and Sprague Branch Libraries are open to the public from 9 a.m. to 9 p.m., Monday through Thursday; 9 a.m. to 6 p.m., Friday and Saturday; and closed Sunday. Chapman Branch is open to the public from 12 noon to 9 p.m., Monday through Thursday; 9 a.m. to 6 p.m., Friday and Saturday; closed Sunday.

Summer hours (June, July, August) for all Branches are 9 a.m. to 9 p.m., Monday; 9 a.m. to 6 p.m., Tuesday through Saturday; closed Sunday.

Any request for a change in the number of hours to be worked must be made to the Personnel Office through the immediate supervisor. The Office will recommend action to the Director as the needs of the Library warrant.

Evening, Saturday and Sunday work may be required of any staff member. A full-time salaried employee is ordinarily not scheduled for more than two evenings a week and every other Saturday and every third Sunday, but may be so scheduled as circumstances necessitate. Schedules of employees working less than 40 hours per week may vary.

In the event of retrenchment as provided above, the administration may find it necessary to readjust working schedules to provide a maximum of public service within the limits of staff reduction. Such action may include regular evening assignments in excess of the usual two evenings, reduction of morning hours, assignment of staff to two or more agencies, reassignment of staff from nonpublic to public agencies, or such other working schedule arrangements within a 40 hour week which will meet the Library public's needs.

The work day for Library staff members in public service areas is from 9 a.m. to 6 p.m., or 12 noon to 9 p.m., unless the operation of the department requires that someone be there at 8:30 a.m. Nonpublic areas begin their business day at 8 a.m. and end at 5 p.m.

When the Library is opened on Sunday (October through April), staff hours are from 1 p.m. until 5 p.m. This means staff is at a service desk ready to work at 1 p.m., not just arriving at the Library.

Lunch periods are usually an hour in length, although the schedules of individual agencies might require less time in order to meet that agency's needs. Regardless of the length of the lunch hour, the employee will normally work the eight hour day.

"Breaks"

A staff member may take a rest period not to exceed a maximum of 15 minutes (including time in transit) per each four hours worked. Break periods may be taken only when there will be no interference with good public service and divisional routines. Break time is not cumulated or combined, nor is it added to meal time or taken to leave early, or to make up time.

Time for Voting

For official public elections, full-time salaried staff members may use up to one hour of Library time to vote, if necessary. This must be prearranged with the head of the department or branch.

Transportation Costs and Time

Bus fare or mileage and traveling time are allowed when transfers to other agencies break into the regular schedule of a staff member. This includes only official library business such as book talks and school visits.

Branch library staff members who come to the Main Library for official business during the working day other than regularly scheduled meetings are reimbursed for extra bus fare or mileage. However, a staff member who lives downtown and stops at the Main Library before driving to the branch or vice versa is not compensated for extra mileage or carfare since no extra expenditure is involved. Parking and traffic tickets cannot be reimbursed by the Library. Parking fees may be paid with prior approval of the Business Office and only for Library business.

Staff members regularly assigned to branches are expected to pay their own transportation to their regular place of work and are compensated only for extra travel.

Mileage will be calculated . . . . and all requests for reimbursement . . . . must be submitted to the Business Office on the proper form.

For trips of more than one hundred miles, the Library Administration may opt to pay for gas expenses only rather than mileage. All such trips must be approved in advance by the Administration.

ABSENCES

Emergency Absence

Emergency absence or any other unplanned absence is reported to the immediate supervisor or the agency as soon as possible. If necessary, a long distance phone call must be made or a telegram must be sent. A staff member who does not inform the supervisor may find his/her position filled by another upon return.

Vacations

The following two vacation categories have been set up in accordance with other libraries and standards set by the American Library Association. Professional staff members with a library science degree at the master's level receive 22 working days (176 hours) vacation annually.

All other full-time salaried staff receive a ten working day (80 hours) vacation. Those who have worked for the Library two to five years will receive 15 days (120 hours). An additional day is given (up to 22 days) for each year worked after five years.

Vacations are calculated on a year running from the beginning of the fifth pay period (September 1) through next year's fourth pay period (August 31). Accrued vacations, according to the full periods worked, may be taken at any time within the current calendar year with approval of agency head. However, it must be taken in no less than four (4) hour blocks of time.

New staff members are granted a proportionate vacation credit beginning with the first full pay period worked, but are not allowed vacation time until after 12 full pay periods (6 months) are worked.

Part-time salaried employees receive a proportionate amount of vacation calculated from the basic weekly schedule. Hourly employees receive no vacation with pay. Vacation allowance is not determined from *any* overtime worked.

Vacations may be taken at any time within the current calendar year with the approval of the supervisor and at the convenience of scheduling. Supervisors should be informed a month in advance or as soon as possible, by the employee wishing to take a vacation.

Each agency head will stagger vacations so that only a minimum number of staff members are away at any one time, thus leaving enough staff to cover the schedules. Staff may be borrowed from other agencies only in extraordinary circumstances and with the consent of the Deputy Directors concerned. The schedules of hourly employees should not be increased to cover desks, but their hours may be rearranged within two pay periods. If such scheduling is not possible the supervisor will work out a schedule where the hourly employees work a minimum number of additional hours. This schedule then needs to be approved by the Director, or Director of Personnel before becoming effective.

Instructions concerning vacation procedure along with a sheet showing vacation time due each individual are sent out from the Business Office in April. The Agency Head will have first choice of vacation, followed by each staff member in order on the basis of seniority with the library system.

Vacation benefits are to allow each employee time away from work for rest, recreation, and the pursuit of non-employment objectives. Payment for vacation time accrued in lieu of taking vacation leave will be not permitted except on termination of the employee. Vacation cannot be held from one calendar year to the next without the written permission of the Director.

Leaves of absence without pay of more than 15 days throughout the year reduce the amount of vacation proportionately.

If a legal holiday occurs during a vacation period, an equivalent number of vacation hours will be due the employee.

Upon an employee's resignation that individual's unused vacation time will be paid in a lump sum with the final check or used to extend the employment period and taken as a vacation. When people who have resigned return for employment at the Library they will accumulate vacation time at the same rate as a new staff member.

Hourly employees are not eligible for a paid vacation but may apply for a leave of absence without pay (see below).

Legal Holidays

Eleven legal holidays are observed by the Library.

The Library will be closed for the following holidays:

New Year's Day	January 1
President's Day	Third Monday in February
Memorial Day	Last Monday in May
Independence Day	July 4
Pioneer Day	July 24
Labor Day	First Monday in September
Thanksgiving Day	Fourth Thursday in November
Christmas Day	December 25

The usual weekly day off is scheduled in addition to the time allowed for a legal holiday. Part-time salaried staff members receive a proportionate amount of time for legal holidays. Substitutes and other employees who work at an hourly rate do not receive any compensation for holidays.

When legal holidays fall on Sunday, the following Monday will be observed.

The Library will be open for the following legal holidays:

Arbor Day	Last Friday in April
Columbus Day	Second Monday in October
Veteran's Day	November 11

Salaried employees regularly scheduled to work on one of the above days will be given an equivalent number of hours off within a two week period before or after the holiday. Part-time salaried employees, those working twenty (20) hours or more per week, will take pro-rated compensatory time.

New staff members and persons returning from extended leaves of absence of five (5) working days or more without pay must work before a legal holiday in order to get credit for the holiday.

In lieu of Lincoln's Birthday, one day of personal leave will be allowed each year. This day must be scheduled in advance with the supervisor's approval and as scheduling permits.

The Library closes at 1 p.m. on Christmas Eve and 6 p.m. on New Year's Eve. Because the Library Board of Directors cannot give a bonus at Christmastime, the Board does grant this half day (4 hours) "shopping period" to all full-time salaried employees. Part-time salaried employees receive a proportionate amount. This time is normally taken on Christmas Eve, December 24th, when the Library closes at 1 p.m. Those individuals whose vacation includes, or whose regularly scheduled day off is, December 24th must take the "shopping period" at another time during December. The total week's working hours remain the same for those on duty at these times. When Christmas and New Year's fall on Saturday, the Library will be closed on the following Sundays. When Christmas and New Year's fall on Monday, the Library will close at 1 p.m. on Saturday, December 23rd, and at 6 p.m. on Saturday, December 30th. It will remain closed until Tuesday, December 26th, and Tuesday, January 2nd.

The Library will be closed on Easter Sunday. No compensation will be given for Sundays when the Library is closed.

Religious Holidays

Upon arrangement with the supervisor, a member of a religious group which has special observances on days other than legal holidays (Good Friday or Yom Kippur, for example) may be absent on the member's own time. If desired, the time may be made up at the discretion of the supervisor . . . .

Sick Leave

Sick leave is granted to all salaried employees at the rate of one (1) day per month during the first year and one and one-quarter (1¼) days per month thereafter (15 days per year). Although time accumulates from the date of employment, an employee is only eligible to take paid sick leave at this rate after working for one (1) month. At the beginning of each fiscal year, unused sick leave cumulates (up to 135 days). If there is not sufficient cumulated sick leave to cover an employee's illness, vacation time may be used or a deduction will be made from the employee's salary.

Sick leave is used in the following conditions: absence due to the employee's illness, injury, or exposure to contagious disease which could be communicated to other employees and to absence due to illness in the employee's immediate family. Sick leave is allowed for dental and medical appointments that cannot be arranged on the staff member's day off. Supervisors must be notified in accordance with above.

If a salaried employee is ill and unable to work on one of the legal holidays that the Library remains open for service, that employee has the following two options:

1. Be charged with a day of sick leave and still be eligible for a compensatory day according to regulations on undertime and overtime.

2. Have no sick leave charged and the day the employee is ill be entered on the records as the compensatory day.

An employee who is unable to work four hours on Sunday, will, unless further illness precludes it, work 36 hours during the week, and be charged with a half day sick leave. If time is not taken during the week, no sick leave is charged.

If the employee is ill on the compensatory day given for the Sunday work, there is no further time due. This is the same as if the employee were ill on his/her regular day off.

In addition to sick leave the Library offers thirty working days hospitalization leave each year to all salaried members of the staff. Such hospitalization leave may be used only during the period that the employee is actually confined in a hospital. Hospitalization leave is not accumulated and cannot be transferred from one year to the next.

The Personnel Office may request a doctor's certificate to substantiate a request for sick leave in frequent, unusual, or patterned absences, or a city nurse may call on the employee. Abuse of sick leave is grounds for dismissal.

Any employee who has accumulated to his/her credit thirty (30) days of sick leave and has been employed with the Library for at least three (3) years may choose to convert a portion of the yearly sick leave grant to vacation under the following plan:

If the employee has used one sick leave days during the previous calendar year, he/she shall be entitled to convert five days for use in the following year. Such converted sick leave days shall be permitted as vacation days in addition to any other vacation award to which the employee is entitled.

If the employee has used one sick leave day, he/she shall be entitled to convert four days; two sick leave days, three converted days; three sick leave days, two converted days; four sick leave days, one converted day; and if five sick leave days are used, no converted vacation days will be allowed. For conversion purposes only, a fraction of a day of sick leave will be counted as a full day of sick leave.

The balance of the sick leave days allocated but not converted to vacation days as permitted above, less the number of days used during the calendar year as sick leave days, shall be carried forward as accumulated sick leave days to the maximum of 135 days.

Death in Family

One to four days leave is allowed for a death in the immediate family or household. One additional day may be allowed, when requested, to be taken from sick leave, compensatory time, or vacation time. If there is no such time available, full deduction will be made for the additional day(s). Part-time salaried staff receive proportionate time. For record keeping purposes, a leave of absence form should be filed with the Personnel Office at the earliest convenience.

The immediate family is interpreted to include father, mother, grandparents, sister, brother, husband, wife, son or daughter, and in-laws of the same degree of relationship.

Time may be allowed when needed, for the death of a relative outside the immediate family or of other persons where the closeness of relationship warrants. Such time up to three days may be taken from compensatory time, or vacation time, and if necessary from sick leave. If no such time is available, full deduction will be made for these hours or days.

If schedules permit, time may be allowed during a scheduled working day to attend funerals of staff members, retired staff, and members of their immediate families.

Leaves of Absence

Leaves of absence without pay may be granted for maternity, adoption, illness, travel, or graduate education and/or work experience that would benefit the Library. All leaves without pay, except military, are permissive, considered individually, and must be approved by the immediate supervisor, the Personnel Office and the Director before being granted. Requests for such leave must be submitted in writing on the approved form at least one month before the leave is to begin. Leaves without pay do not accrue vacation, sick leave, or holiday time.

Hourly employees not eligible for paid vacation may apply for a leave of absence without pay for vacation purposes. Requests must be submitted on a leave of absence form and entered on the vacation sheet.

Leaves of absence, except for military service, do not exceed one year. For approved leaves of over three months, a written statement of intention to return must be filed with the Personnel Office at least 30 calendar days before the date of expiration of the leave. The absence of this request implies an automatic resignation. If it is necessary to exceed a leave, a request may be submitted to the Personnel Office, at least 30 calendar days before the date of expiration.

For leaves of over 60 calendar days, every effort will be made to fill a vacated position for the period of the leave only. If it becomes necessary to fill a vacancy with a permanent appointee, the employee on leave will be placed on a reinstatement list at the expiration of the leave and will be offered the first vacant position for which he/she is qualified. An employee on the reinstatement list may refuse any position except the one vacated when the employee went on leave.

An employee who is granted a leave of absence to attend library school will be given preference in consideration for appointment to a professional position, but no definite promise can be made. If the employee wishes to be reinstated to a former paraprofessional or clerical position, he/she may be placed on the reinstatement list, pending a professional opening.

Maternity Leave

No uniform period of absence for confinement before and after delivery shall be required, but the commencement of leave for pregnancy, and the return to work, shall be determined by the employee and her supervisors in harmony with the advice of the employee's doctor.

Where sick leave is available to the employee, its use may be authorized for absence due to pregnancy under the same requirements as apply to other use of sick leave, including the requirement for proper medical verification as to the necessity for the absence. Where paid leave is not available, leave without pay shall be granted, upon written request of the pregnant employee, for necessary absences due to pregnancy, the same as for other medically required absences.

An employee shall not, in any case, be separated involuntarily solely because of pregnancy, but shall upon written request, be granted sick leave or leave without pay under the conditions as outlined above.

Military Leave

The Law provides that "inductees and enlistees who serve on active duty as distinguished from training duty, for not more than four years, are entitled to reemployment if they apply within 90 days after discharge or from hospitalization after discharge for a period of not more than a year."

Veterans returning to the Library will be given positions in the same grade they held on leaving to enter the service. They will be given credit for increments they would have earned within the grade. Time credit for the period of military service is granted by the Library and the Utah State Retirement System.

Leaves of absence with pay up to 15 working days a year, and without reduction of time credit, will be granted members of reserve units which require annual training periods.

Jury Duty

Staff members are required to serve on juries when called. All employees are entitled to receive and retain statutory juror's fees paid for jury service. No reduction of an employee's salary shall be made for absence from work resulting from jury duty for a total of seven days during the employee's term of jury service, whether consecutive or not. If the employee is required to serve for more than seven days, the matter of salary reduction shall be presented to the Board of Directors by the Library Director for determination. If the employee is required to report for jury service and is then excused, he/she shall immediately return to work or forfeit the day's pay.

Attendance at Professional Meetings

Staff members wishing to attend meetings and conferences sponsored by professional library or library related organizations of which they are members should make application on a leave of absence form to the Personnel Office at least one month before the conference. The application must have the approval of the staff member's immediate supervisor. This is leave with pay. For meetings, workshops, etc., compensatory time may be granted. Compensation in time or money may not exceed the regularly scheduled work hours for that day.

As a general rule, attendance should not exceed fifteen working days in any calendar year for all meetings and conferences. When a conference covers less than a week, it may be necessary to use the weekly day off for part of the conference time. A week at a conference cannot exceed the regular working week in the amount of time credited. Staff members are expected to travel over weekends whenever possible.

For attendance at the annual ALA conference, priority in assignment of funds will be given to: (1) a Board Member, (2) the Director,

(3) either the Assistant Director or a Deputy Director on a rotating basis, (4) a staff member at large, selected as described below. Any further funds available may be divided among those staff members who have elected to attend.

Staff members at large are selected by the Administration on the basis of written applications sent to the Personnel Office by March 31st. Applicants must be current members of ALA. In making its decision, the Administration will consider an applicant's professional qualities, potential, and participation in professional activities.

Attendance at pre-conference institutes, ALA Mid-Winter meeting, and other conferences or workshops is allowed under the rules given above if the Director believes it would benefit the Library. In such cases application in writing may be made to the Director for financial assistance which will be approved, or disapproved, within the limitations of the budget.

Guidelines for Financial Assistance to Attend Seminars, Workshops, Specific Courses of Study, Etc.

These guidelines are designed to clarify the circumstances when the granting of library funds to a staff member for attendance at job-related workshops, mini-courses, conferences, seminars, etc., would be appropriate. They expand, but do not supersede, the policies set down elsewhere in this document.

In addition to granting leave with pay, the Library may pay tuition and/or traveling expenses, or a portion thereof, for staff to attend workshops, conventions, or other educational activities within the following limitations:

1. Budget considerations.
2. The degree to which the content of the educational opportunity (in the opinion of the Administration) will benefit the employee in making his/her contribution to the Library.
3. The nature of the educational opportunity, e.g., the Library cannot subsidize the formal education of its staff. Hence, no leave with pay or other financial consideration will be given for classes, workshops, etc., for which the individual receives credit toward a degree.

All requests for financial assistance must be made in writing through the appropriate channels at least two weeks prior to the event.

APPENDIX A: AFFIRMATIVE ACTION PLAN

Policy Statement and Commitment

It will, at all times, be the policy of the Salt Lake City Public Library to practice equal employment opportunity to all persons without regard to race, creed, religion, color, sex, national origin, age in the case of individuals below the age of 65, and when they do not interfere with job performance, physical or mental handicap, and individual life style. This will include but not be limited to the following: employment, transfer, recruitment, termination, training, compensation, benefits, and promotions.

In order to implement this Affirmative Action Policy, an Equal Opportunity Employment Officer will be appointed by the Director of the Library. Adherence to this policy will be the responsibility of this Officer; however, it is recognized that a total commitment by all employees is necessary for the effectiveness of the program and achievement of the goals of the plan.

Approved by the Board of Directors of the Salt Lake City Public Library at its regular meeting on June 15, 1977.

> Signed by the President, Board of Directors,
> and the Library Director.

Dissemination of the Affirmative Action Plan

Internally
1. The Affirmative Action Plan signed by the Library Director will be distributed to all employees, and will become an integral part of the Library's Personnel Code.
2. A policy orientation session for all supervisors will be held, and progress and achievements of the Plan will be discussed at least four times a year.
3. Presentation and discussion of the Plan will be an integral part of all employee orientation and training programs.
4. Equal Opportunity Employment posters and policies will be posted in key areas of the Library, including the Business Office, Assistant Librarian's Office, Information Desk, and staff rooms.

Externally
1. The Library will advertise all job openings through classified advertisements in the local newspapers and/or the national professional journals. All advertisements will indicate that the Library is an Equal Opportunity Employer.

2. A special effort will be made to list employment opportunities with college placement bureaus, Utah State Employment Agency, women's organizations, and minority groups such as SOCIO, NAACP, Indian Center, Utah State Employment Security Office, etc.
3. A copy of the Plan will be sent to the American Library Association. Copies will be sent to other library associations, organizations, and library schools upon request.

Responsibilities for Implementation of the Affirmative Action Plan

Responsibility for overall implementation of the Affirmative Action Policy will be held by the Director of the Salt Lake City Public Library as governed by its Board of Directors. An Equal Employment Opportunity Officer will work with the Personnel Director and also department heads in monitoring, coordinating, and implementing the Affirmative Action Policy. Department Heads are directly responsible for implementing the Affirmative Action Policy within their respective departments. Every staff member will be responsible to live up to the letter and spirit of the Affirmative Action Policy. Noncompliance with the ideals expressed in this Policy will be subject to reprimand.

Board of Directors
The Board of Directors of the Salt Lake City Public Library has the authority to enact an Affirmative Action Plan and to instruct the Director to carry out this plan. Any change in the Affirmative Action policy will be submitted to the Board for its approval.

Director
The Director shall instruct by a written statement all employees to comply with the Affirmative Action Plan. Within 90 days after the end of each calendar year, the Director shall report to the Board of Directors the condition of staff utilization at the beginning of the year, the achievement of goals, and the status of all employees who have had personnel actions during the year. The Director shall appoint an Equal Employment Opportunity Officer from among the full time staff members who shall assist in monitoring the Plan within the Library system.

Personnel Director
The Personnel Director shall be responsible for the external dissemination of the Affirmative Action Plan and shall collect and

maintain in a reasonable order all employment data, disseminate legal information, and make known the Library's desire and commitment to employ members of minority groups through regular and frequent contacts with community groups, employment agencies, and the media. He/she shall report quarterly to the Director on the achievement of the goals of those aspects of the Plan which are his/her direct responsibility.

The Personnel Director shall be responsible for the posting of all vacancies for the information of the staff, and shall encourage and counsel present staff to make application. On an annual basis, the Personnel Director shall update the Staff Profile. [See Table IV in actual policy.]

Equal Employment Opportunity Officer

The Equal Employment Opportunity Officer shall have the responsibility of monitoring procedures in order to eliminate discriminatory practices within the employment system, and shall be responsible for the internal dissemination of the Affirmative Action Plan. This Officer shall report quarterly to the Director on the progress made toward the achievement of the goals of those aspects of the Plan which are his/her direct responsibility. Of major importance shall be the Officer's position as a liaison between management and the employee. He/she shall deal with Affirmative Action questions and grievances brought to his/her attention by individuals of the staff.

The Equal Employment Opportunity Officer shall also head a committee of staff members to provide a broadened base for improvement of policies and programs. This committee shall be comprised of no fewer than five staff members who represent a cross-section of agencies and positions in the Library. Their charge shall be to review, revise, and update the Affirmative Action Policy on a yearly basis.

The Equal Employment Opportunity Officer shall be appointed by the Director and shall be other than the Personnel Director. Since this Officer will have duties that are more extensive than his/her job description, he/she shall be compensated by a professional fee set by the Library Board. This fee will be evaluated on a yearly basis. The Equal Employment Opportunity Officer is subject to the same disciplinary action of all employees who do not comply to the spirit and letter of the policy.

Coordinators, Department and Branch Heads

Supervisors shall have the responsibility to implement the Affirmative Action Plan in their units as part of their prescribed duties. They shall be expected to cooperate with the Equal Employment

Opportunity Officer and the Personnel Director in the achievement of goals.

Library Employees

All Library employees will comply with the spirit and the letter of the Affirmative Action Plan. Any employee who willfully violates the intent of this Plan shall be subject to appropriate disciplinary action including reprimand, suspension, and/or dismissal.

Utilization Analysis

The Library as an educational institution recruits all staff from both local and national levels. The following places for recruitment may be contacted depending upon type and needs of the opening at hand: the Utah State Employment Offices; local university and college placement bureaus; graduate library schools, especially those in the Midwest and West coast area; business colleges; Utah Trade Tech; the Rehab Center at the State Board of Education. Advertisements are also placed in local newspapers; in various library journals and magazines; in library employment "hot lines," especially those in the West. Contacts are often made with the Utah State Library for its placement service information. Attempts are made to contact minority groups within the community.

The Salt Lake City Public Library receives many applications directly through walk-in applicants and through the mail. These applications are grouped according to the background qualifications of the applicant and whether they have been submitted for full-time or part-time employment. They are then placed in current files to be called for interviews when positions are open.

In order to provide for upward mobility, notices of all vacancies are posted on staff bulletin boards, and staff are encouraged to make applications to the Personnel Office.

Professional personnel staff members are drawn from both the national and local work markets. Paraprofessional, clerical, and custodial employees are most frequently drawn from the local area.

Information and statistics concerning the population of Salt Lake City may be found in the 1970 U.S. Census. However, for this document, figures compiled by the Utah Department of Employment Security are as follows [these tables follow in the policy but are omitted here]:

    I. Population Statistics for Salt Lake City by Ethnic Status

    II. Categories of Library Employees by Rank and Minority Status

III. Minorities by Ethnic Status at Library

IV. Staff Profile.

The Staff Profile (Table IV) indicates that there are some areas of employment that need improvement, while other areas are adequately represented. For instance, when comparing the statistical makeup of the Library staff to the Salt Lake City population, the Library staff is under represented in the minority categories consisting of black, American Indian, and Spanish Americans. However, the Library has a higher percentage of Oriental and female employees than is representative of the Salt Lake City population in general.

As of November 1976, the Library employees represented in the minority category comprised 5.6% of the total staff; this compares to a minority population in Salt Lake City of 9.3% of the total population. In recent years the turnover rate in the professional and administrative categories has been small. Efforts will be made to improve the areas in which the number and percentage of minorities are low.

Goals and Timetables

The Library will evaluate the Affirmative Action Plan annually and attempt to retain and/or increase the number and percentage of minorities in accordance with the availability in the labor force in Salt Lake City and in the nation for professional positions.

Long range plans are for an increase in the number of Black and Spanish Americans in all categories and an increase of males in the paraprofessional, office clerical, and technician categories. In addition, efforts will be continued through in-service training and educational opportunities to upgrade current staff into higher level professional and other supervisory positions.

Internal Auditing

The Library will have an internal audit system which will be established to measure the effectiveness of the Affirmative Action Plan. An EEO-4 Report will be completed annually by the Assistant Director and forwarded to the Federal Equal Employment Opportunity Commission. This is an annual audit of the employment of minorities, men, and women. This report will be relayed to the Library Board through the Director at a regular meeting of the Board.

All supervisors will be requested to make notations on reasons for selection or rejection of all applicants referred by the Personnel Office. These notations will become a part of the personnel file of current staff, and will be available upon request to the applicant. The applicant will also be made aware of means of improvement so he/she may be more eligible for future employment opportunities. The notations on reasons for selection or rejection will be compiled in a monthly report submitted to the Library Director.

APPENDIX B: POSITION CLASSIFICATION SCHEDULE SUMMARY

Class Title	Grade	Requirements
PROFESSIONAL		
Librarian I	17	BA, or BS, paraprofessional post
Librarian II	20	MLS degree, entry level for professional staff
Librarian III	23	MLS degree, Assistant Agency Head, Specialized Library Tasks
Librarian IV	25	MLS degree, Agency or Branch Head
Librarian V	28	MLS degree, Deputy Director
Assistant Library Director		MLS degree, extensive experience
Library Director		MLS degree, extensive library and management experience
PARAPROFESSIONAL		
Library Assistant I	11	HS graduation, 2 years college and junior status
Library Assistant II	14	HS graduation, 2 years college and junior status, some experience
Library Assistant III	16	HS graduation, 2 years college and junior status, considerable experience, some supervisory duties
PUBLIC INFORMATION		
Public Relations Director	22	BA or BS, courses/experience journalism and public relations
TECHNICAL		
Printer	11	HS graduation, experience/courses in printing
Bookmobile Driver	15	HS graduation, experience as library clerk, a driver's license
CLERICAL AND RELATED		
Library Aide I	4	Pages, usually high school students, age 16
Library Aide II	9	Clerical, HS graduation, typing
Library Aide III	11	HS graduation, experience as library clerk, some supervisory duties and responsibilities
Clerk Typist I	9	HS graduation, typing, routine typing and clerical duties
Clerk Typist II	11	HS graduation, typing, contact with public
Secretary	16	HS graduation, stenographic, typing, clerical tasks
Accounting Supervisor	24	HS graduation, business and accounting classes and experience, supervises business office
Computer Operator	17	HS graduation, experience and training in computer operations

BUILDING OPERATIONS AND MAINTENANCE

Custodian/Maintenance	17	Building and grounds cleaning and maintenance experience, HS graduation preferred
Building Superintendent	26	Extensive experience in building maintenance and equipment, supervise maintenance staff, HS graduation desirable

SAINT JOSEPH PUBLIC LIBRARY
(Saint Joseph, Missouri)

Staff Manual
(Revised March, 1979)

TABLE OF CONTENTS

Conditions of Work
  Hours
  Schedules
  Overtime
  Rest Period and Lunch Hour
  Lateness and Disciplinary Action
  Miscellaneous
    Dress. Gum chewing. Personal telephone calls. A change of address.
Leaves of Absence
  Sick Leave
  Vacation Leave
  Holidays
  Leave of Absence Without Pay
  Attendance at Workshops and Conferences
  Maternity Leave
  Jury Duty
  Military Leave

FOREWORD

This manual has been prepared in consultation with the department heads and with the approval of the Board to inform the staff of the St. Joseph Public Library of certain policies pertaining to their employment, and, subsequently, to the total operation of the library. This document will supercede any previous ones dealing with personnel matters.

Like most codes of human conduct, this staff manual does not deal with every situation or answer every question. It is also bound in a loose-leaf folder, which means that it can easily be changed at any time. For this and other reasons the director welcomes your suggestions for its improvement.

Signed by the Director.

ORGANIZATION OF THE LIBRARY

Position Classification

Each position in the library, with the exceptions of the director, the secretary-bookkeeper, and the custodian of the main library, falls into one of three levels: department head, assistant library or clerk-typist, and page or custodian. The responsibilities and duties of jobs within a particular level or classification are similar throughout the system, and remuneration shall be made on the basis of the responsibilities of the job itself, the education and background of the person holding it, and the staff member's length of service at the library. All positions are subject to frequent review at the initiative of the director or at the request of a department head or staff member.

Process and Implementation of Change

All staff members are encouraged to make suggestions for the improvement of library services. They should discuss recommendations with their department heads, who should, when appropriate, refer them to the director for further review. Any problems or complaints involving or originating from the public should also be brought to the immediate attention of the department head, who should, when appropriate, inform the director.

EMPLOYMENT PRACTICES

Recruitment

The authority and responsibility for the selection and appointment of the director rest solely with the Library Board, whose activities are governed by the Revised Statutes of the State of Missouri and the Charter for the City of St. Joseph. The director shall be responsible for the selection and appointment of all other staff positions.

Selection of a Person to Fill a Vacant Position

When a position becomes vacant, the director shall prepare a written statement containing both a job description and employment requirements concerning experience; special training, skills and/or education; and other relevant skills, aptitudes, or interests.

The director shall maintain a file of applications and when a position falls open shall consider these applications after first giving ample and appropriate considerations to persons already employed by the library. The director shall advertise all professional positions in any or all of the following places: local newspapers, publications of the Missouri Library Association and the Missouri State Library, placement offices of graduate schools of library and information science and professional journals. The term "professional" as it is used in this manual refers to a person holding a Master's degree in library science from a graduate institution accredited by the American

Library Association. Non-professional positions shall be advertised locally when suitable candidates cannot be found from within the staff or the file of applications. The director and the department head concerned shall interview a minimum of three persons for each available position.

Procedures for recruiting and appointing the director shall be determined by the Board.

Appointment

The director shall notify a successful candidate by a letter which shall include the working job title or classification and location of the place of work; the beginning salary; the name and title of the applicant's immediate supervisor; the date on which the candidate should report to work; and a request for a written acceptance of the position to be addressed to the director. All unsuccessful candidates who have been interviewed for a particular position shall be notified in writing of a negative decision.

A new staff member shall be given a copy of the personnel manual and shall be asked to read it before beginning regular duties.

PERSONNEL ACTIONS

Probation

Each non-professional staff member shall complete a probationary period of three months, after which the immediate supervisor must indicate to the director in writing the employee's suitability for continued service. If during the probationary period in the department head's estimation, the employee demonstrates an inability or an unwillingness to perform satisfactorily the duties of the position, he or she may be dismissed by the director after being given two weeks' notice.

Professional staff members must complete a probationary period of six months, following which the director shall make a written evaluation of the staff member and discuss it with him or her. If after the six months' probation period the director decides to terminate a professional staff member, the latter shall be given one month's written notice.

Performance Evaluations

All staff members, both professional and non-professional, shall be evaluated annually for the purposes of assessing competence and encouraging self-improvement, giving them an opportunity to discuss the satisfactions and problems of the job, and improving the operations and services of the library. The department head will initiate the process using a form prepared by the director. The evaluation shall rate the staff member on such issues as promptness in reporting for work; knowledge of and the quality of performance of specific duties and responsibilities; initiative; capacity to develop and to improve; ability to work with both fellow staff and the public; and appearance. The staff member and the department head will discuss the latter's written evaluation with the director, after which the evaluation will be signed by the three parties and placed in the staff member's personnel file in the office of the director. If the staff member does not agree with the evaluation after the discussion, the right of appeal extends through the director. The director will review performance evaluations when considering a staff member's eligibility for a promotion, salary raise, reassignment, or dismissal.

The director's performance may be reviewed by the Board at their request.

Resolution of Grievances

All employees of the library are expected to work with their colleagues in a spirit of cooperation and harmony. However, occasionally problems develop. Misunderstandings between staff members, between a staff member and a department head, between a staff member and the director, or between a department head and the director should be resolved whenever possible at the level at which they occur. If two or more parties cannot reach a satisfactory resolution of a problem, they should be resolved whenever possible at the level at which they occur. If two or more parties cannot reach a satisfactory resolution of a problem, they should refer it to the next higher level of administration. Only after all other lines of communication have broken down should an internal difficulty be referred to the Library Board. If a problem should reach the Board, the parties involved should present written documentation of it.

Remedial or Disciplinary Actions

If in the opinion of the department head and/or the director an employee is not meeting performance standards or is violating the terms of employment, remedial or disciplinary action may be necessary. In most cases informal discussion initiated by the department head should suffice. Failing this, the problem shall be referred to the director, who may place necessary documents relating to the difficulty in the employee's personnel file. Abuse of sick leave, consistent tardiness, or unauthorized absence from work will at the discretion of the director result in the library's docking the staff member's pay.

Personnel Records

A personnel file kept in the office of the director for each staff member shall contain documents relating to the employee's recruitment and appointment; requests for leave; performance evaluations; and written grievances. Letters of reference; memoranda relating to performance; and records of attendance at job-related workshops or courses may also be contained in the file. The director will be responsible for each file's contents, and an individual staff member may have access to everything except recommendations which have been specifically designated as not to be shown to a staff member. A staff member may ask for and receive from the director a review of the file's contents and may appeal to the Board the director's decision not to show him or her a particular item. After a staff member leaves the library's employ, his or her personnel record will be transferred to the library vault and kept indefinitely.

Separation from Service

The separation of a staff member from service to the library shall take one of the following forms: resignation, lay-off, disability, death, retirement, or dismissal.

A permanent staff member who separates from service to the library for any reason shall receive payment of all salary earned to the effective date of the resignation. If the employee has been with the library for at least twelve months, payment shall be made for vacation leave accrued.

Resignation

A non-professional probationary or permanent staff member shall submit a resignation in writing to the director with a copy to the department head. The letter should contain the effective date of and the reason for resignation. Under ordinary circumstances, two weeks' (or ten working days') notice must be given by non-professionals and four weeks' (or twenty working days') notice by professionals. A full-time staff member who fails to give the required notice shall forfeit accrued vacation time.

Lay-off

If, because of lack of funds, the library must lay off a staff member, he or she shall be given at least two weeks' notice. Whenever possible, a staff member terminated for this reason will be considered for other positions within the system and given priority over applicants from outside the system.

Disability

A staff member may be separated from service for disability when he or she cannot perform the duties of a particular position because of physical or mental impairment. The director may require an employee to undergo an examination by a physician at the employee's expense to determine his or her ability to perform required duties.

Retirement

A staff member cannot be made to retire because of age before she or he reaches seventy. Permission to continue working past the age of seventy may be granted by the director on a yearly basis. A staff member wishing to appeal the director's decision in such a matter may have a hearing before the Board.

Dismissal

The director may terminate a staff member who does not meet performance standards or violates terms of employment after remedial action has been taken. A professional staff member shall be given one month's notice, and a non-professional two weeks'. A staff member who feels unjustly terminated may within a week of receiving notice request in writing to the President of the Board a full hearing of the Board. After such a hearing the Board shall make a final decision on whether or not to retain the staff member.

Dismissal of the director shall be by Board action only. The director shall serve at the pleasure of the Board.

SALARY ADMINISTRATION

Procedure for Determining Salaries

The director shall determine salaries based on the state of the library's budget, the requirements of particular positions, and the background and education of people holding them.

Other Salary Factors

Time Cards and Schedule of Paydays

Each staff member fills out a time card every two weeks and submits it to the department head for approval a week before the paycheck is issued. Paychecks are distributed by the secretary-bookkeeper every other Thursday and cover the two-week period ending the Sunday before the payday.

Deductions

Automatic payroll deductions are made for state and federal taxes and Social Security. Full-time personnel are also required to participate in the Missouri Local Government Employees Retirement System (LAGERS) after seven months of employment. Deductions may also be made for participation in the City's Blue Cross/Blue Shield health plan and a United Way donation. A credit union is also available through the City of St. Joseph.

EMPLOYEE BENEFITS

Health Benefits

A Blue Cross/Blue Shield health insurance plan is available to full-time staff members. The City of St. Joseph pays for the individual's share of the plan.

Staff members interested in this plan should consult the secretary-bookkeeper, who has an informational manual on the program, forms on which to sign up for the plan, and claim forms.

Retirement Benefits

All full-time staff members are required to participate in the Missouri Local Government Employees Retirement System (LAGERS) after seven months of employment. A LAGERS newsletter provides members with information on benefits.

CONDITIONS OF WORK

Hours

Central Public Library Hours	
Monday through Friday	9:00 a.m. to 9:00 p.m.
Saturday	9:00 a.m. to 6:00 p.m.
Children's Department	
Monday through Saturday	9:00 a.m. to 6:00 p.m.
Branch Hours	
Monday through Saturday	10:00 a.m. to 6:00 p.m.

The normal work week for a full-time staff member is forty hours. However, since almost all units of the system are open more than forty hours per week, individual schedules will vary according to departmental needs. All employees in public service areas will be expected to work an equitable number of evenings and Saturdays, and full-time staff members working from 1 p.m. to 9 p.m. with an hour off for dinner will receive credit for eight hours' work. Staff schedules on the Bookmobile, in the branches, and in Technical Services also vary somewhat.

Schedules

The department head is responsible for preparing and submitting to the director a weekly schedule by the Friday preceding the week in question. The department head is also responsible for informing the director's office of any changes in the schedule. A staff member is expected to adhere to the schedule and to notify the director's office when she or he expects to be more than fifteen minutes late. A staff member should also report illness as soon as possible to the secretary-bookkeeper and should make arrangements for notifying the department head.

Overtime

Under ordinary circumstances staff members will not be expected to work overtime. When working overtime is necessary, the department head shall report it to the director and make arrangements for the staff member to take equivalent time off as soon as possible after he or she has worked the extra hours.

Rest Period and Lunch Hour

A staff member is allowed a fifteen-minute rest period for every four hours of work. Under ordinary circumstances rest periods should be scheduled at the middle of the four-hour period at a time convenient for the department. The department head may rule on any exceptions to this practice.

A staff member working eight hours is entitled to one hour for lunch.

Lateness and Disciplinary Action

Staff members are expected to report for work on schedule and to adhere to the fifteen-minute limit on rest periods and one-hour limit on lunch time. Lateness of any kind must be made up under the direction of the department head, and excessive tardiness will be reported to the director, who has the authority to dock a staff member's pay for continued abuses.

Miscellaneous

Dress. Staff members are expected to dress neatly in clothes which are appropriate for their work. The Board of Directors have decided that the following clothes are unacceptable: bare-shouldered or sun dresses; blue jeans; shorts; culottes; and barefoot thongs. Hose or knee socks must also be worn.

Gum chewing is not permitted.

Personal telephone calls should be made on the library lines only when absolutely necessary and should be of short duration, especially when made from a public service desk.

A *change of address* should be reported immediately to the director's office.

LEAVES OF ABSENCE

Sick Leave

Sick leave is leave with pay to be taken in the event of the illness of a staff member; the illness or death of a member of an employee's immediate family; or a medical appointment which cannot be made during a staff member's regular time off. If a full-time staff member does not wish to draw sick leave for any of these purposes, she or he may make up the time lost.

After a new full-time staff member has worked three months she or he begins to accumulate sick leave at the rate of one day per month. A maximum of sixty days of sick leave may be accumulated. No sick leave may be taken until earned.

Vacation Leave

After a permanent, full-time staff member has completed six months' service with the library, she or he shall be eligible for a vacation.

Permanent, full-time, non-professional staff members earn vacation time at the rate of 5/6 of a day per month, totaling 10 working days per calendar year. Permanent, full-time, professional staff members earn vacation time at the rate of 1 ¼ days per month, totaling 15 working days per calendar year. Permanent, full-time, non-professional staff members who have completed five years of service are entitled to 15 working days of vacation per calendar year.

Under no circumstances shall vacation time be taken before it is earned.

Vacations are planned in consultation with the department head, subject to final approval from the director.

Under ordinary circumstances all vacation leave should be taken within six months after it is earned. Permission to accumulate vacation from one year to the next shall be granted by the director only in unusual situations.

Holidays

All full-time personnel receive the day off with pay on the following holidays: January 1, Memorial Day, July 4, Labor Day, Thanksgiving, and Christmas. Although the library will remain open on Washington's Birthday, Veteran's Day, and Columbus Day, full-time employees will receive compensatory time off for those days. In addition, a "shopping" day is granted each full-time employee at Christmas.

A holiday falling within a vacation period or on a regularly scheduled day off shall not be counted as vacation time. A holiday falling on a Sunday will, under ordinary circumstances, be celebrated the following Monday. Part-time personnel may make up regularly scheduled work time lost because of a holiday.

Leave of Absence Without Pay

A leave of absence without pay may be granted by the director provided that a request is submitted in writing at least thirty days in advance of the date of the proposed leave. The term "leave of absence" for part-time personnel is any single leave of more than two weeks' duration. Full-time personnel must draw on accrued vacation before applying for a leave of absence without pay, which for them would be defined as any time off in excess of earned vacation which cannot be made up within a regular departmental schedule.

Attendance at Workshops or Conferences

The library encourages the development of staff members by participation in workshops and conferences. Attendance at such activities, when approved by the director in advance, shall count as time on the job.

Maternity Leave

A staff member who becomes pregnant will be granted accrued vacation and sick leave. At her request she may also be granted a leave without pay to be taken before or after childbirth, not to exceed four calendar months. At the end of that period she may be reinstated in her former position, or one similar to it, or terminated at her request.

Jury Duty

A full-time staff member called for jury duty or subpoenaed as a witness in a trial shall receive full pay during any such time served, provided that compensation from the court is turned over to the library. A staff member wishing to take vacation leave and retain the jury fee may do so.

Military Leave

A full-time staff member who is a member of a military reserve unit of the United States when ordered to a training session shall be granted a leave of absence with pay not to exceed fifteen working days. Such a leave shall not be counted as vacation time.

LOWER MERION LIBRARY ASSOCIATION
(Ardmore, Pennsylvania)
Personnel Guide
(Revised April, 1976)

INTRODUCTION

As an employee of the Lower Merion Library Association you assume certain responsibilities. One of these is a commitment to the citizens of Lower Merion Township to provide the type of service one can expect from a first class library system. Your attitude and the manner in which you handle yourself when meeting the public contribute to the impact which you make on a citizen. This becomes a part of the criteria by which the Township is judged. Thus, YOU are an important and vital member of the Lower Merin Library Staff. Your handling of your responsibilities and the way you deal with both the library users and your fellow employees determine how successful the Lower Merion Libraries will be in meeting their objectives.

The Lower Merion Library Association consists of the Director's Office; the Processing Center; Ludington, the main library; Bala Cynwyd, the one regional library; and Ardmore, Belmont Hills, Bladwyne and Penn Wynne, the local area libraries.

The Association is the designated agent of Lower Merion Township to provide library services for the residents and taxpayers of the Township. The financial support for the service comes principally from the Board of Commissioners as an appropriation from the General Fund—about 80% of the total library budget. Local support is also needed (about 16%) which comes from local fund drives, gifts, fees and fines. There is also a "per capita" State allocation—4% of the total library budget.

GENERAL EMPLOYMENT INFORMATION

The Director of Libraries is in charge of personnel in the Lower Merion Township Libraries and along with your Head Librarian is your primary consultant when questions arise concerning your status or classification as a Township library employee. The Director of Libraries is responsible to the Township Manager and the Township Personnel Director.

Upon submitting an application for Township library employment, you will be required to have an interview with the Director, the Head Librarian, and in some instances, the Personnel Chairman of the local board of trustees. In addition, you will be asked to submit a list of references as designated on the written application. When you are hired, you are asked to accept the standards of a loyalty oath as required by state law.

The Director of Libraries and the Personnel Director maintain a cumulative record for each employee in the Township's library service. Every change in status as an employee is reported and recorded. The complete history of your career with the Township libraries is recorded in this manner.

POSITION CLASSIFICATIONS

Professional

In general, these positions require persons who have knowledge of library work and an accredited degree. A head librarian or head of a department must be a full time employee. The professional classification consists of the following positions: Director of Libraries, Assistant Director of Libraries, Coordinator of Reference Services, Coordinator of Children's Services, Librarian IV (Cataloger), Librarian III, Librarian II, and Librarian I.

Non-Professional

These positions, being similar to other departments in the Township, do not require any library training to qualify. This classification consists of the following positions: Library Assistant II, Library Assistant I, Administrative Secretary II, Administrative Secretary I, and Senior Page, Junior Page, Custodian.

The organization of the Lower Merion Township libraries is described in the classification plans which are available in each library. A statement of qualifications and duties for each position are a part of this plan. However, as new positions are created and responsibilities change in present positions, these changes are then incorporated in the present plan.

PERSONNEL PRACTICES

As a new *full time* employee, you are a probationary appointee for the first three months. At that time, your job performance will be reviewed by the Director of Libraries and the Township Personnel Director. Upon satisfactory performance, you receive permanent employment status. Employees shall be entitled to receive benefits after the completion of three (3) months continuous employment.

As a *part time* employee you are paid on an hourly basis for time worked as scheduled and are not eligible for Township benefits unless specifically provided for.

Neither the Township nor the Township Library Association shall discriminate against or in favor of any employee on account of race, color, creed, national origin or sex.

Salary Schedules

The pay plan of the Library Association consists of a salary schedule for each class of position, with rates of pay so adjusted that they reflect the level of difficulty and responsibility of each class of position. The salary schedules are in line with those of other Township employees and, as closely as possible, to those recommended by Pennsylvania Library Association and American Library Association.

Hours of Work

Full Time: These are employees who have been hired to fill permanent job vacancies and regularly work the schedule each week, as determined by the head librarian. A typical schedule is as follows: 7 ½ hours per day: 37 ½ hours per week as scheduled by your head librarian, lunch hour – 1 hour, 5 workdays per work week, and 2 evenings per week and every other Saturday required.

Part Time: These are employees who are employed to perform specific jobs of a permanent nature which require less work time. The Head Librarian is responsible for establishing the work schedule for these employees.

Sunday Hours: Between September and June, *all* employees are required to work a minimum of 3 Sunday afternoons at the Ludington Library. The Sunday working hours are 1:00 P.M. to 5:00 P.M.

Pay Procedure

All employees are paid every other Friday . . . .

Payroll Deductions

There are several *deductions* that the Township is required or authorized to take from your pay. They are: deductions for Federal and State Income Tax, deductions for Lower Merion Township Occupational Privilege Tax, deductions for Social Security, deductions for Life Insurance and Retirement, and deductions for other reasons which may be required or authorized from time to time. These deductions explain why you will find a difference between your pay rate and your "take home" pay.

Overtime and Compensatory Time

Generally, working hours will be limited to the normal schedule. Occasionally, the services provided by the Township Libraries will require beginning work before the normal scheduled time or remaining at work after the normal scheduled hour. When these emergencies or peak load periods occur, cooperation and the extra hours of work to complete the job are expected. Under normal circumstances, you will be given compensatory time off for these extra hours of work. The extra time for this work *cannot* be cumulative nor be reimbursed in less than *one hour* units, and must be authorized by the Head Librarian approving the extra work.

Payment for overtime work must be authorized by the Director of Libraries and the Head Librarian who approved the extra work.

Sunday Hours.

A *professional employee* is granted compensatory time off for Sunday hours worked, subject to the approval of the Director of Libraries.

A *full time non-professional employee* who is required to work a Sunday afternoon is paid time and a half for these hours.

A *part-time employee* who is required to work a Sunday afternoon is paid at the regular hourly rate.

Coffee Break

Coffee breaks are to be limited to 10 minutes and are a privilege offering opportunity for mental and physical refreshment and improved efficiency, rather than a "social right." Coffee break time is not to be regarded as "time off" or to be cumulative for any reason whatsoever.

Late to Work

Punctuality is expected at all times. However, if you are going to be late to work or late returning from lunch hour for any reason, you must call your immediate supervisor, explain the circumstances surrounding your absence and advise him or her when you expect to arrive. Habitual lateness will be reason for a deduction from salary or cause for dismissal.

EMPLOYEE BENEFITS

The following are provided and paid for by the Township and effective at completion of the 3 month continuous service.

Life Insurance

Full-time Township library employees are protected by a $5,000 group life insurance plan. Additional coverage is available as explained in the Township Insurance Booklet.

Health Insurance

Medical protection under a group insurance policy with Blue Cross/ Blue Shield is provided by Lower Merion Township. *Full-time employees* and their families are covered at no cost to the employee. *Part-time employees* who work 20 hours or more per week receive individual coverage at no cost with the option to enroll family members at the prevailing group rates and at the employees' expense. These costs will be billed on a quarterly basis through the Township's accounting department.

By joining the Township group plan, you obtain certain premium advantages, since premium payments are lower when the insurance is taken on a group basis instead of individually.

Hospital Medical Insurance

Blue Cross Co-Pay Preferred 365, Blue Shield Prevailing Fee 100, Major Medical—$25,000 Maximum, Blue Shield Basic Dental Program, Co-pay Prescription Drug Program, and Vision Care. Township pays full monthly premium for full-time employees, spouses, dependents to age 19 and dependent students to age 23 . . . .

Workmen's Compensation

Employees absent from duty due to on-the-job injury are covered by Workmen's Compensation insurance and receive full pay according to the basic rate of pay received from a standard work week. Any compensation payments made directly to Township employees are to be endorsed over to the Township. The Township will also pay such employees full compensation for any waiting period provided under Workmen's Compensation Law.

If you are absent from work due to an accident and are covered by Workmen's Compensation insurance, and willfully fail to fulfill all of the conditions necessary to receive Workmen's Compensation benefits, you are not entitled to any payments from the Township until such conditions are fulfilled.

RETIREMENT

The Township sponsors a retirement program for all its *full time employees*. Participation in this retirement program is mandatory. It is impossible to set forth all the details here. You may consult with the Director of Libraries or the Township Personnel Director for further details. While participating employees are required to contribute part of the cost of this plan, the Township will pay by far the greater cost of providing the benefits to which you will be entitled upon retirement.

Retirement Policy

Mandatory retirement is to occur at normal retirement date (i.e., age 65 for salaried personnel). In exceptional cases, an employee may be retained in an *acting* capacity to a limit of two years at the discretion of the Director of Libraries and the Township Personnel Manager.

A retiring employee may be considered for any part time position available within the system—the salary to be as already established for that part time position. A former head librarian may not take a part time position in the library where he or she had been head librarian. A part time employee reaching the age of sixty-five may be asked to remain on a yearly basis, subject to annual review, until age seventy, when he or she would normally retire.

A program for continuing preretirement planning has been established, to commence for each employee one year prior to retirement date. Personal interviews will be held with the employee, the Personnel Director and the Department Head. Interviews will include discussion of financial planning, insurance review, and other matters of concern to the employee, relevant to retirement.

In the event of your death BEFORE reaching retirement age, your beneficiary will receive the total amount that you have contributed, plus current rate of interest per year, compounded annually.

In the event of your death AFTER you have retired, your beneficiary will receive the difference between the amount you have received as retirement payments and that which you have contributed, plus current rate of interest, compounded annually.

If you should terminate your employment before reaching retirement age, you have two options from which to choose: You may have your contributions returned to you with interest. You may leave your contributions and interests with the insurance company and receive basic benefits, beginning at your normal retirement date, if you are vested by service and age (i.e., 12 years of service and age 55).

Social Security (Federal Insurance Contributions Act)

In addition to the Township's retirement plan, all employees are covered by the Old Age and Survivors Insurance Program (F.I.C.A.). The benefits you receive from Social Security, upon retirement, are dependent upon your total wage earnings and laws applicable to Social Security. The regular Social Security Tax is deducted from your salary as required by Federal law.

Paid Vacations

Full-Time Professional: 4 weeks after 1 year of continuous service; 5 weeks after 23 years of continuous service.

Full-Time Nonprofessional: 2 weeks after 1 year of continuous service, 3 weeks after 7 years of continuous service, 4 weeks after 15 years of continuous service, and 5 weeks after 23 years of continuous service.

Part-Time: 2 weeks with the *budgeted* weekly pay after two (2) years of continuous service, 3 weeks with the *budgeted* weekly pay after ten (10) years of continuous service.

The time of year you take your vacation will be determined by your head librarian, in conjunction with the Director of Libraries, according to the needs and activities of the library. An attempt will be made to grant your vacation at the time you prefer. However, the activities of the library receive top priority. In order that library services and activities be maintained at peak efficiency for the public, no two persons in the same library can be on vacation at the same time without approval from the Head Librarian. Seniority is the guide in this situation.

Plan your vacation as early as possible. You should give your head librarian your vacation requests by the end of April.

Vacation time is not cumulative from year to year, except in *most unusual* circumstances (and then with approval from the Director of Libraries and the Township Personnel Director) and then only until the next year and no longer.

Should you leave the Township service before one year of continuous service, you are not entitled to any vacation time or vacation pay. Should you leave the Township service for any reason, after one year of continuous service, you will receive normal vacation time or its equivalent in pay on a pro-rated basis as follows: employee leaves in January, 20%; employee leaves in February, 40%; employee leaves in March, 60%; employee leaves in April, 80%; and employee leaves in May – December, 100%.

Holidays

The Township Library Association grants a certain number of paid holidays. They are New Year's Day, January 1; President's Day, 3rd Monday in February; Good Friday; Memorial Day, last Monday in

May; Independence Day, July 4; Columbus Day, 2nd Monday in October; Labor Day, 1st Monday in September; Thanksgiving, 4th Thursday in November; Christmas Eve Day, December 24; Christmas Day, December 25.

If the holiday falls on Sunday, it will be observed the following Monday. If so scheduled, you must work the day before and the day following the holiday to be eligible for the paid holiday. When an authorized holiday falls within the vacation period, time equivalent to the authorized holiday will be granted, in addition to the regular vacation.

When an authorized holiday falls at a time when the library is kept open, compensatory time equivalent to the authorized holiday will be granted at the discretion of the head librarian and according to library activities.

Vacation pay will be granted to part time employees whose scheduled workday falls on a holiday.

Paid Sick Leave

"Sick leave" is defined as an absence of an employee from work by reason of illness or accident which is non-work connected and not compensable under the Workmen's Compensation Laws of Pennsylvania. Sick leave not used in any calendar year may *not* be cumulated from year to year. Sick leave shall be granted only for bona fide incapacity. Any fraud on the part of an employee in accepting sick leave pay under other circumstances shall be cause for dismissal.

All *full-time* employees shall be granted sick leave as follows: first 3 months, no sick leave; after 3 months, up to 7 working days; after 1 year, up to 30 working days; after 5 years and up, up to 60 working days. The Director of Libraries reserves the right to require a medical certificate.

All *part-time* employees: *no* paid sick leave.

Personal Business

Full time employees may request and be granted three (3) personal holidays of their choice provided seventy-two (72) hours advance notice is given whenever possible in writing and there is no conflict with the work schedule of the library. Regular full time employees who have completed the probationary period shall be paid at the regular straight time rate for the number of work hours regularly scheduled provided that such employees work the entire scheduled workdays immediately preceding and immediately following the holiday.

Death in Family

If there is a death in your immediate family—parents, children, spouse, or a relative living in your household—where your attendance at home is required, you may be granted three days leave with pay. This three day leave is not charged against your vacation or sick leave. To be eligible for this benefit, notify your supervisor or department head at least within the first two hours of the first working day that you are to be absent. If more than three days are required, they may be granted at the discretion of the Director of Libraries and may be charged against vacation or sick leave. If the death occurs outside the Township limits, you may be required to submit evidence of death for which a leave of absence has been requested.

Jury Duty

You may be called upon for jury duty, and if this should happen, you will be granted a leave of absence for the period you serve on the jury. This leave of absence will not be charged against your vacation or sick leave privileges. For the time you serve on the jury, you will be given full pay, according to the basic rate of pay usually received for a standard work week, minus the standard rate of pay received as a jury member.

Other Leaves

Requests for leave of absence without pay must be in writing and directed to the Head Librarian. The letter should be explicit and factual and state the period for which the leave of absence is requested.

The Director of Libraries and the Head Librarian will consider the circumstances and, at their discretion, may or may not grant permission to do so.

Absence Without Leave

Any leave, other than those previously covered, will be considered an unauthorized absence. Such leaves will be without pay and subject to disciplinary action. An absence of three (3) consecutive days without leave shall be considered a resignation. Upon receipt in writing of the circumstances and facts for the unauthorized absence, if conditions warrant, disciplinary action taken by the Director of Libraries and the Head Librarian may be modified by a subsequent grant of leave with pay.

TERMINATION PROCEDURES

Resignation

If, for any reason, you should decide to leave the Township Libraries' service, notify your supervisor at least two weeks prior to the last day you expect to work. Resignations MUST be submitted in writing. Upon termination of service you will receive, on the payday following your last day of work, all earnings due you, including accumulated vacation pay. There may be some benefits, however, such as pension repayments, to which you are entitled, but will not be paid at that time. These payments must be cleared through the insurance company. In this case, the insurance company makes the repayment directly to you and, therefore, it may be a short time after leaving the Township's service before you receive all payments to which you are entitled.

Dismissal

Normally, the dismissal procedure consists of the performance evaluation process, warning, and 2 weeks dismissal notice. However, should events indicate a need for immediate action, the Director of Libraries has the authority to dismiss any member of the library staff. The advice and counsel of the Library Board of Trustees and/or the Township Personnel Director will be obtained when advisable. A complete report of the reasons and actions taken will be made in writing to the local Library Board and the Library Association Board.

Cut-Back (Financial Exigency)

There may be occasions when the Township may have to reduce its work force, although this happens very infrequently. It is the Township's policy to consider both seniority and quality of service performed in determining its separation policy. Employees receive two weeks notice in case of a reduction in force, reduction in hours, or reduction in salary.

GENERAL INFORMATION

Inclement Weather

Snow beginning during the night: Director will consult with the Township on road conditions and take into consideration the closing of schools. If there has been no decision from these two by 7:00 a.m., then decision is left to the judgment of the Director, who will then notify staff. If conditions improve during the day, the Director may call the head librarian and recommend reopening during that day. The same plan will be followed in any other natural or weather emergency.

Snow beginning after the libraries have opened: The Director of Libraries, after consulting with the Township on road conditions, may call the Head Librarian of each library and recommend that the library close.

Political Activities

You may not discuss your political opinions with patrons of the library. No appointment or promotion will be dependent on your political activities or opinions.

Development and Training of Staff

The Township Library Association encourages the development of its employees through individual initiative on the job and attendance at courses and meetings sponsored by the District Library Center and the State Library Bureau of Development. Time off is granted at the discretion of the head librarian and the Director of Libraries for attendance at specific courses or conferences which are concerned with professional development and advancement. As far as possible, the privilege of attendance at such meetings is rotated among members of the staff. You will be paid your regularly scheduled base pay for such attendance, plus travel allowance.

On-the-job training is conducted by the head librarian. Regularly scheduled staff meetings require your attendance and you will be reimbursed in either time off or pay. A minimum of 4 staff meetings a year is required. Departmental heads meetings are held weekly. Attendance is required. These are held during the normal working hours as scheduled by the head librarian.

Educational Refund

The Township encourages all employees to further their development and effectiveness on the job by partially reimbursing tuition for work related study programs. The Township will reimburse an employee 50% of the cost of tuition (Lab Fees, Registration and Books included) up to a maximum of $300.00 per school year. Tuition reimbursement is subject to the approval of your immediate department superior, Director of Library, Personnel Director and Township Manager's office.

Information and application for Employee Tuition Refund can be secured from the Personnel Department through your department supervisor.

Complaints

Staff reports to Head Librarian. If you have any complaint that cannot be adjusted by the Head Librarian, the Head Librarian then reports to the Director of Libraries.

Staff Questions and Problems

Any questions and/or problems should be discussed first with your head librarian. If further discussion is required, it is then taken to the Director of Libraries, who in turn can call on the Township Personnel Director.

Performance Evaluation

The purpose of the performance evaluation is to indicate employee progress, to show areas for improvement, to aid in promotion purposes, to serve as an aid in salary administration (merit raises). All regular staff members are usually evaluated once a year. Non-professional staff persons are evaluated by the Head Librarian, the professional staff by the Director of Libraries; in conjunction with the local library board. The entire performance then is reviewed by the Township Personnel Director. The evaluation is in written form, followed by a personal interview in private, with the Head Librarian. Any staff member can appeal an evaluation rating through the Director of Libraries and the Township Personnel Director. The individual reports are kept in the Personnel file (private), but may be seen upon request by the person rated.

The Role of the Township Personnel Director

The Director is responsible for the following areas of Township management: In conjunction with Department Heads, the recruitment and selection of all Township personnel; Medical, health, safety and training programs for the Township; Position classification; Wage and salary administration; Benefit programs; and Township personnel policies and practices with regard to wages, hours and conditions of employment.

Staff Privileges

Staff Quarters

In each library, efforts are made to provide staff with an area away from the public, for rest and relaxation. The area is routinely cleaned by a custodian, but the staff is solely responsible for its general neatness. You are expected to wash, dry and put away your own dishes, to dispose of your own aging food supplies BEFORE they become noticeable, and to leave the sink, stove and dining table clean after each use.

Parking

Whenever possible, sufficient parking has been provided for staff and visitors on business. This is usually separate from the parking for patrons.

Book Purchasing

All staff members have the privilege of purchasing books through the Lower Merion Library Association Processing Center at the regular library discount. Each book must be ordered on the standard library order form, clearly marked with the name of the individual purchaser and library.

Loan of Materials

All staff members also have the privilege of borrowing library materials on which there are no other demands. Such materials MUST BE CHARGED OUT, but they may usually be kept beyond the normal loan period. Fines will not be charged. Any material in demand will, of course, be returned promptly by staff, whether or not that material has been formally reserved.

Staff Obligation

Dress and Manner

The dress and manner of the staff contributes directly to the overall impression a library makes on the community. As a member of the library staff, therefore, you are expected to dress and conduct yourself at all times in a way suitable to your age, position, work to be performed and any other special facts which may be pertinent. In case of doubt, consult your supervisor.

Attitude Toward Public and Other Staff Members

More important than dress is the employee's professional and personal conduct in his associations with fellow workers and library patrons. This is manifested through strict adherence to the accepted standard of accuracy, courtesy and good taste. Rudeness or loss of temper with the public is never permitted. It is important that you, as an employee, recognize your role as a public relations representative of Lower Merion Township and the Library System. In your dealings with the public, both off the job as well as during business hours, you must show respect and regard for the reputation of the Township, the Library System and your fellow workers.

Work Performance

An essential element of courtesy and cooperation is good work performance. Lateness in coming to work or in returning from a break, carelessness which results in mistakes, slowness which results in tasks left undone—all these place an unjust burden on fellow workers and detract from the quality of service given the public. You owe the library, the public and your fellow workers a full day's work of the best quality of which you are capable. A salary increase is a reward for improvement in the quality of your work, and not a reward for years of service.

Working in the spirit of the aforementioned rules of conduct will result in smoothly operating libraries which are a pleasure to patron and staff alike.

Selections
from
Policies

Affirmative Action, Equal Opportunity Statements

SPOKANE PUBLIC LIBRARY
(Spokane, Washington)

Affirmative Action Program

EQUAL EMPLOYMENT OPPORTUNITY POLICY

Spokane Public Library will continue the policy of appointing, transferring, promoting, and assigning work on the basis of the most qualified people available to perform the many tasks necessary in providing high quality services to the citizens of the City of Spokane at reasonable costs.

This includes providing equal opportunity to all applicants for employment and all employees; and administering all personnel practices such as recruitment, hiring, promotions, training, discipline, and privileges of employment in a manner which does not discriminate on the basis of race, color, religion, ancestry, national origin, sex or age (except where sex or age is a bona fide occupational qualification as defined by the State of Washington Human Rights Commission), marital status, the presence of a physical, mental, or sensory handicap, or liability for service in the Armed Forces of the United States, e.g., military service or reserve training.

This policy is in accord with the laws of the United States and the State of Washington, and reaffirms the Spokane Public Library's continuing commitment to provide equal opportunity to all employees and applicants for employment with respect to selections, terms and conditions of employment, assignments, training, promotions, and compensation.

Dissemination of Policy

1. Dissemination to all Library employees annually.
2. Discussion of policy at meetings involving Library supervisory personnel at least every six months . . . .
3. Incorporation of appropriate materials in Library supervisory training programs and Library employee orientation programs.
4. Encouragement of Library supervisory staff to attend and participate in conferences, workshops, seminars on affirmative action and interviewing techniques which are job related and nondiscriminatory.
5. Inclusion of policy and related information in policy manuals, publications, and communications prepared by Spokane Public Library. All Library vacancy notices and employment advertisements shall contain the phrase, "Equal Opportunity Affirmative Action Employer."
6. Notification of policy to City Hall Affirmative Action Office, Washington Employment Security, high schools, academic institutions utilized for recruitment, agencies concerned with employment/training of minorities and handicapped, and the Washington State Library.
7. Notification of union officials of the Spokane Public Library's Equal Employment Opportunity Policy and Affirmative Action Program.
8. Posting of Equal Employment Opportunity Policy on Library bulletin boards, both public and staff.
9. Inclusion of statement relating to Equal Opportunity requirements of various federal executive orders where appropriate in Library contracts, order forms, leases, etc.
10. Afford maximum practicable opportunity for minority business enterprises to participate in contracts and to act as suppliers of goods and services to Spokane Public Library.
11. Provision of copies of the Spokane Public Library's Affirmative Action Program to the public at cost and upon request.

Responsibility for Policy Implementation

The Library Director, as authorized by the Spokane Public Library Board of Trustees, has the overall responsibility for insuring that the Library's Equal Opportunity Policy is aggressively implemented by all levels of management. The Library Director will review the policy and the Affirmative Action Program to insure completeness and effectiveness.

Recruitment

Spokane Public Library will continue to seek out minority applicants through regular contacts with the following: Washington State Employment Security; educational institutions, both private and public; related library agencies or institutions; agencies which provide special training, counseling, etc., for minorities and handicapped; minority group organizations; and referrals from minority group Library and City employees.

Hiring Practices

Most Library positions are open and may be filled from either outside or within the Library. All job applicants are invited to file a Library application for employment. They are held two years, or as instructed by the applicant, in a chronological sequence. A data card, filed alphabetically, provides name, date of application, educational attainment level, desire for part or full-time work, and any other limitations indicated by applicant.

Library vacancy notices are circulated simultaneously among: internally with Spokane Library's various facilities; minimum of three (3) applicants in the file are notified . . .; sources of recruitment.

A walk-in, who has heard about a specified opening and wishes to apply, is considered if that person surpasses the qualifications of either the pre-filed applicants notified or the existing staff applying for the opening.

Transfer and Promotion

All Spokane Public Library vacancy notices are distributed internally and all employees, permanent and temporary, are encouraged to apply for potential promotional openings for which they are qualified. Transfers are encouraged for broadening experiences.

Facilities

All Library work areas, staff rooms, etc., shall continue to be maintained on a non-segregated basis.

Selection Process

Employment standards shall continue to be used only as a guide when considering applicants for employment. When feasible, individuals who fall somewhat below the normal standard may be hired and given an opportunity to display capabilities. Qualifications listed in Library vacancy notice shall be bona fide job requirements. Education and skill requirements listed must be essential to performance of the identified tasks. Interviews of all candidates for a specific Library vacancy are conducted by Library department head/supervisor of area where vacancy occurs. List of applicants together with recommendations are prepared by the Library department head/supervisor. Justifications, which are job related, are specified for first through third priorities.

Complaint Procedure

An *applicant* who alleges discrimination on the basis of race, sex, color, national origin, age (40-65), marital status, or the presence of a physical, mental, or sensory handicap, should follow specified appeal procedures.

1. Discuss it verbally with the supervisor specified in the vacancy notice.
2. If no satisfaction reached, reduce the complaint to writing using complaint form, within 30 days, date and sign it, and submit it to the supervisor.
3. If written reply is not made within 3 working days, or the complainant is not satisfied with the reply, the written complaint should be submitted to the Library Director. Time limits include:
   a. Complaint must be submitted within 5 working days
   b. Library Director must reply in writing within 30 working days.
4. If no settlement is reached in Step 3, the written complaint should be submitted to the chairperson of the Library Board of Trustees for consideration at the first regular Board Meeting following receipt of the complaint.

A *person currently employed* by Spokane Public Library who has a complaint, alleging discrimination on the basis of race, sex, color, national origin, age (40-65), marital status, or the presence of a physical, mental, or sensory handicap should follow the specific appeal procedures. This person's complaint may pertain to scheduling, work assignments, etc. Step 1 would involve verbal discussion with the immediate supervisor. Steps 2 through 4 are identical with those indicated [in the] above [paragraph].

Persons who believe they have experienced discrimination have a number of routes for filing complaints other than the Library Complaint Procedure. A person may file a complaint under any of the options listed below. A person may also file complaints simultaneously under the Library Complaint Procedure and the sources listed below.

1. *The Equal Employment Opportunity Commission (414 Olive Way, Seattle, WA 98101)* enforces Title VII of the Civil Rights Act of 1964 as amended by the Equal Employment Opportunity Act of 1972. The law covers employers of over 15 persons, labor unions, and employment agencies. It forbids discrimination in hiring, firing, or any term or condition of employment because of race, color, religion, sex, or national origin.

2. *Wage and Hour Division: Department of Labor (W. 904 Riverside Avenue, Spokane, WA 99201)* enforces Equal Pay Act of 1963. This act prohibits discrimination because of sex in earnings, including overtime pay and most fringe benefits. It requires equal pay for men and women in the same establishment performing substantially equal work requiring equal skill, effort, and responsibility. The work or job title does not need to be identical.

3. *Wage and Hour Division: Department of Labor (W. 904 Riverside Avenue, Spokane, WA 99201)* enforces Age Discrimination in Employment Act of 1967. This act prohibits discrimination on the basis of age for persons between the ages of 40 and 65.

4. *Washington State Human Rights Commission (Paulsen Building, Spokane, WA 99201)* enforces Washington State Law Against Discrimination. This act prohibits discrimination in employment (hiring, promotion, any term or condition of employment) because of race, creed, color, sex, national origin, marital status, or the presence of a sensory, mental, or physical handicap. Age discrimination (40-65) is also prohibited by State Law.

5. *Federal Revenue Sources.* Complaints may be filed with any Federal agency which supplies money to the Spokane Public Library.

6. *Private Attorney.* You may also use a private attorney to assist you file under any of the above.

Reporting

Monthly reporting procedures will be the responsibility of the Library Director. These reports will measure the effectiveness of the Affirmative Action Program. Weaknesses and strengths will be identified and changes to improve the program recommended.

Goals and Time Tables

Periodically, but at least annually, the employment situation at Spokane Public Library will be reviewed to determine any areas in which greater emphasis is necessary to achieve distribution demonstrative of equal employment opportunity. Where the need is evident, reasonable, specific goals and time tables will be established.

General

All Library management and supervisory personnel are personally and continually required to provide equal opportunity for all employees with regard to work assignments, training, transferring, advancements, and other conditions and privileges of employment. Their responsibilities include, but are not limited to the following:

1. Assisting in the identification of areas in need of improvement and establishment of objectives and goals to implement the Spokane Public Library Affirmative Action Program
2. Cognizance and responsiveness to local minority organizations and community action groups
3. Periodical review of hiring, transfer, and promotion patterns to insure objectives are met
4. Regular discussions with supervisors and employees to be certain Library policies are being followed
5. Review of the recommendations for filing vacancies to insure minorities are given full opportunities for transfer and promotions
6. Provide guidance to Library employees to help them adjust to their work surroundings in order for them to meet job requirements.

Active participation by Library management and supervisory personnel in achieving the goals and objectives outlined in the Library's Affirmative Action Plan shall be a condition of continued employment.

SONOMA COUNTY LIBRARY
(Santa Rosa, California)
Affirmative Action Plan

Responsibility and Authority

Under the general direction of the Library Director, the Personnel Officer has been appointed to serve as the Equal Employment Opportunity Coordinator. The duties of the Equal Employment Opportunity Coordinator are as follows:

1. Insure that all policies covering recruitment, employment and promotion are in accordance with the Library's policy of non-discrimination.
2. Develop appropriate policy statements.
3. Develop appropriate internal and external communications.
4. Assist division heads and supervisors in arriving at solutions to problems in these areas.
5. Assist in the development of programs for increased representation of minorities, women and the disadvantaged, and for the upward mobility of the same.
6. Implement systems that will measure the effectiveness of these programs.
7. Advise the Director of developments in the equal employment opportunity area.
8. Coordinate the activities and quarterly meetings of the Equal Employment Opportunity Committee which will be composed of the Equal Employment Opportunity Coordinator and appointed members.

Education and Orientation of Division Heads and Supervisors

One of the basic concepts of an equal employment opportunity program is that it is a fundamental and continuing management responsibility, the same as any other management function. Since it is to a large degree the attitude, motivation and personal involvement of division heads and supervisors that determine the degree of success of an equal employment opportunity program, activities directed to the education and orientation of division heads and supervisors in minority employment and related problems should be discussed periodically through regularly scheduled meetings between division heads, supervisors and the Equal Employment Opportunity Coordinator.

Job Requirements

Entry level positions shall be periodically reviewed to determine the most realistic and necessary requirements in order to insure minority group candidates, women and disadvantaged persons maximum access to positions.

Medical standards shall realistically relate to position requirements.

Classification specifications shall be periodically reviewed with appropriate division heads and supervisors to insure that selection criteria are related to position requirements.

Those requirements which appear to be barriers to employment of minorities, women and the disadvantaged shall be regularly reviewed, including but not limited to arrest records, educational attainment, continuity of employment history and physical handicaps, and shall be evaluated in the light of achieving the goals of equal employment opportunity.

Validation of Tests

Any and all tests, as now defined in the Equal Employment Opportunity Commission's "Guidelines on Employee Selection Procedures," shall be reviewed for job relatedness. This review of selection procedures should be made by the Equal Employment Opportunity Committee and shall be an on-going project.

Recruiting, Interviews and Certifications

Those responsible for recruiting applicants shall initiate whatever contacts are appropriate to assure minority applicant flow. An inventory of minority applicant flow will be maintained by the Personnel Officer. All personnel involved in recruiting, screening, selection, promotion and related processes will be instructed in methods of avoiding any possibility of bias in personnel actions.

Procedures shall be established and necessary directives issued whereby interviewers and supervisors with appointing responsibilities shall document the reasons for non-employment of any applicant. It is the intent of such procedure that non-selection of any applicant shall be for good and sufficient cause based upon the job performance requirements for which the applicant is being considered, without regard to race, color, religion, national origin or sex.

Internal Audits

Statistical data shall be compiled, maintained and analysed by the Personnel Officer regarding application, examination and employment with the Library in respect to equal employment opportunities. A periodic report will be made at least quarterly to the Equal Employment Opportunity Committee regarding minority and female representation by division and classification, and reviewed by the Committee in the light of achieving the objectives of equal employment opportunity.

Goals and Timetables

The Library will constantly monitor its Equal Employment Opportunity Program for the purpose of determining under-utilization of minorities.

Similar to other management functions, positive action will be achieved through the establishment of realistic goals and timetables. These goals will be established to correct previously determined areas deficient of minority/female representation, training programs, and other similar aspects of employment and upgrading.

Accountability for achievement of established goals and timetables will be with each division head, the same as any other management function.

Review Body

In order to provide an effective review body, the Library Commission shall, in addition to its other duties, monitor and evaluate the Equal Employment Opportunity Program and issue directives to the Library Director and Equal Employment Opportunity Coordinator when specific actions are deemed both appropriate and practical.

SKOKIE PUBLIC LIBRARY
(Skokie, Illinois)
Affirmative Action Statement

Skokie Public Library is committed to provide equal opportunity through its employment practices and through the many activities, programs and services it provides to the community. The Library will continue to make all personnel decisions without regard to race, color, religion, sex or national origin. The Library will continue to offer activities, programs and services that will serve the community without regard to race, color, religion, sex or national origin. The Library will continue to develop and offer activities, programs and services that are sensitive to the emerging needs of all citizens, including members of minority groups.

Furthermore, The Library will undertake an affirmative action program to expand quality of opportunity in employment. And finally, The Library will continue to initiate programs that will increase, on the part of all its personnel, a sensitivity to the interests and needs of those who have historically been discriminated against.

UNIVERSITY OF NEW MEXICO
(Albuquerque, New Mexico)
University Policy on Affirmative Action

Introduction

This will serve to reiterate the policy of the University of New Mexico to work continually toward improving recruitment, employment, development and promotional opportunities for minority employees and for women.

Policy Statement

It is the policy of the University of New Mexico to provide equal opportunity in all personnel actions including employment, compensation, benefits, transfers, layoffs, returns, institutionally-sponsored education, training, tuition assistance, social and recreational programs and advancement, without regard to race, color, religion, national origin, sex, handicap, or age.

One of the most complex problems which confronts the University and our nation today is the absence of true equal opportunity for all people without regard to race, color, religion, sex, age, physical handicap or national orgin.

It is the policy of the University of New Mexico that maternity leave will be granted on the same basis as sick leave. This policy provides that those individuals who take maternity leave will be guaranteed sick leave pay during their absence. Any leave required above sick leave accruals will be granted under our policy for leave of absence for extended illness, injury, or personal reasons. Those who avail themselves of this leave will be reinstated to their original position or one of like status and pay without loss of seniority or accrued benefits other than the sick leave or leave of absence, actually utilized by the employee during her absence. Copies of the University's Sick Leave and Leave of Absence policies are part of the Personnel Policies and Practices Manual.

It is the policy of the University of New Mexico that employment of relatives is acceptable with the limitations specified below:

1. No supervisor may employ a member of his immediate family. Nor may any supervisor employ a member of the immediate family of any of his line supervisors without the advance approval of the President.

2. Relatives, regardless of employment rank or classification, may be employed in a separate department, but no relative can be employed in the same department where one of his relatives holds supervisory rank or has hiring authority.

3. A department is defined as an organization reporting to a Dean or Director.

4. Relatives not holding supervisory rank or having hiring authority may be employed in the same department.

5. Relatives are defined as members of a person's immediate family and includes parents, spouses, children, brothers and sisters.

6. If there is a change in the family relationship or rank which would violate the above policies, the situation must be corrected within six (6) months by the transfer, resignation, or discharge of one or more of the employees so related.

The University of New Mexico has no policy which discriminates against an individual because of church affiliation or religious beliefs. The University of New Mexico has no policy which discriminates against an applicant for a staff or faculty position or a current staff or faculty member in selection, promotion, or the granting of tenure because of church affiliation or religious beliefs.

Recruitment of Staff Personnel

The Personnel Director is to engage in a sensitive recruitment effort with local community groups interested in the placement of minorities and women and to solicit help from these organizations in encouraging minority groups and women applicants to interview for employment. All regular, as well as innovative recruitment sources, are continually informed of the Affirmative Action policy. Regular contact is made with all known minority and women's organizations. These sources are used on a regular basis in all recruiting along with any additional minority and women search sources we can locate and develop.

Policy on Managerial Responsibility for Program Implementation

Vice Presidents, Directors, Deans, Managers, Department Chairpersons and Supervisors are responsible for controlling activities within their respective areas of responsibility to assure accomplishment of the Affirmative Action Program and its goals. Their work performance evaluations will include an evaluation of their Affirmative Action efforts as well as other criteria. It must be emphasized, however, that the responsibility for Affirmative Action is not limited to upper-level administrators, but extends to all levels at the University, and particularly to all employees with any personnel duties.

While there have been civil rights laws enacted during the past decade to assure such equality, many individuals and institutions have been negligent in meeting the requirements of these laws to the extent that equal opportunity for all people, in fact, is not a reality.

Consequently, the denial of equal access to opportunities for development and growth has permitted discrimination to continue in a variety of forms. This means that proposed remedies must go beyond the mere announcement of an equal opportunity policy. We must recognize and accept our responsibility to design and implement programs which strike at the total problem rather than make simply overt manifestations. In a similar manner, women have found themselves locked into sexual role stereotypes which have acted to exclude their full participation in the mainstream of the working world. Attitudes towards women have prevented women from realizing their full potential and achieving equality within the institutions of society.

We must, therefore, strive aggressively to insure the entry and growth of minorities and women in our work force until it is emphatically clear that equality of opportunity in the University is a fact as well as an ideal.

To achieve ultimate effectiveness in this matter, our efforts toward equal opportunity for all people in our employment must extend above and beyond the letter of the law, that is, total commitment to this goal on the part of all personnel.

Handicapped as an Included Protected Group

[Detail omitted]

Bona Fide Occupational Qualification

[Detail omitted]

Authority Vested in Director, Affirmative Action Program

This policy will be administered for the University by the appointed Director, Affirmative Action Program, who, in this capacity, will report directly to the Office of the President. Progress reports will be submitted to the Office of the President on a regular quarterly basis by the Director, Affirmative Action Program.

THE UNIVERSITY OF TENNESSEE
(Knoxville, Tennessee)
Equal Employment Opportunity and Affirmative Action

Objective

To set, define, and communicate broadly the policy of The University of Tennessee, Knoxville concerning fair employment practices and equal employment opportunity for all UTK employees and applicants for UTK employment.

Procedure

The University of Tennessee, Knoxville offers equal employment opportunity to all its employees and to all applicants for UTK employment without regard to race, religion, sex, age, national origin, or veteran status, as required by federal, state, and local laws, executive orders, and regulations pertaining to fair employment practices. UTK is also prepared to make reasonable accommodations to allow employment of handicapped individuals. This policy extends to recruitment, employment, promotion, UTK-sponsored training programs, educational opportunities, compensation, leave, tuition assistance, transfers, lay-offs, return from lay-offs, demotions, terminations, social and recreational programs, use of University facilities, and treatment as individuals. This policy is binding on all UTK employees engaged in any of the processes or programs listed above.

UTK views this policy as being basic to the institutional commitment, not merely a means of complying with orders, laws, and regulations to which it is subject.

The following procedures have been established in order to implement this policy:

1. Advertising copy prepared to announce available positions at UTK shall comply in all regards with federal, state, and local regulations pertaining to equal employment opportunity. In the case of faculty, administrative, and professional advertisements, copies of advertisements placed are to be maintained on file by the head of the unit advertising the vacancy. The UTK Personnel Office will place all advertisements for clerical and supporting position vacancies and will maintain on file copies of all such advertisements.

2. Sources of referral utilized by UTK units are to be informed in writing of this policy and UTK's intention to seek out and employ

qualified applicants without regard to race, color, religion, sex, age, national origin, handicap, or veteran status. A copy of such notification shall be maintained on file by the head of the unit contacting the source of referral, in the case of faculty, administrative, and professional positions. The UTK Personnel Office will notify sources of referral for clerical and supporting positions and will maintain on file copies of the notifications.

3. Employment decisions shall be based solely upon an individual's qualifications for the position for which he/she is being considered.

4. Promotions shall be made in accord with the principles of equal employment opportunity. Only valid, job related requirements for advancement will be established.

5. No employee shall be excluded from participation in any University sponsored activity or denied the benefits of any University program on the grounds of race, color, religion, sex, age, national origin, or veteran status. The University is prepared to make reasonable accommodations to allow participation by the handicapped in its programs, activities, and benefits.

6. Evaluation of supervisors' and managers' work performance will include a review of their equal employment efforts and results, as well as other criteria.

7. Reports required by federal, state, and local agencies with regard to equal employment opportunity and affirmative action shall be submitted by the Office of the Vice Chancellor for Planning and Administration, which will also maintain the reports on file.

UTK deans, directors, managers, and supervisors shall be appraised of this policy in writing and shall be reminded of its provisions at least once a year. A record shall be made of such notices by the Affirmative Action Coordinator. Employee Handbooks, the Faculty Handbook, the Affirmative Action Plan, and other appropriate documents shall contain this policy. This policy shall be posted in conspicuous places throughout the campus and shall be on file in the office of all budgetary unit heads.

In support of the intent of this policy, UTK has issued an Affirmative Action Plan. It shall be the responsibility of the Office of the Vice Chancellor for Planning and Administration to monitor the effectiveness of the implementation of this policy by monitoring the provisions of the Affirmative Action Plan.

Any UTK employee or applicant for UTK employment who feels that he or she has been discriminated against in any manner affecting his/her employment relationship because of race, sex, religion, national origin, age, handicap, or veteran status is entitled to seek relief through the following procedure. This EEO complaint procedure is available for use by all UTK employees or applicants for UTK employment, including employees or applicants for employment who are UTK students. In addition, any employee who feels that he or she has been discriminated against on the basis of sex, as covered by Title IX of the Higher Education Amendments of 1972, is entitled to seek relief through the following procedure:

1. In the event a complaint cannot be resolved, the complaint should be submitted in writing to the Affirmative Action Coordinator. (This procedure is not intended to discourage efforts to resolve complaints through regular administrative channels.)

2. The Affirmative Action Coordinator will report the complaint to the Vice Chancellor for Planning and Administration (UTK Affirmative Action Officer and EEO and Title IX Compliance Officer) who will request the appropriate Vice Chancellor to attempt, through the appropriate Dean or Director, to resolve the matter informally.

3. If informal resolution is not possible, the Vice Chancellor for Planning and Administration will appoint an investigative committee to assist the Affirmative Action Coordinator in investigating the complaint. The members of each committee will have the qualities of impartiality and fairness and will be UTK employees.

4. The Affirmative Action Coordinator will interview the complainant and, together with the investigative committee, conduct an investigation; including interviewing and taking statements from appropriate individuals and review of appropriate documents. The investigation will include a hearing if (a) the investigative committee deems it necessary or (b) either the complainant or the party against whom the complaint has been lodged requests it. If a hearing is held, it will afford both parties the opportunity to present evidence and testimony in their favor and to be confronted with evidence and testimony against them.

5. The Committee will reach a conclusion as to whether discrimination has or has not been present as charged and prepare a statement giving (a) the conclusion and (b) the evidence which supports the conclusion reached. The Affirmative Action Coordinator will transmit the committee's statement, as a recommendation, to the Vice Chancellor for Planning and Administration, together with the investigation files.

6. The Vice Chancellor for Planning and Administration will review the committee's statement and the investigation file, make a determination, and transmit the decision to the complainant in writing.

7. If the complainant feels that a satisfactory resolution has not been achieved, he or she may appeal to the Chancellor, in writing, within ten days following receipt of the decision of the Vice Chancellor for Planning and Administration.

8. The Chancellor will review the matter, make a determination, and notify the complainant in writing of the decision.

9. Appeals from the Chancellor's decision should be directed to the Executive Assistant to the President of the UT system, who serves as the University-wide Affirmative Action Officer, within ten days following receipt of notification of the Chancellor's decision. The By-Laws of the University (Article V, Section 7) provide that any individual may ultimately appeal to the Board of Trustees, through the President.

Complaints must be filed with the Affirmative Action Coordinator within 180 days of the alleged discrimination.

WHITTIER COLLEGE
(Whittier, California)
Equal Opportunity

It is the policy of Whittier College that it will take affirmative action in the selection of individuals for employment, promotion, training, transfer, and work assignment; in the establishment and review of individual salaries; in the determination of other conditions of employment; and that race, color, national origin, religion, age or sex will not be a consideration.

Individual opportunity with the College is based strictly on merit, ability and performance as measured and evaluated by the College. The College endeavors to provide opportunities for each employee to realize his or her potential and to assist him or her to reach a level commensurate with his or her ability and ambition.

UNIVERSITY OF PORTLAND
(Portland, Oregon)
Affirmative Action Statement

The University of Portland is a private institution of higher learning, Christian in orientation, Catholic in tradition. Rooted in the Judaeo-

Christian heritage, the University seeks to provide an environment that encourages and facilitates the intellectual, spiritual, cultural, and social growth of its students. Within the University there exists integral theological programs of study as well as voluntary programs of pastoral services.

The University intends to preserve its nature and to foster its distinctive characteristics through the employment of personnel at all levels who desire to support and espouse its ideals and its philosophy of education. It requires that all who are associated with the University recognize and understand the nature and special characteristics of the institution. Although members of the regents, administration, faculty, or other staff are not required to agree with the theological or pastoral presence and activities at the University, they are presumed to respect them, to be able to support them, and to find them compatible with their own functions within the University.

The Congregation of Holy Cross possesses a special relationship with the University, which stems from their founding of the institution in 1901, their 66 years of direct control of the institution, and through the Deed and Trust Agreement they currently have with the governing board. The Board of Regents desires to preserve and foster this special relationship through the continued presence of the Holy Cross Community within the University in responsible capacities and in sufficient numbers. Accordingly, special consideration is given to qualified members of the Holy Cross Community, and the Board encourages the Holy Cross Community to present interested and qualified candidates, not only for faculty positions, but also for administrative positions, and most especially for the office of President of the University.

With these distinctive characteristics and special considerations understood, it is the policy of the University of Portland:

1. To provide equal employment opportunity for all employees and applicants for employment, regardless of race, color, national or ethnic origin, physical handicap or sex.

2. To admit qualified students of any race, color, national or ethnic origin, physical handicap or sex to all the rights, privileges, programs and activities generally accorded or made available to students at the school. The University does not discriminate on the basis of race, color, national or ethnic origin, physical handicap, or sex in administration of its admissions policies, educational policies, scholarships and loan programs, athletic programs, and other school administered programs.

3. To take affirmative action to determine deficiencies, analyze corrective measures, and implement programs to eliminate any dis-

crimination as to race, color, national or ethnic origin, physical handicap, or sex in its employment practices or admission practices.

Administration

The Executive and Financial Vice President has been appointed by the President as University Compliance Officer for Non-Academic Personnel. The Director of Administrative Services, as Director of Personnel, will be responsible to the Executive and Financial Vice President for developing, implementing and updating the plan.

The Vice President for Academic Affairs has been appointed by the President as the University Compliance Officer for all Academic Personnel.

Recommendations concerning Equal Employment Opportunity and the Affirmative Action Program will be made to the appropriate Vice President, who when necessary will receive the support of the President and the Executive Council.

All Deans and Department Heads share responsibility for program implementation. All supervisors will insure that members of minority groups and women receive proper consideration in hiring, promotion, transfers, pay, terminations, and other personnel actions.

All Deans, Department Heads and other Administrative Supervisors are responsible for reporting their compliance with the University's Affirmative Action Program. Deans and Department Heads must submit their compliance reports to the Academic Vice President and the general Administrative Supervisors must submit their compliance reports to the Executive Vice President. These Vice Presidents, in turn, will make a formal annual compliance report to the President.

Policy Dissemination

Policy dissemination will include but not be limited to the following means:

1. A letter from the President stating the University's policy on EEO and the Affirmative Action Program will be distributed to all employees presently employed and all new employees as they are hired.

2. All outgoing purchase orders will advertise the fact that the University of Portland is an Equal Opportunity Employer.

3. Employment applications will state the EEO principle.

4. Posters will be placed on all bulletin boards, specifying the EEO policy.

5. All contracts for goods and services will have EEO clauses contained therein.

Recruitment

Our recruitment efforts will follow the guidelines as set forth in our Preamble. In addition, first consideration will be given to current employees who are interested and qualified for a particular opening.

If no qualified person is found from our internal staff, then an outside search will be initiated.

Academic Personnel. The outside recruiting area for academic personnel will be as broad as is feasible. A group of colleges and universities having graduates in the discipline required will be notified of the position opening. Also, outlets such as the *Chronicle of Higher Education* and other pertinent, professional educational publications, known to reach a wide group of applicants, will be utilized. Equal Employment Opportunities will be emphasized.

Non-Academic Personnel. The outside recruiting area for non-academic personnel will generally be considered the vicinity of Portland, Oregon . . . . Notice of all openings will be made by local newspaper advertisement, the State Employment Office, local minority group employment offices, and campus mail.

Selection and Placement

All job classifications are open to all persons on a qualification and merit basis with no distinctions being made between male or female, married and unmarried persons, and minority groups. Any testing of applicants will be limited to devices validated for the position being applied for.

Training and Education

The University does not possess a formal training program as such. However, it often allows inexperienced staff personnel to develop their skills on the job. For those employees who are interested, there are several public and private schools in the metropolitan area where employees can learn new skills or increase proficiency in old skills in order to advance their value to the University.

Promotion and Transfer

All promotions and transfers within the University of Portland are made on the basis of merit and follow the guidelines as set forth in our preamble. Specific procedures and criteria for promotion in faculty rank are set forth in the Articles of Administration. Procedures and criteria for non-academic personnel promotion are related to the particular position open. Vacancies are promulgated to all personnel within the University and interested and qualified candidates are given full consideration.

Promotion-transfer flow data will be kept on a current basis. It will be reviewed annually to see if the University is conforming with its Affirmative Action Program.

Open Door

All Department Heads, Deans and other supervisors have an open-door policy where employees can bring grievances, problems, and suggestions. If the problem cannot be resolved at the given level, it should be appealed to a higher authority to insure that any discrimination, if existing, is eliminated. The established channels of authority at the University for respective employees should be followed.

Salary Administration

All jobs are classified and salary ranges assigned in relation to the job requirement. The salary received by the job incumbent is dependent on the individual's experience and proficiency without regard to race, color, national or ethnic origin, sex, or other discriminatory tool. Special emphasis is placed on insuring that wage rates of minority group and female employees do not discriminate in any way.

Application Flow Data

The University will maintain application flow data on all of the appointments made at the University in the various work categories. This data will be reviewed on an annual basis to see if it conforms with the Affirmative Action Program of the University.

Goals

The specific goals are contained in the analysis section of this document. They will be reviewed annually, based on October 1 statistics, to determine progress and reestablish corrective actions and new goals.

The Executive Vice President and the Academic Vice President are responsible for auditing the entire Affirmative Action Program. They will be responsible for assuring that the various Compliance Officers throughout the University make annual reports concerning their activities toward Affirmative Action.

Selection of Staff

EL PASO PUBLIC LIBRARY
(El Paso, Texas)

Recruitment

Formal recruiting is accomplished by the Assistant Director and every possible effort is made to obtain the best qualified applicants for the El Paso Public Library.

El Paso Public Library is not under El Paso Civil Service; however, the Library Board has directed that the Library follow the practices and procedures of the City Civil Service System as set forth by the City Personnel Department when consistent with established library practices and procedures. All library position vacancies must be approved by the Mayor and the City Council. A requisition for each vacant library position must be sent to the City Council for approval before the library can formally recruit for the vacant position....

Professional vacant library positions are announced to the local staff by the Assistant Director. The position announcement contains the job specification, the position description and the closing date for applications. The position announcement is posted on the staff bulletin board and sent to all Coordinators, Section Heads, and Branch Heads.

When possible, professional library vacancies are filled by promotion from the present qualified library staff. If no qualified applicants are forthcoming from the present library staff by the internal closing date for applicants, the professional vacant position is announced nationwide. The position announcement is sent to City Personnel office, Texas Employment Commission, UTEP Placement Office, EPCC Placement Office and to the Placement Offices of all accredited library schools, state libraries and jobline offices.

All applications are screened by the Assistant Director to check for minimum requirements, MLS degree from an accredited library school and required post graduate experience. The qualified applicants' resumes, placement files and references are reviewed with the Director of Libraries, Coordinators and/or the immediate supervisor to select the best qualified applicants which are invited to travel at their own expense to El Paso for a personal interview by the Library Management Team. The Library Management Team consists of the Director of Libraries, Assistant Director, Coordinator of Public Services, Coordinator of Extension Services, Coordinator of Technical Services and the Coordinator of the Trans-Pecos System Libraries, if the vacancy is a Systems position.

Each applicant is evaluated by each member of the interview team. After the final closing date for interviews, the interview team reviews the qualifications of the applicants interviewed and a tally is taken of each interviewee's ratings of the top applicants. The applicant receiving the top rating is offered the vacant position.

The selected applicant is notified by phone, if possible, and a letter of confirmation is sent. The other applicants are notified by letter that the vacancy has been filled. All of the other applicants for the vacant position that are not interviewed and/or not qualified are informed that the position has been filled.

All applications for vacant positions are maintained in the personnel files for one year to be considered for future vacancies.

The Director of the Libraries is selected by the members of the Board of Directors. The Assistant Director of the Library is selected by the Director of Libraries.

RIVER BEND LIBRARY SYSTEM
(Coal Valley, Illinois)

Appointment

The Board of the River Bend Library System is responsible for the establishment of positions on the staff of the library. The position's title and classification will be established and the Director authorized to fill the position. The Director will select the best qualified applicant and report to the Board the person selected for Board approval.

At times the library may need to cover a position between appointments or to accomplish a specific task on a temporary basis. In these cases the Director may make a temporary appointment and seek Board approval at the first meeting after the appointment. These appointments will accrue only Annual Leave and Sick Leave benefits.

The Director is empowered to employ a satisfactory substitute when for any reason a regular staff person is absent.

MT. LEBANON PUBLIC LIBRARY
(Mt. Lebanon, Pennsylvania)
Appointment

The Head Librarian is appointed by the Board of Library Directors. Appointments to other full-time positions are made by the Head Librarian with the approval of the Board of Library Directors. Part-time professional librarians, library assistants, clerks and shelvers are appointed by the Head Librarian. Pages are appointed by the supervisor of pages with the approval of the Head Librarian. The appointment of part-time employees will be reported by the Head Librarian to the Board of Library Directors at the Board's next regular meeting.

VIKING LIBRARY SYSTEM
(Fergus Falls, Minnesota)
Application and Appointment

A written System application form shall precede employment. References are required. A resume must accompany all applications for the professional positions.

Applicants are interviewed by the Director and immediate supervisor. The final decision on hiring will be made by the Director.

Before the employee has served six months, the supervisor will complete an evaluation of the employee's work performance. If the rating is satisfactory, the employee will receive permanent status. Probation may be extended for one 3-month period by the Director.

WINNETKA PUBLIC LIBRARY
(Winnetka, Illinois)
Selection of Staff

The members of the staff are selected on the basis of merit with due consideration given to educational, personal, and physical qualifications as well as the training, experience and aptitude for the position. Race, creed, sex, age, national origin, or marital status shall have no bearing in the consideration of a candidate. Because the library is a public service institution, personal qualities as well as professional should be considered in the hiring of library staff. These personal qualities include a sense of purpose, understanding of people, a sense of humor, dedication to service, and awareness of community needs. Members of immediate families of Board members or present employees cannot be hired on a full time permanent basis.

It is the Library Director's duty to select and to supervise the staff, in accordance with the powers vested in her/him by the Library Board. However, in case of serious unresolved conflicts of any nature, all staff members have the right to request a hearing before the Board. The Library Director and the Board of Trustees should be notified separately in writing of the nature of the grievance and a hearing requested of the Board, to be scheduled at the earliest convenience of Board, Library Director, and employee.

SKOKIE PUBLIC LIBRARY
(Skokie, Illinois)

RECRUITMENT

The Library will attempt to reach all groups in recruiting to fill position openings in accordance with the affirmative action policy. . . .

Announcement of vacancies will be posted on the Staff Room Bulletin Board. Minimum age for employment shall be in compliance with the Illinois State Labor Laws.

SELECTION AND APPOINTMENT

Selection of the employee is based upon educational qualifications, technical skills as well as personality, ability, and aptitude for the position. Appointment to the staff is made by the Chief Librarian who submits the name of the employee to the Board of Directors for approval. A pre-employment physical examination at the expense of the Library may be required for new employees.

PIKES PEAK
REGIONAL LIBRARY DISTRICT
(Colorado Springs, Colorado)

RECRUITMENT

The purpose of recruitment is to use all sources of advertisement to reach qualified applicants interested in the job. To accomplish this, vacancies will be announced simultaneously in-house and through outside channels. The best qualified applicant will be hired for the position.

Recruitment In-house

Announcements of vacant positions will be distributed to all library agencies normally through the weekly intercom. The announcement will include the closing dates of the application period, methods of submitting applications, pay range, classification and abbreviated job description.

Recruitment Outside the Library

The Personnel Resources Officer will maintain unsolicited applications on file for six months. Newspapers, specialized periodicals, job lines, college placement bureaus, specialized sources such as Goodwill, Rehabilitation, CETA, and the State Employment Office may all be used to reach qualified applicants.

Applications

Staff members should submit in writing to the Personnel Resources Officer a request to be considered for the job vacancy advertised. This should include identifying information as to vacancy classification level, department and division. Staff members may, at any time, submit in writing to the Personnel Resources Officer request for transfer or promotion to another position and will be considered for appointment to such vacancy when it occurs . . . .

SELECTION

The best qualified applicant is selected for appointment to the library staff. Applicants need to meet qualifications necessary for the job in the area of education, training, skills, special knowledge, and ability to work with the public and with other staff. The Personnel Resources Officer will screen all applicants to see that they meet minimum qualifications for the job. This may be done through interviews, examinations (oral and written), appraisal of the information contained in the application, reference inquiries and other measures of ability as may be considered appropriate.

Rejections

Applicants may be rejected if (1) they do not meet minimum qualification standards for job vacancy, (2) the application contains a false statement, (3) they are addicted to the use of narcotics or intoxicants, (4) they are physically disabled to the extent of not being able to perform the required duties, and (5) they are not sixteen years of age. Applicants not meeting the minimum requirements will be notified as to reason by the Personnel Resources Officer.

Referral

After initial screening by the Personnel Resources Officer, qualified applicants for librarian and Management Team positions will be referred to the Director for selection and appointment. Qualified applicants for non-professional employment will be referred to department heads for selection and appointment.

Promotions

Promotions are based upon evidence of satisfactory performance and promise of future development as reflected by service ratings, and upon educational, technical and personal qualifications. Length of service, unaccompanied by increased efficiency and interest in the profession, is a reason against rather than for promotion. Seniority is a determining factor only when two candidates have equal qualifications.

Acting Appointments

If a position is temporarily vacated, a staff member may be placed on an acting assignment in the position. A record is kept on the performance of the employee while so assigned and filed in the personnel record.

Appointments to any library position must be submitted to the Personnel Resources Officer ... and be signed by the Department Head and the Director prior to the person starting to work. The employee must sign an acceptance of appointment ... prior to beginning work. Employees appointed to permanent positions will be on probation during the first six months.

TOLEDO-LUCAS COUNTY PUBLIC LIBRARY
(Toledo, Ohio)

RECRUITING

The Library as an equal opportunity employer seeks to find the best qualified candidate for each position as a vacancy occurs. Recruitment is carried out by sending a staff notice to each agency in the system which describes the responsibilities of the position as well as the qualifications and the salary. This notice is to be posted on staff bulletin boards for every staff member to examine. Advertisements are also sent to library journals and/or local newspapers. Contact is also made with library, business or other appropriate schools.

Grade I positions are not advertised unless some special feature of. that position makes it seem desirable to call it to staff attention.

A written application must be on file in the Personnel Office.

APPOINTMENTS

All appointments are made by the Director and confirmed by the Board of Trustees. The letter of appointment issued by the Personnel

Officer indicates the position, the grade, the pay, the starting date and the probationary period of the new employee. An identification card is issued which serves as a library card as well. It must be surrendered at termination of employment.

SONOMA COUNTY LIBRARY
(Santa Rosa, California)
Appointment Procedure for Librarian III (Specialist)

Authority

The position classification of Librarian III has been established by the Library Commission and ratified by the Board of Supervisors for the assignments in the Library requiring the highest degree of professional skills, but not necessarily involving supervisory responsibilities. In order for an appointment to be made, a vacant Library III position must exist or a new one created. A vacant Librarian III position will be filled by a Librarian II appointment only when the need for this level of assignment remains.

Fair Employment Practices

All of the following procedures shall be exercised in such a way that appointments shall be made without discrimination as to sex, race, age, religion, political activity, national origin, citizenship, or lifestyle.

Persons with histories of physical or mental illness, narcotic or alcoholic addiction, arrests or convictions shall not be excluded from consideration for appointment under these procedures.

Candidates for Appointment

Vacancies to be filled in budgeted positions of Librarian III shall be filled by direct appointment by the Library Director. Each such vacancy will be considered individually in consultation with the Librarians IV and the Personnel Director to determine need and qualifications required for the specialty of the position to be filled. All eligible Library employees will be considered in addition to applications from specialists received in response to advertisements placed in national media.

Documentation

The Director, Librarians IV and Personnel Director shall have available to them the following information regarding each candidate:

1. A standard application form submitted for the position, containing complete information regarding education and experience.
2. For a Library employee, his current performance rating.
3. For other candidates, letters of recommendation, including at least one from the current or most recent employer.
4. Any letter or other written statement which the candidate may have submitted for the position stating specifically his qualifications in the specialty under consideration.

Oral Examination

The Director shall examine each candidate in turn involving Librarians IV as appropriate. Any question may be asked which is appropriate to the requirements of the position or the candidate's interest in it. No questions shall be asked regarding factors which by law may not be considered in appointment procedures.

Appointment

The Director shall make a determination upon the appointment after consultation with the Librarians IV and the Personnel Director.

UNIVERSITY OF PITTSBURGH LIBRARIES
(Pittsburgh, Pennsylvania)
Appointment

Recommendations on appointment shall be made by a sub-committee of the Peer Review Committee (PRC) . . . .
Vacancies will be advertised in accordance with University policy and Affirmative Action guidelines. The search process cannot be initiated until prior approval has been granted by the Provost upon

reviewing the preliminary recruitment statement, which describes specifically how recruitment and selection will occur. This statement, from the Director, will include a description of the position to be filled; a list of the requisite qualifications and, when appropriate, salary ranges; the means to be employed in searching for qualified candidates for positions (such as calls, trips, inquiries to organizations, and appropriate professional and other publications in which the position will be advertised); the expected duration of the recruitment phase, and any criteria to be employed in evaluating applicants for recommendation for appointment. Information concerning faculty librarian vacancies will be forwarded to the Office of Affirmative Action for advertising throughout the University.

The Director(s) and/or the supervisor(s) involved shall examine all applications received, and forward appropriate applications to the Search Committee. These applications will then be reviewed in accordance with the Faculty Recruitment Procedures and the recruitment statement. When the interviewing process is completed, the sub-committee chairpersons will then provide the supervisor and/or the Director with a list of the top candidates, ranked in order of recommendations, with an accompanying rationale. The decision shall be made by the Director and the appropriate supervisor(s), and they will then inform the sub-committee chairperson regarding their reasons for selection or rejection of the candidates.

Before an offer of appointment is tendered, the decision and a completed description of the recruitment process will be submitted to the Provost, who will consider whether sincere attempts were made to identify minority persons who are qualified, and whether all applicants were given fair consideration. If the process is found to be satisfactory, the Provost will tender an offer of appointment to the recommended candidate, and if not, the process may be reopened.

INA DILLARD RUSSELL LIBRARY
GEORGIA COLLEGE
(Milledgeville, Georgia)

Employment Procedures for Faculty Positions

All initial faculty [including librarians'] appointments must be approved by the Board of Regents of the University System of Georgia, including full time, part-time and temporary appointments. Faculty appointments are initiated by the chairperson of the academic department involved who has the primary responsibility for complying with the Affirmative Action program of the University System as presented by the U.S. Department of Health, Education, and Welfare. All faculty appointments are approved in advance by the Dean of the College and the President.

Departmental chairpersons and Search Committees are obligated to publicize their position vacancies in as specific terms as possible and advertise the vacancy in all media available to the discipline that would normally be used by applicants of all races and both sexes to secure official information on available openings.

When the applicant pool has been narrowed to contain only the final list of candidates for the position, there should be represented in the final group members of both sexes and from black and white ethnic groups. If no women and black applicants are represented, then the search must include the procedure involving the Applicant Clearing House of the University System. Department chairpersons contact the Affirmative Action Officer . . . to initiate the Applicant Clearing House process. After the position has been filled, the unsuccessful applicants contained in the final selection group shall, with their permission, be supplied to the Applicant Clearing House on a form furnished by the College Affirmative Action Officer.

All records of the search, advertisement, vitaes of applicants, letters of correspondence, etc. (everything related to the hiring process to fill any vacancy or new position) must be maintained intact for a minimum of three calendar years from the date of filling the appointment. No position may be filled until the proper forms are completed certifying that a deliberate and comprehensive effort was made to obtain applications from all qualified persons. Forms for keeping track of these efforts are obtained from the Office of the Dean of the College. The departmental chairperson must document to the satisfaction of the College Affirmative Action Officer that a deliberate and comprehensive effort was made to find women and black persons qualified to fill the position and that the decision making process used no discriminatory practices in violation of state and federal laws. The spirit as well as the letter of the law must be adhered to. Once the College Affirmative Action Officer certifies this fact to the department chairperson, the chairperson may recommend to the Dean that the College proceed to enter into contractual agreement with the best qualified candidate.

An Affirmative Action record must be kept on file for each applicant for an announced position vacancy. Forms for this purpose are obtained from the Dean's Office. Unsolicited vitaes received when there is no vacancy in the department should be kept on file for three years.

If a position vacancy occurs during that period, qualified candidate vitaes should be reviewed, activated, and, if possible, the candidate should be notified . . . .

LIBERAL ARTS COLLEGE
(Anonymous)
Recruitment and Review Procedures

An appointment to the faculty is made by the President, subject to the approval of the Board of Directors. The procedures leading to such appointments include the following steps.

Notice of Vacancy and Advertising

Notice of a faculty vacancy is given to a department/division by the Vice President for Academic Affairs. Upon notification that a vacancy exists, the department/division establishes a search committee, if needed, and prepares a vacancy notice in cooperation with the Vice President for Academic Affairs. The notice of vacancy includes at least the following information: title and rank, position description, effective date of appointment, salary range, anticipated dates for recruitment and selection, deadline for applications/nominations, minimum and desired academic/professional preparation, specific qualifications and competences sought . . . . The notice of vacancy is reviewed and approved by the Vice President for Academic Affairs and the President. Following such approval the notice is distributed to individuals, professional societies, departments of colleges and universities, and other agencies in an attempt to identify possible candidates. A copy of the notice of vacancy is sent to every candidate for the position.

Vacancies are also advertised in newspapers, magazines, and periodicals which might provide a vehicle of communication with prospective candidates. Such advertising . . . states the college's guarantees of non-discrimination based on race, color, sex, and national origin. The text of any such advertisement is reviewed and approved by the President.

Formal Application

Formal application for a faculty position is made through the use of a form. Included in the form is a statement on *Institutional History and Philosophy*, to which each candidate is asked to respond. References are contacted and a file is developed for each candidate. If the applicant has compiled a placement file, a copy of the file is requested. The files are maintained in the Office of the Vice President for Academic Affairs.

After the initial contact, applicants with whom the college wishes to conduct further explorations are sent materials describing the college. Included in these materials are the college catalog, a copy of the current class schedule, information concerning the accreditation status of the college, a statement of institutional philosophy and mission, a statement on procedures for faculty evaluation and promotion, a statement on academic freedom and tenure, and information on salary schedules. A copy of the Faculty Handbook is made available. Other materials are shared as the case requires. The purpose of sharing such materials is to fully inform the candidate about the nature of the college and to enlist his/her participation in evaluation of the degree of convergence between his/her own skills/goals and the needs/goals of the institution.

Review of Applications

Initial review of applications is at the departmental or divisional level. If the department agrees on a recommendation of one or more candidates for campus interviews, that recommendation is presented to the Vice President for Academic Affairs, who will determine whether or not such an interview should be authorized. Normally, a candidate will not be brought to the campus for such an interview unless there is strong evidence that he/she is sufficiently well qualified to be offered the position. The primary function of the campus interview is not to screen candidates but to reach agreement concerning an appointment. Any campus interview will include meetings with departmental/divisional faculty, the Vice President for Academic Affairs, and the President.

Selection and Appointment

The appointment of a full-time faculty member by the President is made only after he has received the advice of the Vice President for Academic Affairs. The advice of the Vice President for Academic

Affairs is made, in turn, only after he has received the recommendation of the department/division chairperson or the search committee. In case of a conflict of recommendations, an attempt is made to develop a consensus through conference. The final power of appointment rests with the President, subject to the approval of the Board of Directors . . . .

UNIVERSITY OF MISSOURI–ST. LOUIS LIBRARIES
(St. Louis, Missouri)

Guidelines and Procedures for Recruitment and Hiring of Permanent Academic Staff Members

The ultimate objective of the search process is to select the best possible applicant for a position, in a fair, equitable, and open manner, in compliance with the University of Missouri Affirmative Action Guidelines. This objective requires the active involvement of the academic staff. The search committee is responsible to the academic staff and the Director of Libraries for conducting the search according to established guidelines and procedures. At the outset of its work the committee should decide the kinds of documentation (resume, application forms, letters of recommendation, etc.) it will request of the candidates and the criteria to be followed in evaluation of each candidate. The criteria should be objective, consistent and equitable. All candidates, whether they are external or internal to the libraries, should be accorded the same treatment in the screening and interview process. The final selection of the candidate will be made by the Director of Libraries and will be forwarded for approval to the appropriate administrative officers.

Formation of Search Committees

Search committees will be appointed by the Director of Libraries from volunteers from the academic staff. The committee will consist of three or more members of the academic staff, one of which must be the division head of the division in which the vacancy exists, if possible. Any academic staff members accepting appointment to the committee should automatically disqualify themselves as real or potential nominees. A chairperson shall be designated by the Director of Libraries and will be responsible for administering these guidelines. Specific duties of the chairperson are enumerated [below].

Charge to Search Committees

The Director of Libraries shall instruct the committee in writing at the time of the first meeting as to the following:

1. Approximate date for submission of a list of nominees and the proposed date of appointment.
2. Number of finalists to be recommended, and whether or not to rank the finalists.
3. Salary range allotted for the position.
4. Budgetary allowance available for the recruitment process.
5. Any unique concerns with respect to the position.

The committee shall have access to the Director of Libraries to clarify the committee search charge whenever necessary. The Director of Libraries will make available secretarial help as needed.

Responsibilities of the Committee

The search committee will complete the Notification of Full-Time Position Vacancy Form and forward it to the Affirmative Action Office. The committee shall obtain a written position description from the supervisor. The committee will write position advertisements as needed using the position description as a guide. The ads should include the following information and will be submitted to the Director of Libraries for approval: a full account of the responsibilities of the position, minimum qualifications as to educational background and experience, special competencies desired of the applicants, minimum salary level, appointment date, closing date for receipt of applications, name of chairperson to whom application should be submitted, and statement of adherence to Affirmative Action/EEO guidelines.

Minimum postings of job advertisements for academic positions will be done on a state-wide basis and are to include the following agencies: the UMSL Job Register, Missouri State Library, Missouri Division of Employment Security (this is done by the Affirmative Action Office), Missouri Library Association, University of Missouri-Columbia School of Library & Information Science, local newspapers including St. Louis *Post Dispatch* and St. Louis *Argus*, and St. Louis Public Library Clearinghouse.

Additional minimum postings for positions at the division head level or above should include at least three of the following: ALA

Placement Service, *LJ/SLJ Hotline, American Libraries, Library Journal, ACRL News, Chronicle of Higher Education*, and minority caucus newsletters (required posting). For positions requiring special qualifications, additional advertising should be done in relevant sources.

The Library's in-house file of applications should be checked for six months back and letters sent to qualified candidates informing them of the position. All applications should be courteously and promptly acknowledged. This communication should include a request to fill in and return the Ethnic origin card to the University's Affirmative Action Office. Within one week after the closing date the committee will evaluate the applications received and place them into three categories according to pre-established criteria.

Category A: Applications submitted by persons that do not meet minimum or appropriate qualifications. These persons will be notified that they will not be considered for the position.

Category B: Applications submitted by persons that meet minimal qualifications but which are not strong candidates for the position. These persons will be notified that their applications are being kept in the pool for further consideration.

Category C: Applications submitted by persons that appear to be strong candidates. The committee may request from the candidate the following appropriate information which may be deemed necessary: references and/or permission to contact references, verification of degrees, and any other pertinent information within the Affirmative Action/EEO guidelines. Upon receipt of complete information the search committee will select the finalists to be interviewed for the position.

Selection Process: The number of candidates selected will depend upon the requirements of the position, the number of applications received and the number of finalists desired.

Interview Process: The committee will plan an interview schedule which will be as consistent as possible for each candidate. The schedule will include an interview with the Director of Libraries and an interview with the search committee in conjunction with any academic staff members who wish to participate. For positions at the division head level and above, additional activities may be scheduled as appropriate. The candidates to be interviewed will be notified of the interview schedule in advance. Interview schedules should take into consideration the personal needs of the candidates. The committee shall circulate the interview schedules and the candidates' resumes to the Director of Libraries and the academic staff members.

Final Evaluation of Candidates: The committee should consider and evaluate with all deliberate speed the interviewed candidates. If a satisfactory list cannot be compiled, the committee will select additional candidates for interviews or may re-open the search as deemed necessary by the committee and the Director of Libraries. The list will be ranked if previously requested by the Director. The Director will make the final selection and notify the committee of his/her decision and forward the decision with appropriate documentation to the Affirmative Action Officer.

Final Letters of Notification: The Director shall send letters of determination to all candidates interviewed. The committee will send appropriate letters of determination to all remaining candidates involved in the search procedure.

Responsibilities of the Search Committee Chairperson

To schedule meetings of search committee, keep all files of documents and submit reports required by the library and Affirmative Action Office, place all advertisements, send and receive all correspondence with candidates, be responsible for all communication with the academic staff and Director of Libraries, and be responsible for scheduling interviews and hosting candidates while they are on campus.

Employee Evaluation, Tenure, and Grievance Procedures

CENTRAL NORTH CAROLINA REGIONAL LIBRARY
(Burlington, North Carolina)

PROBATIONARY PERIOD

All appointments and promotions to positions in the service of the Central North Carolina Regional Library shall be for a probationary period of six months. Employees serving a probationary period following initial employment in a permanent position shall receive all benefits provided in accordance with this resolution with the following exceptions or as otherwise provided:

The employee may accumulate leave but shall not be permitted to take vacation leave during the probationary period unless the denial of such leave shall create an unusual hardship. Vacation leave may be granted to such employee only with the approval of the Director. The employee, if dismissed during the probationary period, shall not be eligible for terminal pay for accumulated vacation leave.

Employees serving a probationary period following a promotion shall continue to receive all benefits provided in accordance with this resolution and under supplementary rules and regulations.

Before the end of the probationary period, the staff member's work performance is reviewed and evaluated by his supervisor and his strengths and weaknesses discussed with him. New staff members are given orientation in the operation of the library, its objectives and history as well as instruction concerning their duties. All new staff members are expected to familiarize themselves with the rules and practices of the library system. If the new staff member fails to give a satisfactory performance and is not to be continued in service after the probationary period, he is to be given at least one month's notice prior to the expiration of his probationary period. The library is not obligated to retain a probationer throughout his probationary period if his performance is not satisfactory or further training will not be of any help. In such cases, the employee shall receive two weeks' notice before termination. At the time of permanent employment, the performance rating of the probationer is reviewed and the decision for permanent appointment is made by the Director.

REINSTATEMENT

An employee who has been separated because of a reduction in force or who has resigned while in good standing shall be credited his previously accrued sick leave if he is reinstated within five years. If the reinstated employee shall have continued to be a member of the North Carolina Local Governmental Employees' Retirement System, he shall receive credit for all accrued contributions to the time of his separation.

PROMOTIONS AND TRANSFERS

Promotions and transfers within the existing library staff are considered when a vacancy occurs, although the library is free to seek candidates from other sources to fill the vacancy with the best qualified person. Promotions are based on satisfactory performance service ratings, educational, technical, and personal qualifications. Length of service is not a determining factor except in the case of equal qualifications of candidates.

PERSONNEL EVALUATIONS

In order that a complete record of the job performance of all employees can be maintained, a Personnel Evaluation will be prepared on each employee every six months. Any exemplary work as well as deficiencies in job performance will be noted and explained to the employee. If necessary, the employee will be told what he must do to bring his work up to an acceptable level. The employee is then given a reasonable length of time to improve. If his job performance does not improve, he may be dismissed by the Director. If an employee has a noteworthy deficiency or an exemplary performance, an Individual Personnel Report may be used to delineate the particular incident. The employee must sign and date all Personnel Evaluations and Individual Personnel Reports when they are permanently in the employee's personnel file. Any employee has the right to see what is in his personnel file. Because these reports ascertain the abilities, performance, and potentialities of all staff members, they will be used to determine promotions, transfers, demotions, dismissals, and any other personnel actions. The Personnel Evaluation that is done on an employee's anniversary date is used to determine the amount of the annual merit salary increment which the employee is eligible to receive.

PARAMUS PUBLIC LIBRARY
(Paramus, New Jersey)
Performance Reviews

The Director shall either personally conduct or receive from other supervisors written periodic evaluations, at least once a year, of the work performance of all staff members. The purpose of such reviews shall be to help employees make progress in their work and learn where they stand in the minds of their supervisors. The performance review must be accompanied by a personal conference in which the employee may examine the review and have an opportunity to ask questions or make comments. The Director may be present at such conferences. Needless to say, these matters are confidential and are not to be discussed with other employees.

Disagreement with the performance rating, or parts thereof, may be voiced, and objections to, or appeals of, an unfavorable rating may be expressed in writing to the Director and the Board of Trustees.

Performance evaluations will be considered as one factor in determining salary increases, promotions, reclassifications or dismissals. These performance evaluations shall be made available to the Board of Trustees for annual salary review.

CRYSTAL LAKE PUBLIC LIBRARY
(Crystal Lake, Illinois)

PROBATIONARY PERIODS

Termination may be initiated by either party during the probationary period for any reason, or no reason, without affecting the work record. The probationary periods are as follows: page and beginning clerical help, three months; department head, supervisor, beginning professional, library technical assistant, and associate, six months; and Administrative Librarian, one year.

EVALUATION

Evaluation of each employee is to be done annually by each supervisor in consultation with the Administrative Librarian. A written evaluation is to be reviewed with the employee and retained in confidential files of the Administrative Librarian, files in which other evaluative materials may be kept. This file is confidential to the individual and to the Administrative Librarian. The evaluation is not performed in conjunction with the annual review of salaries.

Evaluation of the Administrative Librarian is done by the Board of Trustees.

GRIEVANCES

An attempt should be made by the immediate supervisor to handle an employee grievance. If it cannot be worked out, then one or both may submit the grievance to the Administrative Librarian. If it remains unresolved, the aggrieved employee or supervisor may submit the grievance directly to the Library Board president in writing. A written response as to action taken should be returned to the aggrieved party or parties.

SONOMA COUNTY LIBRARY
(Santa Rosa, California)

PROBATIONARY PERIOD

The probationary period is the final phase of the appointment process for all career employee appointments. It is used by the Library Administration to determine the probationary employee's capabilities, compatibility with staff and organization, and adjustment to the philosophy of the Library.

Each appointment, promotion, demotion or transfer to a permanent position shall be subject to a probationary period of not less than six months of work. The Library Director may extend the probationary period for any position to a period not to exceed one year. The probationary period shall date from the time of appointment to a permanent position, but shall not include time served as a substitute, temporary, or student employee.

The permanent status of a probationary employee shall begin on the day following the end of the probationary period, providing the employee has received a satisfactory rating on the Employee's Evaluation Form, *and* a statement in writing from the Library Director that the services of the employee during the probationary period have been satisfactory and that the employee is permanently appointed.

A probationary employee whose performance, attitude or personal philosophy of library service does not meet the standards, requirements and philosophy of service of the Sonoma County Library, may be dismissed at any time during the probationary period without right of appeal or hearing. In case of such dismissal the Library Director shall include on the report of separation a statment of the reasons for dismissal.

ADMINISTRATIVE POLICY REGARDING TRANSFERS

Purpose

The Sonoma County Library, as a countywide agency, provides numerous benefits to the residents of its service area. Among the most significant of those benefits is a large and diverse staff whose individual aptitudes and competencies can be utilized in positions and locations most suited to them and therefore to the service to be provided.

As the Library system expands, its staffing patterns must of necessity change. As the Library develops new services and technologies it will require from each employee the ability to accept new methodologies, new responsibilities, and new assignments, whether in the same or another facility.

In the course of their service individual employees are expected to become more knowledgeable and competent in their own and related areas of work, through training, experience and continuing education, thus adapting themselves to the expansion and changing requirements of the institution.

Appointments

All professional appointments are made to the staff of the Sonoma County Library with initial assignment to the Central Library in order that individuals may become familiar with the specialized resources and staff available as direct backstop service for all other facilities and extension programs. Other employees also are appointed to the staff of the Sonoma County Library, but may, depending upon the level of work and responsibilities involved, receive initial assignment to a large branch which can provide appropriate experience and supervision.

All individuals are selected on the basis of their demonstrated competencies, potential for development, and flexibility in matters of job assignment.

Reasons for Transfer

Individuals are transferred to fill vacancies, which may be caused by retirements, resignations, other transfers or the creation of new positions. Because of the specific number of positions allocated to the Library, a vacancy must be filled when it occurs.

Individuals are transferred to provide a necessary balance of staff in a particular facility. Nonbalance of staff between adult and children's services, between experienced and inexperienced personnel or incompatibility within the confines of a single facility or department to the extent that service suffers, may require one or more transfers in order to strengthen the service and provide necessary leadership.

Individuals are transferred to enhance their experience, increase their knowledge of the Library, and expand their skills. Individuals are valuable to the Library as employees, and eligible for advancement, in proportion to their breadth of knowledge and variety of skills. Such development can only come about through exposure to several working situations in more than one facility.

Individuals are transferred where this is necessary to provide advancement. When opportunities arise for advancement, present employees will always be given careful consideration. Promotions, especially for extension personnel, almost invariably involve transfers to other facilities.

Employees' Preferences

Whenever possible an individual's desire for a transfer, or for a particular transfer, is accommodated. This must be matched, however, with qualifications for the position to be filled. In matters of transfer, employees must be frank in expressing interest or lack of interest in order to have their desires seriously considered. A request for a transfer for purely personal reasons cannot be granted if the result would be the involuntary and unwise transfer of another individual.

Other Considerations

Individuals are not transferred when serious physical or economic hardships to them would result. If an individual can demonstrate that such hardship would result due to commuting or moving of residence, such a transfer will not be made.

Individuals are not transferred for disciplinary reasons. No position or facility in the Library is unimportant to the service which the institution provides. It follows, therefore, that when an individual is not performing satisfactorily the problem for the Library cannot be cured by a transfer to another position.

It sometimes happens, however, that a person whose performance is below standard can show improvement through transfer to another assignment which is more suitable to the individual's abilities, or provides an opportunity for more careful performance evaluation. When this possibility exists it will be utilized in an attempt to avoid dismissal.

Posting of Vacancies

Every effort will be made to notify staff of impending vacancies in advance of the date on which it is necessary to make a decision on a transfer or recruitment. However, it is absolutely necessary to fill vacancies promptly where public service would be adversely affected by a delay. Therefore it is not always possible to post notice and provide an open filing period. This is particularly true when a transfer creates a second vacancy, and sometimes a chain reaction of vacancies, within the system.

TACOMA PUBLIC LIBRARY
(Tacoma, Washington)
Grievance Procedures

Purpose

Misunderstandings and problems arise from time to time in any employment situation. It is the intent of this policy to solve these as expeditiously as possible. Because informal discussion may not resolve the problem and in order to facilitate a uniform and equitable procedure, the following steps should be followed to whatever level necessary to achieve a resolution of the grievance.

Definition

A grievance is an allegation by an employee that there has been a breach, misinterpretation or improper application of City or Library policies, practices or procedures; or an arbitrary or discriminatory application of terms and conditions of employment.

Procedures

1. Oral discussion with immediate supervisor.
2. Written statement of problem and request for resolution to the supervisor with a copy to the Assistant Director.
3. Discussion with department head or branch librarian.
4. Hearing with the Assistant Director or other person designated by the Director.
5. Request for a grievance panel.
6. Resolution by the grievance panel will be forwarded to the Director whose decision will be final subject only to appeal rights.

Grievance Panel

A three member grievance panel will be selected from the list of permanent library employees. One member will be selected by the Library Director and one by the grievant. These two members will then select a third member.

Appeal Rights

When the grievance involves discrimination, reduction in rank or pay, suspension or termination, a permanent employee may appeal by requesting a hearing before the Board of Trustees.

Conclusion

The grievance may be concluded by mutual decision at any step of the procedure. There shall be no reprisal by reason of the involvement of any person in the grievance procedure.

TOLEDO-LUCAS COUNTY PUBLIC LIBRARY
(Toledo, Ohio)

PROBATION

All employees are on probation during their first year regardless of position or salary. Each new employee and each employee in a new position is evaluated quarterly by the supervisor the first year. This evaluation of the strengths and weaknesses of the performance in the job is discussed, written up by the supervisor and signed by both the employee and the supervisor.

The Annual Brief Rating Report follows the three quarterly reports. Both the supervisor and the employee fill out the annual evaluation forms individually and after discussing the evaluations, sign the reports. The reports are reviewed by the supervisor of the reporting supervisor and filed in the Personnel Office. An evaluation by the appropriate supervisor and the Personnel Officer determines whether or not the appointment should be continued. Performance evaluations are made annually after the first year.

In those rare instances when a decision cannot be made on an individual's performance within a year the probationary period may be extended, but not beyond a second year.

Performance evaluations are made annually after the first year. The purpose of the evaluation is to provide: an opportunity for each employee to discuss the job and the strengths and weaknesses of the performance of the job, with the supervisor; a basis for awarding salary increases, promotions, etc.; and a basis for preparing future letters of reference for the employee.

PROMOTION

Requests for promotion to a vacant position which is classified at a higher grade may be submitted by any interested employee who meets the qualifications of the higher grade and the specialization required by the specific vacancy. When a position is reclassified and the person holding the position is qualified and satisfactory, it is not considered as a vacancy and will not be advertised. If because of a reclassification a vacancy is created, that position will be advertised.

TRANSFER

Request for transfer may be made by an employee for such valid reasons as an interest in a special subject area or kind of work, convenient location, personality conflict, etc. Every effort will be made to accommodate a personal request insofar as it does not detract from library service, infringe on someone else's rights, and providing a suitable vacancy occurs. The timing depends upon the needs of the Library.

Request for transfer may be made by the Library for such valid reasons as covering staff shortages, maintaining staff balances, development of personnel, personality conflict, etc. It is expected that staff members will share the Library's concern for the excellence of the total library service, which would prompt such a request. No transfer will be made without the concurrence of the employee and both supervisors involved.

GRIEVANCE PROCEDURE

Purpose

The Board and Association intend that the grievance procedure as set forth herein shall serve as a means for a peaceful settlement of all disputes that may arise between them concerning the interpretation or operation of this policy without any interruption or disturbance of the normal operation of the Library.

Definition

1. A "Complaint" shall mean the discussion that is initiated with the immediate supervisor by the employee in an effort to informally resolve a matter causing dissatisfaction.
2. A "Grievance" shall mean an unresolved complaint by an employee or a group of employees based upon an event, condition or circumstance under which an employee works, allegedly caused by a violation, misinterpretation, or inequitable application of established personnel policy, or any provision of this policy.
3. An "Aggrieved Person" shall mean the person or persons making the complaint, either individually or through the Association.
4. A "Party in Interest" shall mean the person or persons making the complaint and/or any person who might be required to take action or against whom action might be taken in order to resolve the grievance.
5. The term "days" shall mean working days excluding Saturday, Sunday and holidays that the Library is closed.

General Principles

The primary purpose of the procedure set forth in this policy is to secure, at the earliest level possible, equitable solutions to complaints or grievances of employees or groups of employees. Both parties agree that proceedings under this article shall be kept as informal and confidential as may be appropriate.

It shall be the firm policy of the Library to assure to every employee an opportunity to have the unobstructed use of this grievance procedure without fear of reprisal or without prejudice in any manner to employment status. Any Association officer or member of the Personnel Relations Committee of the Association who may normally be involved in the Association's handling of a grievance proceeding shall disqualify him or her self from a grievance proceeding if he or she is the grievant's immediate supervisor or a party in interest to the grievance.

The failure of an aggrieved person to proceed to the next step within the time limits set forth shall be deemed a waiver of any further appeal concerning the particular grievance; provided, however, in the event that new facts are obtained which were not previously known but which, if they had been known, might have influenced the disposition of the grievance, the presentation of such information to the parties in interest shall constitute grounds to re-open the grievance at the level at which it has been terminated.

At any level the failure of the Library's representative to communicate a decision to the grievant within the specified time limits shall permit the grievant to proceed to the next level.

It shall be the general practice of all parties in interest to process grievance procedures during times which do not interfere with assigned duties; provided, however, in the event it is necessary to hold proceedings during regular working hours, an employee participating in any level of the grievance procedure, on his or her own behalf, or on behalf of the Association, with any representative of the Library, shall be released from assigned duties without loss of salary.

Grievances shall be processed as rapidly as possible. The time limits provided at each level shall be considered as maximum and every effort shall be made to expedite the process. Time limits, however, may be extended when mutually agreed upon in writing.

Grievances will follow the grievant's chain of supervision except that the Personnel Officer may also be involved at any step in order to facilitate the amiable and equitable resolution of the grievance. The progression of a grievance that passes through all possible steps would be: first level supervisor, agency head, administrative head together with the Personnel Officer, Director, Board of Trustees and mediation.

An employee may approach the Personnel Officer or the Association for help during or before level one of the grievance process if he or she has difficulty in talking with the immediate supervisor.

In the event that an individual who has been dismissed for cause feels that he or she has been treated unfairly, he or she shall have 10 days in which to make an appeal. This appeal shall be in writing and shall state the reasons why the individual feels he or she was treated unfairly. After such re-evaluation if no amicable solution is reached the Director shall forward it to the Board's Personnel Committee for consideration as provided by the grievance procedure starting at the Board level.

Informal Complaint

An employee with an informal complaint shall, within either ten days of the occurrence at issue or the employee's awareness of the situation involving the complaint, first discuss it with the immediate supervisor. This may be done individually or with a representative of the Association or with the assistance of the Personnel Officer. The objective of the discussion shall be to resolve the matter informally if possible.

Steps in Grievance Procedure

Grievance at Beginning and Higher Supervisory Levels

If the informal meeting does not resolve the matter to the satisfaction of the employee, he or she shall within the five days following the informal meeting put the complaint into writing. The complaint shall then be considered a grievance. This may be done with the Association or with the assistance of the immediate supervisor or the Personnel Officer. The written grievance should contain the name(s) of grievant(s), description of the facts of the matter causing dissatisfaction, summary of efforts made to resolve the matter and name of Association representative, if any.

The written grievance shall be given within the five day period to the immediate supervisor and to the Personnel Officer. The immediate supervisor shall have ten days to respond in writing to the grievant. The response of the immediate supervisor may be to forward the matter to the next level supervisor if the matter exceeds the immediate supervisor's scope of authority. Conferences may be called by the immediate supervisor to determine and review facts if necessary.

If the grievant is not satisfied with the written response, he or she shall have five days to forward a request for a hearing to the next level supervisor with a copy going to the next higher level supervisor and to the Personnel Officer. This request shall include copies of the grievance as originally written and the response received from the preceding supervisor. The request will also state any reasons which would support raising the grievance to the next level supervisor. The receiving supervisor shall have ten days in which to review the matter, hold hearings if necessary, and to make a written response with copies to the Personnel Officer, to the next level supervisor and to the Association representative, if any. The grievant may raise the grievance in this manner through the levels of supervision listed in paragraph 7 under *General Principles.* The Personnel Officer shall participate in any hearings that may be called should the grievance advance to the administrative head or higher level.

Grievance at Director's Level

If not satisfied after completion of level two, the grievant has five days in which to make a written request to the Director for a hearing. The Director shall have ten days within which to adjudicate the matter and make a written response with copies to the Personnel Officer, appropriate supervisory personnel, and to the Association representative, if any.

Grievance at the Board Level

If the grievant is still not satisfied he or she has ten days in which to make an appeal to the Personnel Committee of the Board of Trustees.

After receiving the appeal the Personnel Committee of the Board shall instruct the Director to arrange a hearing between the committee and grievant and his or her representative, plus such other parties in interest as may be called for. The committee will render its decision on the case in writing to the grievant with copies to the Director, the Personnel Officer, the supervisors involved, and to the Staff Association Personnel Relations Committee, if involved. The Personnel Committee of the Board shall have twenty days following receipt of the grievant's appeal in which to hold the hearing and study the matter. The Personnel Committee will then make its recommendation in executive session to the full Board at the next regular meeting of the Board. The Director or Personnel Officer shall notify the grievant, the Association, if it is involved, and the supervisors of the Board's decision.

Grievance at Mediation Level

If the grievant is not satisfied with the final action of the Board, and no further discussion is mutually agreed to, the grievant shall have five days following the conclusion of any further discussions with the Board in which to request that the Board enter into mediation over the matter. The Board of Trustees and grievant shall enter the matter into mediation through a mutually acceptable mediator from the Labor-Management Citizens Committee. The mediator will act as an impartial third party to assist in identifying common ground upon which agreement can be reached and to facilitate a full exchange of information upon which the Board may re-evaluate its decision.

NATRONA COUNTY PUBLIC LIBRARY
(Casper, Wyoming)
Handling of Complaints or Appeals

Should an employee feel he or she has been treated unfairly, the Library provides recourse through the following grievance or complaint procedure. Typical grievances might involve wages, job classifications, promotions, terminations, transfers, working conditions, and supervisory directives.

Within 3 weeks of the incident generating the complaint, an employee should first try to resolve the matter with his immediate supervisor. The supervisor will also inform the Director of the grievance, the action taken by, and the decision arrived at by the supervisor.

If dissatisfied with the supervisor's decision, an employee may appeal to the Director within two weeks of the supervisor's decision. The employee and supervisor should each submit separate, signed statements to the Director relating the facts of each side. The Director, employee, supervisor, and a representative from the staff association, if requested by the employee, will meet together in an effort to resolve the matter. The representative from the staff association will be appointed by the chairperson of the association. The Director will furnish his decision in writing to the employee and supervisor within one week after the Board meeting.

If there is dissatisfaction with the Director's decision, final appeal may be made to the Board of Trustees during its next meeting. The Director, employee, supervisor, and staff association representative will meet together with the Board in an effort to settle the matter. The Board will give its decision in writing to all four parties within one week after the Board's meeting.

Time allowances may be waived by mutual consent of the parties.

EARLHAM COLLEGE
(Richmond, Indiana)
Review of Librarians

Five-Year Review

Each professional librarian shall undergo an assessment every five years until one shall have attained the age of 60.

Early in the year in which assessment is to occur, the librarian and the Provost will have a short conference to work out specific details of the assessment. They will determine the membership of a committee of three (to include one other librarian and a Faculty Affairs Committee member) who will make a final reading and evaluation of the dossier. The Provost and faculty member will also reach agreement on the persons from whom other materials will be requested. A dossier will be collected. Ordinarily it should contain the following:

1. A self-evaluation. This is probably the most important document in the file, and it is assumed that the faculty members will

devote considerable thought to its preparation. While it could review past accomplishments and weaknesses, it should be primarily forward-looking with a detailed statement of the member's professional and personal plans, aspirations, and needs for the following five years.

2. Letters from colleagues, including the Library director (unless he or she is a member of the Committee). These should be from colleagues both in and outside the Library, and also those in the profession at large.

3. Additional documentation considered relevant. This might include copies of publications or proposals to granting agencies, reports of a professional nature, summaries of meetings attended, talks given, descriptions of professional activities, etc.

4. Letters from students, present and past, which speak to the criteria listed below under "Two-Year Review."

Consultation and Report

During the fall term the committee will consult and work with the librarian being assessed, preferably on a fairly regular basis. Informal discussions with the librarian, observing him/her in various working situations if this is mutually agreeable, and consultation on the preparation of the self-evaluation should ease the tension of such an assessment and should give committee members far greater insight into the librarian's performance than could be obtained by only reading the dossier. Early in the second term the committee will weigh the results of their consultations and materials in the dossier and will forward a written report to the Provost accompanied by the dossier. The librarian being evaluated will receive a copy of this report.

Follow Up and Development

After reading the file and taking into consideration the comments of the committee of three, the Provost will confer with the librarian to determine ways in which the College can contribute in the following years to his or her growth and development. The Director should participate in this conference. Presumably this will include discussion of sabbatical and other leave plans, the possible commitment of special development funds to the librarian, and the like.

Two-Year Review

In addition to the extensive (and time-consuming) five-year review, there should be a shorter two-year review. This review should entail a discussion between the librarian being reviewed and the Library director that is based on forms that have been filled out by the librarian, the Director, one other librarian, and a member of the teaching faculty or administration. The forms should include the following criteria:

1. Performance of Duties.
   Organization of work. Quantity of work. Quality of work. Problem-solving ability. Acceptance of responsibility. Initiative. Recognition of need for and testing of new patterns of work organization. Teaching effectiveness, with individuals and/or classes. Supervising effectiveness.

2. Professional Qualities.
   Depth of professional knowledge. Depth of specialized knowledge. Current awareness of trends. Professional activities. Potential for growth.

3. Personal Qualities.
   Intellectual vitality. Breadth of interests. Helpful attitude toward students and faculty. Flexibility. Attitude toward criticism. Dependability—maintenance of schedule. Cooperativeness with colleagues.

4. Contributions to Community.
   Participation in college governance. Relations with colleagues. Counseling of students. Participation in college programs.

5. Congruence with Earlham College Institutional Identity.
   Support for Earlham College's basic commitment. Support for system of governance. Reflection of values.

INDIANA UNIVERSITY LIBRARIES
(Bloomington, Indiana)

RANKS FOR LIBRARIANS

Criteria for Promotion

The criteria for promotion are (1) performance, (2) professional development, research and/or creativity, and (3) service. Promotion considerations must take into account, however, differences in mission among campuses, and among schools within some campuses, as well as the individual librarian's contribution to his school/campus mission. The relative weight attached to the criteria above should and must vary accordingly. Promotion to any rank is a recognition of past achievement and a sign of confidence that the individual is capable of greater responsibilities and accomplishments.

Affiliate Librarian

Definition and Criteria: The rank for librarians who have a master's degree from an American Library Association accredited library school or the equivalent professional credentials, *or* a graduate degree in other professional or scholarly fields where appropriate, and less than two years of appropriate experience.

This rank shall not be held longer than three years. The second evaluation must be followed by a recommendation resulting in (1) promotion, or (2) a one year terminal appointment, or (3) continuation in rank based on extenuating circumstances (e.g., illness) which shall be explained to justify continuation in this rank.

Tenure: Time spent in this rank is counted toward tenure.

Assistant Librarian

Definition and Criteria: The rank for librarians who have had at least two years of appropriate experience, whose performance has met and fulfills the requirements of operational standards, whose professional development, research and/or creativity, and service have been satisfactory, and who show potential for meeting the criteria for promotion to Associate Librarian.

Tenure: Time spent in this rank is counted toward tenure. In exceptional cases, librarians may be tenured in this rank.

Associate Librarian

Definition and Criteria: The rank for librarians who have excelled in performance as Assistant Librarians and whose professional development, research and/or creativity, and service shows continued improvement.

Tenure: Tenure is normally attained in this rank; however, promotions to this rank may be made before the sixth year without granting tenure.

Librarian

Definition and Criteria: The rank for librarians whose performance as Associate Librarian has been superior, and whose professional development, research and/or creativity or service has resulted in the attainment of state, regional or national recognition in the library profession.

Tenure: Tenure accompanies this rank.

Visiting Librarian

Definition and Criteria: The term "visiting" is used in instances where, (1) an individual is on leave from another place of employment, (2) an individual is employed on a temporary basis, or (3) an individual is being considered for a permanent position or is considering acceptance of a permanent position . . . .

Tenure: This is not a tenure track appointment.

Adjunct Librarian

Definition and Criteria: This title is used when the status conferred by such a title is deemed important and in a variety of circumstances ranging from those in which the appointees are contributing their services gratis, for a limited period and on a part-time basis, to other cases in which the appointees are compensated for part of their time.

Tenure: This is not a tenure track appointment.

Part-Time Librarian

Definition and Criteria: Individuals holding these positions devote only part of their time to the duties of a librarian. They may also be gainfully employed in other activities, either with Indiana University or elsewhere. Thus a full-time employee of Indiana University may still be a part-time librarian. A part-time appointee is also appointed at the rank which would be given were that individual being considered for a full-time position. When an individual is employed in such part-time rank on a continuing or recurrent basis, promotion in rank must go through normal procedures of that unit of the library.

Tenure: This is not a tenure track appointment.

REPRESENTATIVE STANDARDS FOR PROMOTION AND TENURE

Performance

A member of the library faculty must be, first and foremost, an effective librarian in the position she/he fills on the library staff. Evidence of effective accomplishment of professional responsibilities is provided by position descriptions and evaluations made in relation to them. Additional evidence may be provided by descriptions of innovative procedures, publications relative to performance, etc., and evaluation by library users and colleagues.

Professional Development, Research and/or Creativity

A member of the library faculty who is responsive to the demands of his/her profession should make contributions through professional development, research and/or creativity. Evidence might include professional growth through additional formal or continuing education; preparation of scholarly bibliographies, catalogues, indexes or exhibits; presentation of papers or lectures at conferences; receipt of fellowships, grants, awards or other special honors; publication or research including that in process; and attendance at professional meetings, conferences, workshops, etc.

Service

A member of the library faculty is expected to assume service obligations. Fulfilling these obligations enhances the value of the librarian as a member of the university and library community. Evidence of this concern might include such activities as participation in professional or scholarly societies; service on academic, professional or scholarly committees; professional consultation; and community service in organizations outside the university and/or outside the profession which enhances the image of the university (the relative weight attached to this kind of service varies according to the mission of the individual campus).

THE PROMOTION PROCESS

"Advancement within the library ranks shall be by promotion . . . ." Recommendations for promotion in rank are processed as follows:

The Personnel Librarian initiates the promotion process by notifying *all librarians*, their supervisors and, for non-Bloomington units, the appropriate academic officer, that the promotion process should begin.

The supervisors, after reviewing their staff for promotion consideration, notify the individual librarian that she/he is being considered for promotion, and that the professional dossier should be prepared.

If a librarian has not been notified by her/his supervisor that he/she has been recommended for promotion, it is her/his and others' privilege to "submit a recommendation for the promotion of any faculty member including himself or herself. These recommendations shall be properly documented." . . .

When a candidate is not promoted, it is "the obligation of the department chairman (supervisor or dean) to review with the candidate the reasons for the failure to promote, if such a request is made by the faculty member involved." . . .

TENURE

The Principle of Tenure for Librarians

The principle of tenure imposes reciprocal responsibilities on the University as a body politic and on the librarian. The University has the responsibility of maintaining the principles of academic freedom. To discharge this responsibility the University provides tenure in order that the librarian may be secure in her/his professional work. The librarian, on her/his part, is obligated to maintain high standards of professional conduct, research and creativity, and performance in the development and organization of library services, and in the communication of information and knowledge to others . . . .

Granting of tenure to I.U. Bloomington library faculty shall normally constitute promotion to associate librarian for those library faculty not already holding that rank.

Criteria for Tenure

After the appropriate probationary period, tenure shall be granted to those faculty members whose professional characteristics indicate they will continue to serve with distinction in their appointed roles. Tenure considerations must take into account the mission of the particular unit and the individual librarian's contribution to that mission. A candidate for tenure should excel in performance and be satisfactory in the following two categories: (1) professional development, research and/or creativity, (2) service.

Authority for Implementation

The implementation of tenure for librarians is based upon the following statement adopted by the Board of Trustees at its meeting of June 30, 1972: "Subject to the provisions which follow, a person appointed as a *professional librarian* in the Indiana University Library System shall have *Library* tenure after the same probationary period that is applicable to the faculty. In general the same procedures which govern faculty tenure determinations (i.e., probationary period, termination of probationary service, non-reappointment, appeal procedures, etc.) for members of the teaching faculty shall be applicable to professional librarians." . . .

Notice of Terms of Initial Appointment

Before a librarian is appointed to library rank in the University, the initial salary, rank, years as a librarian elsewhere creditable toward tenure, and duration of the initial appointment and of the probationary period shall be stated in writing and placed in the possession of the University and the librarian. The librarian shall also be advised in writing, before or at the time of the initial appointment, of the criteria and procedures employed in recommendations and decisions about reappointment and the award of tenure specified in the *Academic Handbook* and library documents. The librarian shall acknowledge in writing at the time of acceptance of the appointment that the conditions and terms of the initial appointment, as well as the criteria and procedures for reappointment and tenure, are agreed to.

Credit Toward Tenure

Credit toward tenure for previous experience shall normally not exceed three years; however, in exceptional cases, tenure may be conferred at the time of initial appointment. (It should be explained to applicants that acceptance of the maximum of three years credit at the time of appointment may not work in her/his favor since review for tenure will begin in approximately two years. This may not be adequate time to prepare for review.) Experience in a professional position without the Master's degree or its equivalent shall not normally be credited toward tenure.

Experience in Other Academic and/or Research Libraries
Service in a professional library position in other academic and/or research institutions may be credited toward tenure.

Experience in Other Libraries
Under ordinary circumstances, credit toward tenure may be given only for previous experience which is directly relevant to anticipated responsibilities at Indiana University. In case of doubt, a job description of the previous position(s) should be requested. Credit toward tenure for experience in other libraries may be granted on a year to year ratio after such experience has been evaluated.

Non-Library Experience
If an individual holds a graduate degree in other professional or scholarly fields, *relevant* non-library experience may be credited toward tenure.

Probationary Period

An individual appointed as a librarian for full-time service shall have library tenure after a probationary period of not more than seven years. Under administrative policies and practices at Indiana University, when a written agreement reduces a librarian's probationary period to less than seven years, this agreement is binding on both parties. The length of the probationary period resulting from any such reduction cannot at a later date be extended to suit the convenience of a librarian or his/her library unit. Since the acquisition of tenure represents a major change in a librarian's status, the librarian to whom tenure is being granted shall be so informed in writing.

Librarians are appointed on a fiscal year basis. When a probationary period expires during a fiscal year, the probationary period will be extended to the end of the year.

Annual Review

During the period of probationary appointment the librarian shall receive an annual review of professional performances. At this time, it is the responsibility of the immediate supervisor to inform the librarian of her/his progress toward meeting the criteria for promotion and tenure. The librarian shall cooperate with the principal administrative officer to insure that the file on which such a review is based contains all relevant materials. Each annual review shall be kept in the file, and a copy given to the librarian.

Notice Requirements

Before any decision is made within a library unit about whether to recommend reappointment or the award of tenure, the librarian shall be notified that she/he is under such consideration and that within a specified and reasonable period of time the librarian may submit materials which she/he believes will be relevant to a consideration of her/his professional qualifications.

The librarian shall be notified as soon as possible of any decision by a library unit not to recommend reappointment or tenure, and the individual shall be notified within stated deadlines of a decision by the University not to reappoint her/him.

At the time that a librarian is notified of a negative recommendation on reappointment or tenure, he or she shall be provided with a copy of the All-University Librarians' Review Board *Final Report* to insure that he/she is fully informed of his/her rights.

Notice of Non-Reappointment

For full-time librarians, notice of non-reappointment shall be given in writing in accordance with the following standards:

Not later than February 1 of the first academic year of service, if the appointment expires at the end of that year; or, if a one-year appointment terminates during an academic year, at least three months in advance of its termination.

Not later than November 15 of the second academic year of service, if the appointment expires at the end of that year; or, if an initial two-year appointment terminates during an academic year, at least six months in advance of its termination.

At least twelve months before the expiration of an appointment after two or more years in the institution.

Review of Decision of Non-Reappointment of Librarians

Upon receiving notice of a negative recommendation or decision on reappointment or tenure, the first recourse of the librarian shall be to request an oral explanation from her/his principal administrative officer.

Upon written request, submitted within thirty days of notification of non-reappointment, to the principal administrative officer, that officer shall provide the librarian within thirty days a written statement of the reasons for non-reappointment. The statement of reasons should reflect careful consideration of the qualifications of the librarian in terms of the professional standards and needs of her/his department, or division, and the University Libraries.

The librarian who believes that a recommendation or a decision that she/he not be reappointed has resulted from inadequate consideration of professional competence or erroneous information may offer corrections and request reconsideration at the level at which the decision not to recommend reappointment was first made.

If the librarian is dissatisfied with the result of a request for reconsideration she/he may petition the Librarians' Review Board for a review of the procedures employed in the decision not to recommend reappointment. The petition must be initiated within thirty days following the receipt by the librarian of the written statement of the reasons for non-reappointment [as specified in the] Librarians' Review Board, *Final Report.*

Before undertaking a review, the All-University Librarians' Review Board may seek to bring about a settlement of the issue satisfactory to both parties. The All-University Librarians' Review Board shall provide copies of its report and recommendations within thirty days of reaching its decision to the librarian, the principal administrative officer of the library unit in which the librarian holds an appointment, the Dean of University Libraries, the campus Chancellor, and other appropriate administrative officers.

Upon finding by the All-University Librarians' Review Board (accepted by the Dean of University Libraries) that the librarian did not enjoy full benefit of the procedures through fault of an administrative officer or body of the University, the University shall, if necessary to avoid prejudicing the rights of the librarian, extend the probationary appointment for one year beyond its normal termination point, or take other appropriate measures agreeable to the librarian.

Recourse by a librarian to the various rights of appeal, review, and reconsideration set forth above shall not be construed as precluding the University's right to give timely notice of non-reappointment as specified [above]. In normal circumstances it is to be anticipated that reconsideration and review will occur before the effective date of termination.

In light of the legitimate educational interests of students, faculty, colleagues, and others, it is the mutual obligation of the University administration and of the affected librarian to observe promptly and fully the above procedures . . . .

AUGSBURG COLLEGE
(Minneapolis, Minnesota)
Promotion in Rank and Tenure of Librarians

The Librarians at Augsburg College shall have the following ranks corresponding and parallel to the ranks of the teaching faculty: College Librarian I, College Librarian II, College Librarian III, and College Librarian IV.

The professional Librarian usually begins his position at Augsburg College as College Librarian I. After not more than five years of full-time service with this rank, when reappointed, he shall be promoted to the rank of College Librarian II. The time of promotion to higher ranks shall be indeterminate.

Promotions shall be based upon six criteria:

1. Educational preparation. The normal requirement for College Librarian I is a Master's degree in Library Science. A College Librarian II is required to have at least one Master's degree. For College Librarian III a second Master's degree or another graduate degree is usually required. The promotion to College Librarian IV normally would demand additional subject specialization, viz., a Master's or a Doctor's degree
2. Performance of academic responsibilities
3. Administrative abilities
4. Participation in college and community affairs
5. Professional interests and activities
6. Personal qualities.

(Detailed information on criteria 2-6 will be found in the Faculty Handbook.)

College Librarians shall acquire tenure according to the same regulations and provisions as the teaching faculty of the corresponding ranks.

CALIFORNIA STATE UNIVERSITY AND COLLEGES
(Long Beach, California)
Personnel Plan for Librarians

[Reprinted below is the new (1978) Librarian Personnel Plan of the California State University and Colleges. It differs from the previous plan in several respects. The major changes are discernible from the prefactory material. The Personnel Plan covers the 19 campuses in the California State University and Colleges (CSUC) system.]

Introduction

Since 1961, efforts have been made to recognize in personnel policies the evolutionary nature of librarianship and the academic functions of librarians in the CSUC. Personnel plans in the form of classification and qualifications standards, regulations covering tenure rights, appointment procedures, probationary service, etc., have been revised and updated periodically after consultation and systemwide review.

There have been changes over time in the type of work performed by academic librarians as campuses have modified organizational structures of the libraries; have more closely coordinated the holdings and advisory services of the library with academic program planning and curricular offerings; and have instituted new technologies in the operations of the library. Equally important in the process of change has been the increasing professional development of the librarians, their conscientious efforts to encompass academic and educational objectives in their library work, and their concern for the need for high quality standards to be used in evaluations for appointment, retention, promotion and tenure decisions. Personnel standards and policies have reflected these advancements.

Background

In Title 5 of the California Administrative Code, librarians in the CSUC are identified as academic employees, in the academic-related job category. This designation was reaffirmed by Board of Trustee resolution.

As academic employees, librarians are covered by the same academic tenure regulations as pertain to teaching faculty, including: the same probationary period provisions; the early granting of tenure at the President's discretion; the same regulations covering service credits, terminal year appointments, and notice dates for retention and tenure; and the same policies on consultation and peer judgment in matters of appointment, retention, promotion, tenure and merit step adjustments.

Librarians are covered by the same academic grievance and disciplinary action procedures as faculty . . . .

Librarians participate in academic governance. They are eligible for membership in local faculty senates and councils and they have served in the statewide Academic Senate . . . .

In addition, sick leave regulations for librarians are the same as for all other employees, including instructional faculty. Retirement benefits are the same as for all other employees, including instructional faculty. Librarians, at all levels, accrue 24 days vacation per year—the same rate as for 12-month instructional faculty and academic administrators. While librarians do not have academic year appointments, they are entitled to 10-month appointments with a concomitant reduction in salary. The two months off may be any two consecutive months in a fiscal year. Most, if not all, CSUC libraries now have in operation retention, tenure, and promotion procedures which include a process of peer review and the use of professional evaluation criteria for librarian personnel recommendations.

New Personnel Plan

This personnel plan represents a major change in the method of evaluating professional librarians for advancement. Professional librarian classes are removed from the classification system and incumbents of librarian positions will be evaluated for promotion, through a process of peer review, subsequent review by academic administrators and approval by the President of his/her designee.

Procedures for considering promotion actions for librarians shall be developed by each campus and may be coordinated with procedures for appointment, retention, tenure and merit step increases.

Regulations governing appointment, retention and tenure of librarians and appropriate consultative procedures are covered in Title 5 of the California Administrative Code, Sections 42701, 42702, Article 13 and Article 2.7. Additional information is contained in FSA 71-57 and Supplement #1.

It shall be campus responsibility, using appropriate consultative procedures, to develop promotion procedures, including the organization, selection, structuring and responsibilities of personnel committees; the establishment of general evaluation criteria in accordance with the guidelines in this document; and the development of specific and more detailed criteria for making distinctions among the various ranks of librarians and for evaluating qualifications and professional competence of librarians in promotion considerations. The procedures and criteria shall be subject to review and approval by academic administrators or others in accordance with campus academic personnel policies.

The evaluation of librarians shall include, at a minimum, consideration of such factors as experience, education, professional achievements, university and community service, etc., and in addition, shall include professional competence in the performance of academic library assignments, and professional contribution, growth and development as they relate to library functions and responsibilities.

Professional growth and development are essential in the advancement of librarians. Librarians are responsible for planning career goals and for acquiring pertinent education and training, for pursuing scholarly activities, and taking advantage of challenging experiences. Campuses are encouraged to provide opportunities for, and to facilitate to the extent possible, the professional development and pursuit of career goals of librarians, considering both the needs of the library and the needs of the individual.

Classes for Professional Positions

New classes of positions are established for professional librarians which provide for four ranks within each class. One class is for librarians serving 12-month appointments, and one for librarians serving 10-month appointments.

Librarian–10 month
Assistant Librarian
Senior Assistant Librarian
Associate Librarian
Librarian

Librarian–12 month
Assistant Librarian
Senior Assistant Librarian
Associate Librarian
Librarian . . . .

Processing Promotion Recommendations

Each campus will develop a method for determining when *consideration* for promotion of a librarian is appropriate. Recommendations may be made by the head of an organizational unit, on the basis of an eligibility time schedule, by personnel committee initiation or by other methods. The promotion cycle would typically be the same as that used for teaching faculty.

All promotions must be based on merit considerations. Length of service or time in rank are not sufficient bases for promotion.

Personnel files shall be updated so that appraisers will have current and complete information upon which to base their assessments and, if necessary, their rankings of candidates.

Evaluations by Department Chairs, Division Chairs in the library and library academic administrators are essential in the promotion review.

Librarians are responsible for submitting current information for inclusion in their personnel files for use of the personnel review committees. Such information should include a current resume; a description of special achievements, participation in professional associations, publications, scholarly work; local, regional and national recognition by professional colleagues; campus committee work; etc. The submissions should provide a complete description of contributions made, committee work performed, etc.

The personnel file should also include a statement of responsibilities which is to be used in the appraisal and review process in evaluating professional competence, contributions, and achievements, service and professional growth against functions and responsibilities as they are mutually understood by the librarian and the department or division chair or academic administrator. (These statements are not to be detailed job descriptions; rather they are to provide a frame of reference and an indication of scope and professional level of responsibility.)

It would be desirable for the campus to develop procedures for obtaining recommendations and evaluations from: students, faculty, administrators who have firsthand knowledge of the library services provided by the candidate; professional colleagues who have firsthand knowledge of the candidate's effectiveness in committee work, in team activities, in specific independent or cooperative projects, etc.; and librarians from off-campus who have had an opportunity to assess the candidate's professional activities, publications, scholarly achievements and contributions to the profession.

Review committees should be sure that information in the file is more than a listing of events and provides explanations and evidence of how the candidate's abilities and achievements are demonstrated in or show potential for higher rank professional activities.

The entire appraisal process serves not only as a basis for specific recommendations but provides an opportunity for continuing discussions between the candidate and the department or division chair about the quality of performance, achievements, strengths and weaknesses, courses of action to correct weakness, and paths to follow in career development. Performance and achievements should be measured against organizational and professional objectives and expectations and evidence of progress.

Campuses should incorporate in their local procedures opportunities for the candidate to rebut information in the file, to request reconsideration of a recommendation, etc., necessary documentation and time lines for submission of materials. Campuses also shall determine the levels and sequence of review and recommendations by committees and individual administrators. Department and division chairs shall submit separate recommendations from those of committees. The use of college or university-wide faculty personnel committees is at the option of the campus.

Documentation of promotion actions for professional librarians shall be processed in the same manner as the documentation of faculty promotion actions.

General Characteristics of Different Ranks of Professional Librarians

Campuses shall be responsible for developing specific criteria to be used for determining the characteristics of each of the professional librarian ranks . . . .

In general terms, the ranks may be differentiated as follows:

Assistant Librarian—This is the entry level of librarians with graduate degrees in library science and little or no professional library experience. During the time spent at this rank, the librarian is expected to learn how to apply fundamentals of library science to academic library programs and problems. Generally, librarians would not receive tenure at this rank.

Senior Assistant Librarian—This is the rank in which the librarian with a few years of experience and continuing education and training, performs the full range of librarian activities within a particular function or service with considerable independence.

Associate Librarian—This is the rank in which librarians with typically at least 7 or 8 years' experience and considerable professional achievement serve as specialists in a given subject area or as recognized authorities in a broad range of activities using initiative, judgment and independence in solving unique problems and developing innovative approaches and recommendations. Only tenured librarians or those selected for the simultaneous award of tenure may be promoted to this rank. Librarians initially appointed to this rank will serve the usual probationary period.

Librarian—This is the top rank for librarians who pursue the very difficult problems and provide creative approaches and solutions in areas for which typically there are no precedents. Librarians at this rank usually have at least 10 years of experience and typically are recognized for their professional competence and scholarly contributions in regional or national professional circles. Librarians initially appointed to this rank are subject to the same provisions for probationary period and tenure as are Full Professors.

Positions which include leadership of a department, division, or similar organizational unit along with the performance of professional library activities are to be included in the professional class at the appropriate rank.

The leadership responsibilities involve, for example, interpreting and applying library policy; coordinating services of his/her organizational unit with other library units; recommending budget and staffing needs and monitoring the use of budgeted funds and staff; chairing personnel committees, making appointments and other personnel recommendations; developing new methods for improved service; informing administrators of changing needs in staffing, equipment and policy as those needs relate to changes in workload, changes in direction of campus programs or technological and/or philosophical changes in the profession; maintaining expertise in campus, state, and national trends in education and library science.

Minimum Requirements

The minimum requirement for entry into the professional librarian class is a graduate degree in library science (at least one year beyond the bachelor's level) from an ALA accredited library school, or a school of equivalent quality. Equivalent quality shall be determined by the campus.

The previous systemwide mandatory requirement for a second master's degree or equivalent academic or professional achievement is eliminated. Appropriate advanced degrees for librarians may be considered in the evaluation process. Campuses may utilize educational requirements, including a second master's degree as part of their criteria for promotion, as they see fit, so long as any requirements can be justified as job or career related in accordance with affirmative action regulations and policies. For career advancement, librarians must show professional and academic growth and development as well as competence on the job and professional achievement. The acquisition of appropriate and relevant advanced degrees may be one way of obtaining additional professional knowledge and expertise; other types of education, and/or research or scholarly work may also contribute to professional knowledge and experience which will enhance the librarian's professional development.

Classes of Academic Administrative Positions

Assistant Director of the Library
Associate Director of the Library—12 month
Director of the Library

A new class of Assistant Director of the Library has been added. This class would typically have an organizational title of Assistant Director for . . . .

No tenure is earned in these classes; rather tenure is earned and held in the professional librarian class . . . .

The option for a librarian to be at a 10-month appointment in accordance with Article 2.7 in Title 5 of the California Administrative Code is not provided for incumbents of academic-administrative positions.

Documentation for personnel actions for academic-administrative librarians will be processed like appointment actions for Deans.

Definitions of Levels of Academic-Administrative Librarians

Director of the Library

The Director of the Library, under very general policy direction, is responsible for planning, directing, coordinating and evaluating all facets of a campus academic library, including the development of the collection and the providing of library services to support and enhance the educational programs of the campus, participation in the development of educational policy of the campus, and the development of requests for the necessary resources for effective management of the library.

Associate Director of the Library

The Associate Director serves as full assistant or deputy to the Director in a medium-sized (5,000 or more FTEs) and larger campus with responsibility for sharing with the Director the planning and administration of the library. The Associate Director functions with a high degree of independence and plays a major role in total administration, i.e., program planning, financial and budgetary planning, personnel and management planning including the introduction of new library technologies, and is responsible for program implementation and evaluations of library operations. The Associate Director typically provides technical and administrative direction to the heads of the organizational units and may, in addition, be assigned special projects involving, for example, major acquisition programs, the automation of library services and records. The use of this class is limited to one Associate Director at campuses with 5,000 or more FTEs.

Assistant Director of the Library

The Assistant Director of the Library typically serves as full assistant or deputy to the Director on a small campus (fewer than 5,000 FTEs) or serves as the technical and administrative head of one of the two or three large major program subdivisions of the library. The Assistant Director participates in the overall management of the library, providing advice from his/her area of expertise in administrative and professional matters. The Assistant Director serves on library policy councils to assist the Director with the establishment of policies, resource allocations and long-range planning. He/she is responsible for coordination of operations with those of other segments and programs of the library and with faculty, deans and others in matters dealing with educational policy and programs that relate to the library. Assistant Directors are responsible for the planning and resource management (including budget, personnel, physical facilities and operating expense management) of their organizational segments and for being accountable for operations with considerable delegation of authority. They are responsible for stimulating and facilitating the professional growth and career development of the librarians. Assistant Directors typically provide leadership and direction to the chairs of several departments, divisions or other organizational units and have responsibility for seeing that work is effectively accomplished through them. Typically the staff involved include approximately 20 or more professional librarians, library assistants, and clerical employees. Organizational titles for these positions would typically denote the area administered, e.g., Assistant Director for Public Services, Assistant Director for Administration. The use of this class is limited to no more than three Assistant Directors at campuses of 15,000 or more FTEs, to no more than one at campuses of less than 5,000 FTEs, and no more than 2 at campuses between 5,000 and 15,000 FTEs. Some campuses, because of their style of organization and management, may not choose to use this class. This formula is for classification purposes and does not imply additional staffing.

Minimum Qualifications for Director of the Library, Associate Director, Assistant Director

Knowledge of academic library organization, functions, methods, procedures, and practices; knowledge of current library technical and professional literature, methods and advancements; knowledge of principles of management, including personnel management; knowledge of educational principles and practices of higher educational institutions; ability to formulate and administer library policy and procedures; ability to stimulate, develop and evaluate a staff of professional and non-professional employees; ability to work successfully with and through others in developing recommendations; ability to make decisions with respect to library professional and administrative matters, including budgeting, organization, physical facilities, personnel matters; ability to coordinate library services with the instructional program; ability to gain the confidence and respect of the faculty and adminstrators of the campus; ability to be responsive to the changing needs of the campus and the changing needs within the library; ingenuity and resourcefulness in accomplishing objectives within limitations of money, staff, physical facilities, etc.; recognition and stature in the library profession.

The graduate degree in library science from an ALA-accredited library school, or a school of equivalent quality.

A minimum of five years of professional library administrative experience preferably in an academic setting, with responsibility comparable to that of a librarian in charge of a major activity of a large and dynamic library. (Possession of a doctoral degree in library science or a related field may be substituted for two years of experience.)

Experience as an administrative librarian is usually built on a number of years (e.g., 10) as a professional librarian and the demonstration of professional competence and achievements comparable to those characteristics of an Associate Librarian or Librarian in the professional class.

Special Note

The establishment of two classes of professional librarians in place of the eight previous classes has an impact on the operations of the layoff procedures. In the event of layoff, the time served in any of the previous professional librarian classes shall be accumulated for counting seniority in the new classes.

UNIVERSITY OF MISSOURI–ST. LOUIS LIBRARIES
(St. Louis, Missouri)
Grievance Procedures

The Grievance Panel of the Thomas Jefferson Library has established the following procedures to be handled within the Library for all Library personnel (i.e., Academics, Administrative Service and Support Staff, and Student Assistants).

The responsibility of the grievance panel is to be available to sit on a grievance committee to hear grievances in accord with the Grievance Procedures of the University of Missouri-St. Louis Libraries dated June 23, 1975, and updated July 1976. The panel shall be composed of three academic and three non-academic staff members elected annually by the full-time staff, and one student representative elected annually by the student assistants. Any staff member serving as a member of the Chancellor's Grievance Review Panel would be ineligible to serve on the Library Grievance Panel simultaneously.

Should an employee have a complaint or grievance, it is essential for this person to discuss it with his/her supervisor or the person involved, and try to solve it directly. Should the employee feel it is not possible to discuss the problem with the person involved, he/she can file the grievance with the Panel as specified . . . below.

If a grievance cannot be handled within the line channels of the organization, an aggrieved staff member may present the complaint in writing to any member of the panel, who will contact the person against whom the complaint has been lodged. The latter shall designate a second member of the Panel, who with the first shall choose a third member to serve as Chairperson of a three member Ad-Hoc Grievance Committee to hear that grievance.

The employee shall proceed with the complaint to the Grievance Panel member within ten working days from the date that the problem was deemed unresolved.

After having filed a grievance, the person will be given a date to meet with the committee and present his/her grievance.

If a member of the grievance panel is personally involved in a grievance, he/she will disqualify him/herself from the grievance committee during the investigation of that grievance.

If the committee feels that the problem is one that involves a professional dispute, these will be channeled to the appropriate authority. All others will be investigated and all pertinent information and data will be collected. While investigating the problem, the committee will contact all persons involved in order to get the appropriate facts.

While a grievance is under investigation, no punitive action will be taken against any of the involved persons.

The committee will make a recommendation to the persons involved in the grievance within ten working days from the date the committee was notified of the grievance. The person will be asked to meet again with the committee to be informed of the recommendation. All documents related to the investigation will be kept by the committee in strictest confidence. It will be accessible to the Director upon request.

In case the recommendation of the committee is still unsatisfactory to the employee, the committee will submit to the Director of Libraries its recommendation with regard to the grievance. A copy of this recommendation will be distributed to all parties involved.

If the employee is still unsatisfied with the Director's decision, he/she may proceed in filing the grievance through other channels according to the University Guidelines.

Professional Conduct and Standards

SPOKANE PUBLIC LIBRARY
(Spokane, Washington)

PROFESSIONAL ORGANIZATIONS

All employees are urged to join the American Library Association, Washington Library Association, Pacific Northwest Library Association, and the Spokane Inland Empire Librarians' Association. Anyone wishing to accept a nomination for an office in a professional organization is requested to clear with his supervisor.

PROFESSIONAL CONDUCT

The staff owes impartial, courteous service to all persons using the library. It is important for all members of the staff to remember that in meeting the public they are representatives not only of the Spokane Public Library but also of the City of Spokane. If they are rude, careless, or indifferent, it is not they but the library that is blamed for poor service. It is important to remember that service is an essential part of the library organization. It is the library staff member who must see that the right material and the right person get together at the right time. No distinction between patrons, whether on the basis of creed, race, appearance, social or intellectual status may be shown in a tax-supported institution.

Patrons have a right to expect alert and interested service at all times. It is necessary to remember that any question that is presented is important or the library patron would not have asked. There is no better advertising for the library than a satisfied patron. An appearance of indifference or an attitude of superiority or amusement can undo in a single instance the goodwill which may have been built up through years of friendly relationship with a patron.

Service desk attendants are reminded that while on duty they may not eat food or candy, chew gum, lounge, or sit on the desks. They should keep their voices low and well modulated at all times.

Staff members are requested while on duty or in any way representing the library not to voice opinions about controversial matters of any sort whether political, religious, or social. The Spokane Public Library is an impartial institution supplying, as nearly as possible, material on all aspects of controversial questions, but offering no personal interpretations.

Federal and state laws prohibit an employee from using any official authority or influence to interfere with or affect an election or nomination. Nor may an employee coerce, command or advise another employee to lend or contribute his time, money, or anything else of value for political purposes. State law prohibits solicitation of contributions on any state or local government-owned property. An employee may not be a candidate for elective office in a *partisan* election.

WORTHINGTON PUBLIC LIBRARY
(Worthington, Ohio)
Professional Activities

It is policy to encourage membership by staff members in the Ohio Library Association, the American Library Association, and other professional organizations. Staff members are encouraged to attend appropriate professional meetings, workshops and conferences. The board will pay all reasonable expenses incurred at such meetings, upon recommendation of the librarian.

PARAMUS PUBLIC LIBRARY
(Paramus, New Jersey)
Professional Conduct

The first duty of the Library staff is service to the public. Each patron should be given friendly, courteous and prompt service. No matter what the request, it should be considered important.

Staff members should show proper restraint and tact at all times. Difficult situations, or people, should be brought to the attention of the Director.

The staff should always be alert and approachable. Patrons should not be made to feel that the staff is completely absorbed in work or conversation and thus too busy to help them.

Telephone calls should be answered pleasantly and with identification. Whenever possible, calls of a personal nature should be made on the public telephone.

Each member of the staff owes loyalty to the Library and discretion should be exercised in all public comments.

ROCKFORD PUBLIC LIBRARY
(Rockford, Illinois)
Code of Ethics for Staff Members

The Rockford Public Library was established for the benefit of the citizens of Rockford. Members of the staff should assume an obligation to maintain ethical standards of behavior in relation to the Board of Library Directors, to the library as an institution, to fellow workers on the staff, to other members of the profession, and to the public they serve.

It is the responsibility of all staff members to make the resources of the library known to its potential users. Impartial service should be rendered to all who are entitled to use the library.

All staff members should try to protect library property and to inculcate in its users a sense of their responsibility for its preservation.

Criticism of library policies, service, and personnel should be offered only to the proper authority for the sole purpose of improvement of the library.

Loyalty to fellow workers and a spirit of courteous cooperation, whether between individuals or between departments, are essential to effective library service.

Confidential information obtained through contact with library patrons, or through any other source, should not be repeated.

Acceptance of a position in the library incurs an obligation to remain long enough to repay the expense incident in training. Resignations should be made long enough before they take place to allow adequate time for the work to be put in shape and a successor appointed.

Staff members should recognize librarianship as an educational profession and realize that the growing effectiveness of their service is dependent upon their own development. Staff members should participate in public and community affairs and their conduct should be such as to maintain public esteem for the institution which they represent.

MONTGOMERY COUNTY–NORRISTOWN PUBLIC LIBRARY
(Norristown, Pennsylvania)

Conduct

Library employees should dress appropriately and maintain a friendly, courteous, and business like manner with patrons and fellow employees. The patron should have the library assistant's undivided attention at all times. Discussion of personal affairs, socializing with friends or other staff members during working hours are not acceptable behavior. Discussions of library procedures should be carried on behind the scenes and not in public areas unless circumstances warrant immediate discussion.

If a decision must be made when dealing with the public for which there is no precedent, the department head must be consulted, or in his absence, the librarian in charge.

Personal telephone calls should not be made or received except in case of emergency. A public telephone in the lobby may be used during breaks or meal periods.

Staff members are not permitted to engage in political activity during working hours.

No staff member may be disciplined in such a manner as to embarrass the employee before the public or fellow employees unless the conduct of the employee precludes such consideration.

No one is permitted in non-public areas except authorized personnel. Visitors must stop at the office and receive permission before entering any non-public areas.

Solicitation for any purpose whatsoever is not permitted on library premises by the staff or public with the following exceptions:

- Contributions to the Sunshine Club to provide flowers for a staff member who is hospitalized or seriously ill, may be requested by the library secretary. Contributions are voluntary and staff members are not required to participate.
- Contributions for an employee who has resigned must be approved by the Director. No solicitation will be permitted for a staff member employed less than one year.

All registration files and information related to patron use of library materials are confidential and may be used for library procedures and record-keeping only.

Supplies or equipment must be requested through the department head. Purchases may not be made or charged to the library without permission of the Director.

A staff room is maintained for the convenience of employees and volunteers only, for use during coffee breaks and meal periods. Staff members are expected to wash their own utensils, dispose of unused food, and leave the area in a clean and orderly condition.

CALIFORNIA STATE COLLEGE, STANISLAUS
(Turlock, California)
Standards of Conduct

In protecting the integrity of the California State Service, the law includes standards of conduct with which State officers and employees are expected to comply. In accordance with the requirements of Section 19251 of the Government Code, the following employments, activities, or enterprises of every officer and employee under the jurisdiction of the State University and Colleges are inconsistent, incompatible, or in conflict with his duties as a State officer or employee:

1. The use of State time, facilities, equipment, or supplies at any time for any purpose other than the performance of official business.
2. The performance for compensation other than State salary of any service for any person or public or private agency if such person or agency performs any action which is subject to review, recommendation, or approval by the employee or any of his subordinates.
3. The performance for compensation other than State salary at any time of any service which his State duties require him to render.
4. The acceptance of any obligations on the part of any officer or employee which would prevent him from carrying the responsibilities for which he is employed or the acceptance of any responsibilities which would be in conflict with the purposes of the College.
5. The engaging in any activity which is contrary to a policy of the State University and Colleges or otherwise inimical to its welfare.
6. The willful violation of any law, any regulation of the Trustees, or any directive of the Chancellor respecting his employment or performance of his duties.

Staff Development

MT. CARMEL PUBLIC LIBRARY
(Mt. Carmel, Illinois)
Professional Meetings

Staff members and directors are encouraged to attend professional meetings. Work schedules shall be arranged at the discretion of the librarian, to permit rotation of such attendance by all interested staff members, so long as normal operation of the library is not interfered with. Expenses or salary may be paid by the library for staff members or directors designated by the librarian or the Board as official representatives of the library. Staff members and directors are encouraged to become members of the Illinois Library Association.

WILLIAM RUSSELL PULLEN LIBRARY
GEORGIA STATE UNIVERSITY
(Atlanta, Georgia)

MEETINGS OF PROFESSIONAL AND SCHOLARLY ORGANIZATIONS

The William Russell Pullen Library encourages faculty membership and participation in meetings of local, state, and national professional associations. "Professional Associations" shall be defined as those organizations—library and archival, subject-specialty related, or general—concerned with the acquisition, organization, preservation, interpretation and sharing of information and shall include the American Association of University Professors. "Meetings" shall be defined as the general conferences, special assemblies, workshops, seminars, institutes, committee meetings, and other formally structured discussions of the professional associations. Released time to attend meetings of professional associations will be granted, whenever possible, depending on departmental schedules and workloads. A limited amount of funds may be available to help defray costs of attending meetings of professional associations.

Approval of the department head must be obtained for any released time requested to attend meetings of professional associations. Additionally, approval of the University Librarian must be obtained for any released time requested to attend meetings of professional associations held out-of-town or those meetings which potentially involve reimbursement of funds or authorization to travel.

It is the responsibility of the University Librarian to disburse any available funds and to determine who will attend meetings of professional associations in the event the number of persons wishing to attend is greater than the number who can legitimately be granted released time. The following guidelines, not ranked in order, shall assist the University Librarian in making this decision:

1. Scheduled appearance on the program of the professional association;
2. Representation of the library or the university; for example at SOLINET's functions for membership;
3. Current service as an officer of the professional association;
4. Current service as an officer of a committee of the professional association;
5. Current service as a committee member of the professional association;
6. Degree of relevance of the meeting to a faculty member's professional work; and
7. Membership in the professional association.

FACULTY RESEARCH ASSISTANCE

To encourage our faculty in their research and in recognition of the benefits the library will derive from problem-solving based on sound research, some support is offered in individual research projects. Areas of support include photocopying, clerical assistance, and released time. The following approval route should be followed:

1. The researcher should submit to the University Librarian a prospectus (no more than two pages) succinctly reviewing the most significant literature, outlining methodology, and defining ramifications of research. Type of support requested with any cost data should also be listed.
2. The University Librarian will enlist the aid of one or more readers for the prospectus;
3. The researcher, the University Librarian, and the reader(s) may meet to discuss the proposed research; and
4. The reader(s) will advise the University Librarian on the merit of the proposed research.

The University Librarian will decide whether to assist the proposed research project. Factors in such a decision will include: staffing and financial considerations in the library, the merit of the proposal, the merit of the topic, and the needs of the library.

Both applied and theoretical research will be considered. The potential "publishability" of any effort should be underscored in a request for assistance. It is probable that some proposals may be greeted with loud hurrahs but the resources requested may not be available; in those cases, the researcher may be asked (1) to resubmit his proposal at the beginning of a new funding period, (2) to modify his research so that our resources can accommodate his needs, or (3) to accept what we can provide although we realize that such contribution will only provide some assistance, not even the lion's share.

Inevitably, some proposals are less meritorious than others. One should not take a rejection as a condemnation of one's interest in some topic. The rejection is only the opinion of one or, at the most, several people, so the researcher may wish to refine his/her original idea or pursue another one. The researcher might want to discuss preliminarily his/her research topic with the University Librarian or another colleague prior to doing the necessary work for a prospectus. Sometimes, the difficult part of research is defining and refining the topic, question, or hypothesis, and discussion should help one formulate the necessary questions.

CHERRY HILL LIBRARY
(Cherry Hill, New Jersey)
Staff Development Policy

The Board of Trustees of the Cherry Hill Free Public Library encourages staff attendance at professional meetings that have to do with the work of staff members, to bring to the Library information and ideas gained from programs and contacts with others in the profession on local, regional, state and national levels.

Time Allowances

The absence must be so arranged by the Director that the Library's service is not hampered. Time allowed for attendance at meetings will in no case be a cause for overtime, or extra compensation for part-time personnel, or exceed a normal 7 hour day or 35 hour week. Travel time by the most direct route is to be included in the above statement. If the destination can be reached and return made over week-ends, no allowance for travel is made. Time off for legal holidays that fall during a leave for a professional meeting may be taken either before or immediately after the meeting or at some other time.

Payment of Travel Expenses

Travel expenses such as mileage, room rent, registration fees, meals, tolls, parking fees, and purchased transportation incurred in attending professional library meetings, visits to other libraries, and for travel necessary to accomplish library business, shall be reimbursed to the extent of the approved travel budget for the year.

Eligibility

The number and names of staff members to attend each meeting will be selected on the basis of the nature of the meeting and the funds available. Priority will be given (a) to the professional staff, (b) those participating in or having the greatest responsibility at the meeting, (c) semi-professionals or clerks who have an interest in the meeting. Full-time personnel in priorities mentioned ... will have priority over part-time personnel (those who work 20 hours per week or more).

In-Service Training

The Cherry Hill Free Public Library is willing to arrange adjustment of time in order that full-time employees may take advantage of opportunities for special study, as long as this does not lessen the physical efficiency of the individual or place undue strain upon other employees. For institutes, or work conferences, leave without pay may be granted for periods exceeding one day. Tuition for graduate courses in Library Science will be reimbursed in full upon receipt of a passing grade for the course, subject to the approval of the Director.

Staff Meetings

It is important for the well-being of the Library that complete understanding exists between the staff and the administration and among the individual members of the staff on the policies and programs of the Library and its agencies. The purpose of staff meetings is to present and explain matters of policy; to discuss professional problems; new trends, techniques; to promote progress in the library profession. The staff is urged to suggest questions for consideration, and all staff members are invited to participate in any discussion period. All employees of the Library are members of the staff and are welcome to attend any staff meeting. However, attendance is expected only of those regularly employed full-time or part-time personnel who work more than 20 hours per week.

Staff meetings called by the Director is an assignment and is governed by the same rules of promptness and attendance as regular schedule for full-time and part-time (20 hours or more) employees. Time is allowed for such meetings during regularly scheduled working hours. Part-time staff members, regardless of hours worked, are to be paid or compensating time allowed for attending.

INDIANA UNIVERSITY LIBRARIES
(Bloomington, Indiana)
Staff Development/ Continuing Education Activities [Summary]

Committee Participation

Staff members serve on various committees of the administration, the library units, the Library Faculty and the Support Staff Organization. During the past year, many staff members participated in an internal Management Review and Analysis Program (MRAP) which resulted in a report released early in 1976. The philosophy of consultative management underlies this form of staff input which precedes administrative decision-making.

Conferences, Workshop, Seminars, etc.

Library staff members are given the opportunity to participate in professional association activities and programs often through released time and/or payment of expenses. The individual staff member must submit his request for released time to the supervisor and/or unit head for consideration. Library faculty members may submit requests for travel support to the Faculty Affairs and Continuing Education Committee, the Library Faculty Committee which administers the faculty travel fund. A policy and procedures document for the travel fund is available from the Committee ...

Departmental Meetings

Library unit heads meet with staff members to inform them of current Libraries' programs, policies and problems; to discuss unit matters; and to answer questions. Some units publish minutes of their meetings.

Educational Assistance for I.U. Libraries Employees

The following privilege of fee courtesy shall be extended to all full-time faculty and full-time staff employees on appointment and their spouses, within the limitations indicated:

Fees for a full-time appointed (100% F.T.E.) employee enrolled in 1-6 credit hours in a semester or summer sessions will be assessed at one-half the resident credit hour rate at the campus where the employee enrolls, for the actual number of hours taken. Fees for credit hours in excess of six (6) in a semester or summer sessions will be assessed at full resident rate on that campus ....

Approval of the Department Head will be necessary when classes are scheduled during the employee's working hours. Time taken from work can and will be made up at other than normal work hours at scheduled times determined by the Department Head. It is recommended that, whenever possible, classes be scheduled at the beginning or ending hours of the morning or afternoon work periods, or during the evening.

...Approved ... interim proposal from the Library Faculty Work Environment Committee: "A member of the library Faculty may have up to three hours per week of release time from work for the purpose of class attendance whether for credit or audit. This must be done in consideration of the individual's professional advancement and/or goals of the library and must have the approval of the immediate supervisor. Departmental needs take priority in scheduling time off for classes."

For support staff members, the Flexible Work Week Program provides opportunities for support staff members to enroll in courses while being employed on a full-time basis. Detailed information about this program is available from unit heads and the Library Personnel Office . . . .

In-Service Activities

The Graduate Library School and the University Libraries began in the Fall of 1973 to sponsor jointly a series of convocation programs to which all staff members are invited. The following proposal regarding convocation attendance by the support staff was approved by the Library Administration effective September 9, 1974:

> We, the General Policies Committee of the Clerical Organization of the Indiana University Libraries, propose that the Indiana University support staff members be allowed to attend convocations, providing that they obtain prior permission of their supervisor. Those who attend convocations which relate to their work, as agreed upon by their supervisors, should be allowed to attend without making up work time. However, support staff who are permitted to attend convocations for personal interest reasons should make up the work time missed, with adjustment of work schedules made at the discretion of the supervisor.

In-service training activities relating to automation in general and specifically to OCLC (Ohio College Library Center) program implementation have been sponsored by the Library Systems Development Office and by various library units. Two sections of library management in-service training taught by Indiana University School of Business faculty members have also been held to date, and more management training is planned.

Inter-Departmental Activities

Main library departments and branch libraries are currently responsible for in-service training activities specifically related to the operation of the unit. These have included both inter-departmental and some intra-departmental activities.

News Notes

The *Indiana University Libraries: News* is issued biweekly through-out the academic year for communication within the library system. *Staff News* is published by the Personnel Division on a monthly basis from September through June, and copies are distributed on the second payday of each month to support staff. The *Indiana University Faculty Newsletter* is published monthly by the Office of the President and is distributed to faculty . . . .

Orientation for New Staff

At the time of the completion of employment forms, the Assistant to the Personnel Librarian explains to all new support staff members relevant University employment policies. She also informs each support staff member of the time of the Orientation Meeting conducted by University Personnel where the employee will receive a *Staff Handbook* and other information about the University.

Effective July 1, 1973, a program of orientation for all new library faculty members was begun. This orientation includes explanations of the library system, the main library departments, and the branch libraries . . . .

Unit Orientation

Unit heads, or delegated personnel, are responsible for introducing new staff to the unit itself and to related units. Work routines and flow, procedures, policies, and regulations as well as necessary on-the-job training are a part of one's unit orientation . . . .

Sabbatical Leave Program

The Librarians Sabbatical Leave Program initiated in September 1975, is designed to provide library faculty with the opportunity to devote time with pay to study and research. Details of the programs are stated in a document available from the Library Personnel Office.

Staff Organizations

The Bloomington Library Faculty Affairs and Continuing Education Committee has as one of its functions the planning of continuing education programs. The Indiana University Libraries Support Staff Organization at Bloomington has as part of its purpose the encourage-ment of individual and career development. The Indiana University

Libraries Association (InULA) has a committee assigned specifically to providing continuing education opportunities such as the workshops on participation training, people relations, and grantsmanship held during the last few years . . . .

Tours of Main Library and Branches

Tours of branch libraries and of main library departments are held routinely in the Spring and Fall. These tours include an explanation of branch and departmental functions, resources and services by knowledgeable unit representatives. Library staff members guide the tours between units and are available to answer general questions.

Trips to Other Institutions

Library staff members are given the opportunity to visit other institutions by the library's provision of a University car. For example, a number of library staff have traveled to the Center for Research Libraries. Library staff members are also provided the opportunity to participate in Graduate Library School trips such as those to the Ohio College Library Center and of the Indiana State Library.

TOLEDO-LUCAS COUNTY PUBLIC LIBRARY
(Toledo, Ohio)
Staff Development

In-Service Training

Orientation and training are provided all new staff members according to a planned procedure to encourage uniform training for each person in each of the various job categories. In addition to the orientation given in the Personnel Office and in the employee's home agency, periodic Orientation Days are held at Main Library to acquaint new employees with an overall view of the system once the employee is familiar with the home agency.

In-Service Training programs of various types help individuals improve the quality of their performance and increase job satisfaction and thereby enrich the quality and quantity of the Library's service to the community.

The annual Staff Development Day, designed to widen staff understanding of systemwide concern is considered a normal work day. No one is given travel time or mileage for this day.

Workshops sponsored by the Library or by other agencies may be an effective training tool.

Various types of on-the-job training, demonstrations, and personal instruction suitable to the work assignment are provided at regular intervals to employees at all levels.

Staff Meetings

Regularly scheduled staff meetings are an effective method to keep the staff informed, and promote understanding and cooperation.

An employee required to attend staff meetings away from the home agency, in-service training, or other kinds of meetings for the system is paid [by the] mile or bus fare.

Scholarships and Tuition Grants

Two scholarships of $1000 each are available to help pay the expenses of a year at an accredited library school to qualified persons, subject to the approval of the Board of Trustees. Applications should be filed at the Personnel Office no later than March 30. While no scholarship will be awarded until an applicant has been accepted by a library school, applications should be on file as early as possible so that references, etc., can be carefully checked. A Scholarship Committee selected from the professional staff by the Personnel Officer and approved by Council, meets with the Personnel Officer to interview the candidates, and make recommendations as to their choice to be approved by the Board of Trustees.

Two tuition grants of up to $150 each to provide non-professional staff an opportunity to improve technical skills are available annually to qualified candidates. Applications should be filed at the Personnel Office. A committee appointed by the Personnel Officer, and approved by Council, will interview candidates and make recommendations to the Board of Trustees for approval.

Professional Activities

It is policy to encourage membership by staff members in the Ohio Library Association, the American Library Association, and other professional organizations. Staff are encouraged to be active members of these associations.

When schedules permit, time with full pay is granted to employees attending meetings of library associations of which they are members. Consideration will be given those individuals who have essential program or committee responsibilities, but other staff members are encouraged to attend meetings in their specialized areas of interest. Applications should be submitted on the appropriate printed form to the supervisor, who in turn will forward the applications to the appropriate supervisor for decision by Council and Board approval. Unless notified to the contrary, approval may be assumed. The allowances for expenses for attendance at such meetings or workshops are dependent upon the availability of funds in the budget.

Attendance at other meetings or workshops that may prove helpful for professional development will be handled in the same manner as attendance at OLA, ALA, or other library meetings.

An employee required to attend staff meetings away from the place of employment (home agency), in-service training, or other kinds of meetings for the system is paid [by the] mile or bus fare.

Academic Study

Employees of all educational levels are encouraged to continue their formal education. Whenever possible, without diminishing services to the public or imposing hardship on other staff members, effort will be made to adjust schedule and hours so that an employee can take an educational course.

THE UNIVERSITY OF TENNESSEE LIBRARY
(Knoxville, Tennessee)

TRAINING

It is the policy of the UTK Library to provide training programs for all staff members to develop them for present and probably future job assignments. The Personnel Librarian shall have the primary responsibility for coordinating such training.

Individual departments shall continue to be responsible for the training of their staffs in departmental policies, procedures and skills unique to that department. Department heads should inform the Personnel Librarian about new departmental training activities.

They may also seek the assistance of the Personnel Librarian in the development of departmental programs.

This division of responsibilities also exists for orientation programs, with library-wide orientation the responsibility of the Personnel Librarian and departmental orientation the responsibility of each department head.

TRAVEL POLICY

The UTK Library encourages staff participation in meetings, seminars, symposia, workshops, etc., by funding individual travel whenever possible.

Procedure

Funding for such travel may come from either of the two following sources:

Administrative Travel: The Library must be represented at specific meetings during the course of the year, and administrators or staff are asked to attend these meetings on behalf of the Library. These meetings range from professional association meetings to seminars or symposia. Other kinds of travel supported by the administrative budget are recruiting trips, candidate's travel, etc.

Staff Development: A staff development travel allocation is provided to support the travel costs of individual staff in their attendance at professional meetings. They may have program commitments, hold organizational office, hold committee assignments, or may wish to attend the meeting for professional enlightenment. These reasons differ from administrative travel in that they represent personal professional commitments.

Each spring the Library Administration appoints a Travel Evaluation Committee whose role is to recommend criteria for funding staff development travel requests. Requests from staff which do not meet the definition for administrative travel are reviewed by the Travel Evaluation Committee in light of criteria recommended by the Committee. The Committee then applies the criteria to these requests made by library staff. Based on these criteria staff travel requests are granted as long as funds are available.

ST. JOHN'S UNIVERSITY
(Collegeville, Minnesota)

Continuing Education Through Conferences and Conventions

Members of the faculty and administration who are asked by the President or one of the Vice-Presidents to represent the University at a conference, convention, meeting or academic occasion will normally be reimbursed for reasonable travel expenses incurred. When they are to represent their department at such meetings, the recommendation is made to the Academic Vice President by their chairman.

MORRIS LIBRARY
SOUTHERN ILLINOIS UNIVERSITY AT CARBONDALE
(Carbondale, Illinois)

LIBRARY ORIENTATION

Faculty

Faculty members discuss the terms of their employment during the interview for the position. They will be given a tour of the library shortly after beginning work by a faculty member from [the library], who will also introduce them to their colleagues and tell them about special aspects of Morris Library's operations.

Departmental Visits

A schedule of specific times during which all employees of Morris Library will be invited to visit and receive a detailed introduction to the operations of each department in the library will be arranged each fall semester.

ASSOCIATION MEETINGS, CONFERENCES, WORKSHOPS, AND SEMINARS

Both civil service and faculty are encouraged to be professionally active and to attend meetings, workshops, and seminars which will develop their skills and increase their knowledge. The library will try to support attendance at those events through released time and/or travel expenses. If a staff member is interested in attending a meeting, that person should inform the Fiscal Officer as soon as possible so that the necessary budgeting may be planned. Preference for support will be given to those presenting papers or taking part in the program, association officers and committee members, association members and persons whose attendance at such events will best benefit the library as a whole. A report detailing any information learned at the meeting, conference, workshop or seminar and a record of any sessions attended may be submitted to the Fiscal Officer. A copy of this report will be retained in the attendee's personnel folder . . . .

OTHER TRAVEL

Since people sometimes become so involved in their operations that they fail to see opportunities for improvement, both the library and individual staff members can benefit from visits to the various institutions with which they relate to study new ideas and techniques and to discuss mutual problems. Thus the library will support through released time and/or travel expenses approved visits by either civil service employees or faculty to other institutions, businesses or agencies whose functions complement those of the library. Proposals for such visits may be submitted to the fiscal officer by an individual or a group of library employees. A report detailing the information learned from each trip may be submitted to the Fiscal Officer. A copy of this report will be kept in the traveler's personnel folder . . . .

RESEARCH AND PUBLISHING

The library hopes all its faculty will advance as far up the academic ladder as they are able. Publishing the results of their research is one of the ways in which faculty strengthen their competitive position for promotion. The library supports research and publishing in the same manner as other academic departments. Faculty members requesting time to be spent on research or publishing must complete an "Application for Approval of Research" . . . and submit it for approval to their department head, the Dean and the Office of Research and Projects. In order to obtain funding for a project, one must apply to the Office of Research and Projects. Faculty members should also complete a "Research Assignment" form . . . which must be approved by their department heads and the Dean. On this form a percent of time to be spent on the project is agreed upon and a time for completion of the work is established before it is approved.

MT. LEBANON PUBLIC LIBRARY
(Mt. Lebanon, Pennsylvania)

PROFESSIONAL MEETINGS

Employees are encouraged to attend meetings and conferences of professional organizations. Appropriate employees will be appointed to represent the Library at District and State meetings and conferences. Expenses for travel, meals, lodging, and registration will be paid by the Library within the limits of the budget. Time spent attending such meetings will be considered working time.

EDUCATION AND IN-SERVICE TRAINING

Eligible employees are encouraged to take advantage of workshops and courses of study related to librarianship. Time spent attending State Library sponsored in-service training courses will be considered working time.

ROCKFORD PUBLIC LIBRARY
(Rockford, Illinois)
Communications

The library administration communicates with all its employees as completely as the best interest of the library allows. The usual channels of communication are information bulletins and directives issued by the administrative offices, and supervisory staff meetings. Supervisors are expected to relay information from these meetings to all of their staff members.

These meetings also provide channels through which staff ideas and recommendations may reach administrators, and through which problems and questions may be resolved.

General meetings for all employees are scheduled as the need arises. Staff members are always welcome to attend the regular and special meetings of the Board of Library Directors, unless the session is closed to the public. The SORPL (Staff Organization of Rockford Public Library) officer delegated to speak to the Board has the opportunity to do so at each meeting, as part of the regular agenda.

VIKING LIBRARY SYSTEM
(Fergus Falls, Minnesota)
Staff Development

Staff members are encouraged to become members of civic, educational and professional organizations to as great an extent as job obligations will permit.

Time off with pay may be granted by the supervisor or Director to attend workshops, library association conferences, and other professional meetings. At the Director's discretion, attendance at seminars and short courses is also allowed. Although the administration and Board encourage attendance at professional meetings and conferences, the needs of the System shall have priority. Within its capability, the System will provide assistance toward such expenses as registration fees, travel costs, food and lodging incurred from attendance. Such assistance, of course, is limited, and will vary from year to year. Care will be taken to ensure equitable distribution of available funds and their maximum utility to the individual staff members and the System. Among the factors which may be used in determining the extent or appropriateness of System support are membership in the sponsoring professional organization, committee membership or official status within the sponsoring organization, pertinence of the meeting to the employee's System responsibilities, etc. When such attendance or training is required by the employer, the staff member's expenses will be paid.

Staff meetings will be held monthly to facilitate participation in System policies, procedures and growth. Additional staff and informational meetings may be called as needed.

Supervisors should be aware of their responsibility to encourage and assist in the development of those working under their supervision. This is in the best interests of both the System and the individuals involved.

Personnel Classification

CHAMPAIGN PUBLIC LIBRARY
AND INFORMATION CENTER
(Champaign, Illinois)

METHODS OF DETERMINING RATES OF COMPENSATION

The Library Board of Directors through the Library Director will negotiate with the employee group or their authorized representative as defined...(in case of a collective bargaining unit) for the purpose of establishing wage rates and other conditions of employment that are mutually acceptable. Upon completion of negotiations, the Library Director will recommend to the Library Board of Directors for adoption such wage ranges and other conditions of employment agreed upon by the employees, or their representative, and the director. In the absence of a collective bargaining representative...the Library Director is authorized to develop wage rates and other conditions of employment based on the prevailing rate principle subject to approval of the Library Board of Directors.

CLASSIFICATION AND PAY PLAN

The classification plan shall include all classes, as approved, and from time to time amended by the Library Board of Directors. Each class shall include those positions sufficiently similar in duties and responsibilities, and require such similar education, training, experience, knowledge, and skill that each position in the group has been given the same job title and is filled by the same tests of ability. This job title will be used on all personnel records and transactions. The Library Director shall prepare and keep current class specifications which shall define the duties and the desirable qualifications for the performance of the respective positions, together with the rates of compensation applicable hereto.

Employees of the Library shall be compensated in accordance with the pay ranges contained in the salary scale adopted by the Library Board of Directors. Minimum qualifications for starting salaries have also been established . . . .

The salary scale is subject to annual review by the Board of Directors and may be adjusted periodically according to Board determination and financial position of the Library. Pay ranges give due consideration to education and experience required, relative responsibility and difficulty of positions, availability of qualified employees in particular occupational categories, prevailing rates of pay for similar employment in the Champaign area, the financial position of the Library, and other economic considerations.

Merit Adjustments

Employees will be eligible for merit increases from one designated step in the salary range to the next higher step on their anniversary date of employment subject to recommendation of the supervisor and approval of the Library Director. A merit adjustment is defined as an increment available to an employee who has received a satisfactory evaluation by the supervisor based on a written evaluation of the employee's performance.

Longevity Pay

After completion of 5, 10, 15 and 20 years of service all permanent and continuous employees will receive an additional 2½% of their current base pay per month for each 5 years completed to a maximum of 10% as a bonus for continued service.

Anniversary Date

All employees who began work prior to January 1, 1973 will have anniversary date of July 1, 1973. All employees who began work on or after January 1, 1973 will have the date hired as their anniversary date. This does not include a change from one merit step to another within a classification.

TOLEDO-LUCAS COUNTY PUBLIC LIBRARY
(Toledo, Ohio)
Salaries

Salary Scale and Position Classification

All positions are classified according to the job requirements and responsibilities and remain so classified (regardless of the individual capabilities of the incumbent) until the requirements of the job are changed and the position is reclassified accordingly.

Every position is assigned a grade level and a salary range commensurate with the degree of difficulty and responsibility of that position. The salary range is divided into six steps which provide for salary increases within each grade. The individual starting at the minimum in his/her grade (Step 1) may receive three annual increases in recognition of experience and satisfactory performance in the job. Two further increases (Steps 5 and 6) may be granted at the rate of 3% of the minimum for above average performance or at the rate of 4% of the minimum for outstanding performance.

The Board of Trustees will annually review the salary schedule and determine what adjustments may be made in the schedule.

Anniversary Dates and Increments

As noted above, eligible employees will receive salary increments annually after a full year in a grade at the time of their anniversary date, in accordance with the salary schedule then in effect. Time worked as a substitute or a page is not included in the calculation of eligibility for such increments. Salary increases for pages on the basis of experience and performance are explained in the Page Manual. Employees hired or reclassified between October 1 and March 31 will have an April anniversary date. Those hired or reclassified from April 1 through September 30 will have an October anniversary. Increments are effective at the beginning of the pay period including April 1 or October 1. (Changes in grade brought about by reclassifications may change an individual's anniversary date.)

CENTRAL NORTH CAROLINA REGIONAL LIBRARY
(Burlington, North Carolina)

THE PERSONNEL SYSTEM

Organization Chart

The "Organization Chart" [see below] is hereby adopted as the organization of library personnel as well as the hierarchy and lines of authority of the library.

Merit Principle

All appointments and promotions hereunder shall be made wholly on the basis of merit and fitness. All positions requiring the performance of the same duties and fulfillment of the same responsibilities shall be assigned to the same class and the same salary range. No applicant for library employment or employee shall be deprived of employment opportunities or otherwise adversely affected as an employee because of such individual's race, color, religion, sex, or national origin. All library officials shall give equal opportunity for employment without regard to race, color, religion, creed, national origin, or sex to all persons otherwise qualified.

Responsibility of Director

The Director of the Central North Carolina Regional Library shall be responsible for the administration of the following personnel policies and rules which shall apply to all appointed employees. All matters dealing with personnel shall be routed through the Director who shall maintain a complete system of personnel files and records.

Employees Subject to Resolution

All employees of the Central North Carolina Regional Library shall be subject to all provisions of this resolution. The Director will also be subject to this resolution, and the Board shall be responsible for the hiring, supervision, and termination of the Director in the same manner and under the same conditions that the Director is responsible for all other employees.

THE POSITION CLASSIFICATION PLAN

Adoption of the Plan
The . . ."Position Classification Plan" [omitted] is hereby adopted as the classification plan for the Central North Carolina Regional Library.

Coverage of the Plan
This classification plan shall include all permanent classes of positions (full-time and part-time) in the service of the Central North Carolina Regional Library. The Director shall allocate each position covered by the classification plan to its appropriate class in the position classification plan.

Maintenance of Classification Plan
The Director shall be responsible for the administration and maintenance of the position classification plan. He shall consider any material change in the nature of the duties, responsibilities, working conditions, and other factors affecting the classification of any position. He shall then restudy the position and determine if the classification of the position should be changed. Authority to reallocate the positions to classes on the basis of kind and level of duties and responsibilities is vested with the Director, subject to the approval of the Board.

Classification of New Positions
All new positions shall be assigned to existing classes or to new classes of positions by the Director with the approval of the Board.

THE SALARY PLAN

Adoption of the Salary Plan
The . . ."Assignment of Classes to Salary Ranges" [omitted] is hereby adopted as the salary plan for the Central North Carolina Regional Library, as amended from time to time by action of the board. The salary plan shall include all permanent classes of positions included in the classification plan.

Maintenance of Salary Plan
The Director shall be responsible for the administration and maintenance of the salary plan. Each year prior to adoption of the annual budget, the Director shall, if possible, secure information concerning

the general level of salaries and wages paid and fringe benefits provided in private industry in the area, the salaries paid comparable state and municipal employees, and any change in the cost of living in the area during the fiscal year. The Director shall conduct continuing studies of the internal relationships between classes in order to reduce or eliminate inequities between classes of positions. Based on his findings, the Director shall recommend to the Board increases, reductions, or amendments of the salary plan as he deems necessary to maintain the fairness and adequacy of the salary plan.

Transition to the New Salary Plan

As of the effective date of the adoption of this resolution, all employees whose jobs are covered by this classification plan shall be paid at a rate within the salary range as established for their respective job classifications. No employee shall receive a salary cut as a result of the transition to the new classification plan. Employees being paid at a rate above the maximum rate assigned for the class remain at their present salary as long as it is abvove the maximum rate.

Starting Salary

As of the effective date of the adoption of this resolution, new employees shall be employed at the minimum salary which has been established for the classification in which they are employed except: 1) If the new employee does not meet the minimum requirements of the position and qualified applicants for the position are not available, the Director may designate the employee as a "trainee" to be appointed at a salary below the minimum; 2) Applicants of exceptional experience or training may be appointed at starting salaries above the minimum. The Director shall report all such appointments to the Board at its first meeting following the effective date of the appointment.

Salary of Trainee

A new employee who does not meet all of the established qualifications for a position may be appointed with the approval of the Director at a "training" salary no more than 10% below the minimum salary established for the position. The employee shall continue to receive a reduced salary during the probationary period until the department head and the Director shall determine that the trainee is qualified to assume the responsibility of the position, or until the end of the probationary period when the employee is either discharged or moved to the minimum salary established for the position.

Merit Salary Increments

Employees hired at the minimum entrance salary shall be granted a 5% salary increase after the employee's completion of six months of satisfactory service. Further salary increases above the minimum established for each class of positions shall be granted only in recognition of superior or improved performance. The Director shall each year include funds in the budget proposal for providing merit salary increments.

The Director shall be responsible for devising and administering a personnel evaluation system which will include an annual job performance rating to be used to determine the annual merit salary increment which every permanent employee is eligible to receive. This evaluation will be done by the Director and the appropriate supervisors on the annual anniversary date of each employee. This anniversary date is determined by the date of the employee's hiring, removal from probation, last promotion, and/or last salary increase. The Director will be responsible for determining each employee's anniversary date. These annual merit salary increments will be determined by the Director each fiscal year and will depend on the amount of funds appropriated by the Board for this purpose.

New Class of Positions

When a new class of positions is established as provided in this resolution, the Director shall recommend the assignment of the class at a level in the salary plan. After receiving the Director's recommendation, the Board shall assign the class to the level of the salary plan which it considers appropriate.

Salary of Reclassified Employee

An employee whose position is reclassified to a class having a higher salary range shall receive a 5% salary increase or an increase to the minimum of the new salary range, whichever is higher. An employee whose position is reclassified to a class having a lower salary range will not receive a reduction in salary as a result of the reclassification, except as hereinafter provided in . . .[*Reclassification of Positions*].

Salary of Promoted Employee

An employee promoted to a position in a class having a higher salary range shall receive a 5% salary increase, or an increase to the minimum of the new salary range, whichever is higher. If an employee fails to complete successfully his probationary period following promotion, he shall be reinstated in his former position or in a position in the same class at his former salary.

Salary of Transferred Employee

Salary of an employee reassigned to a position in the same class or to a position in a different class at the same salary range shall not be changed by the reassignment.

Salary of Demoted Employee

The salary of an employee demoted to a position in a class with a lower salary range shall be adjusted to the maximum of the new range or to 5% below his former salary, whichever is lower.

Salary of Part-Time Employee

The salary plan established by this resolution is for full-time permanent service. An employee appointed for less than full-time service shall be paid at a rate in proportion to the percentage of full-time hours that he works each month. For this purpose, full-time employment will be understood as 40 hours per week.

Pay Periods

All employees shall be paid monthly. The monthly pay day shall be the 28th day of each month, except when this date falls on Saturday, Sunday, or a holiday. In this event, pay day shall be the last working day prior thereto. The monthly pay day in December shall be December 20 unless this is a non-working day, in which event it shall be the last working day before December 20.

Effective Date of Salary Adjustments

Salary adjustments approved on or before the fifteenth day of any month shall become effective the first day of that month. Salary adjustments approved on or after the sixteenth day of any month shall become effective the first day of the following month.

Reclassification of Positions

Notwithstanding any other provision in this Article, the Board may, in the interest of the economy and to arrive at a balanced budget, in its discretion, reclassify any position to a lower salary range and require that employees occupying such reclassified positions receive a reduction in salary in accordance with that assigned to the reclassified position.

Longevity Pay Plan

During the first week of December each year annual longevity payments shall be made in accordance with the longevity pay plan to all permanent employees who shall have completed at least two (2) years of continuous service as of November 30th and who shall be in the employ of the library as of *November 30th* of the year in which the longevity payment is made. Payments shall be based on the basic salary of the employee as of *June 30th* of the year in which the longevity payment is made and the rate of payment shall be as follows:

- *1%* of basic annual salary after 2 years of continuous service.
- *2½%* of basic annual salary after 5 years of continuous service.
- *4%* of basic annual salary after 10 years of continuous service.
- *5%* of basic annual salary after 15 years of continuous service.
- *6%* of basic annual salary after 20 years of continuous service.

Social Security, Retirement, Federal and State withholding and other required deductions will be made from all longevity payments.

Leave without pay for a duration of one month or more during the fiscal year in which an employee qualified for longevity payments shall be considered in computing the amount of the longevity payment. Deductions at the rate of 1/12 of the annual gross longevity payment will be made for each month of continuous leave without pay. An employee who is on leave without pay on December 1st will receive his longevity payment upon return to active duty status.

Employees who retire under normal or disability retirement programs of the library during any year in which longevity payments shall be made under this longevity payment plan and who, because of such retirement, shall not be in the employment of the library as of November 30th of that particular year shall, nevertheless, receive a pro-rata longevity payment for that year based on the number of full months of employment from the last November 30th to the date of the employee's retirement. Such longevity payments shall be computed on the basis of the employee's salary at the time of retirement or as of June 30th of the year in which the longevity payment is made, whichever is less.

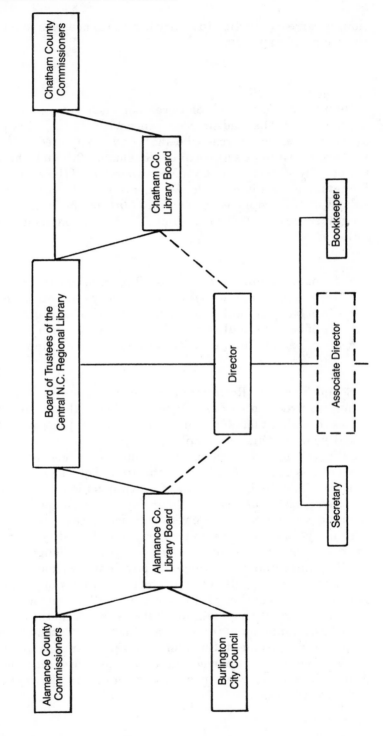

CENTRAL NORTH CAROLINA REGIONAL LIBRARY
(Burlington, North Carolina)

Organization Chart

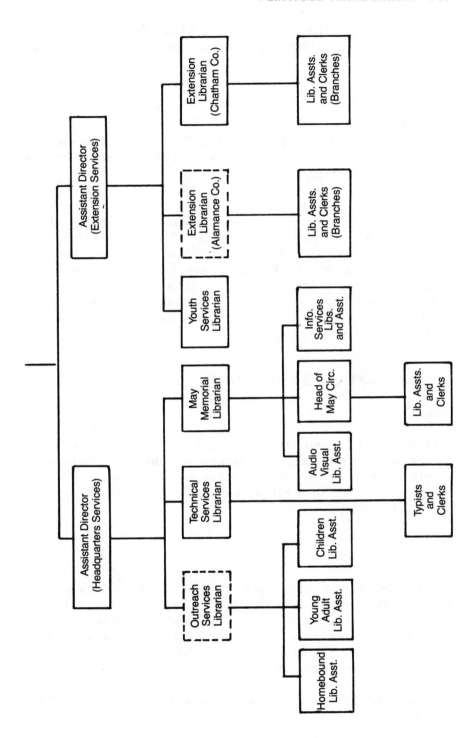

PARAMUS PUBLIC LIBRARY
(Paramus, New Jersey)

STAFF POSITIONS

Full-Time
Professional and non-professional staff members employed full time shall work a 35 hour week and be paid bi-weekly on the basis of their annual salaries.

Part-Time
Staff working less than 35 hours a week, paid by-weekly on hourly basis. *Irregular* part-time employees are defined as those employees working as pages, evening monitors, "on call" or substitutes, and temporary or summer staff. *Regular* part-time employees work a specific schedule of hours each week. Only those scheduled to work an average of 20 or more hours per week receive proportionate benefits of full-time employees. Substitute hours cannot be added to regular hours for purposes of computing benefits.

SALARIES AND CLASSIFICATIONS

Class

All full-time staff members are accorded a job classification. Salary ranges, with minimum and maximum amounts, are set for each classification by the Board of Trustees. Details of job descriptions, requirements and salary ranges are available from the Library Director/Administrative Assistant.

Salaries

Full-Time
Normally, all new appointments to positions classified in a given grade will be paid the minimum salary for the grade. There will be an annual review of all salaries by the Board of Trustees based on evaluations made throughout the year by the Director and supervisory personnel. The following criteria will guide the Trustees in determining salary ranges and increments:

1. Satisfactory job performance, growth, and experience within a particular job category.

2. The extent of supervisory responsibilities.
3. Salaries that other comparable libraries are offering employees in the same or similar classes.
4. Recommendations of library organizations such as ALA, NJLA.
5. Changes in the Cost of Living Index.
6. Outstanding performance of duties over a sustained period of time.
7. The total budget appropriation with which the Library must operate within a given year, dependent on the Borough's approval of funds for the Library.

Salary adjustments will take effect upon approval of the budget by Mayor and Council and shall be retroactive to the first of January. Full-time employees are included in the Borough longevity salary plan. Details are available from the Bookkeeper.

Part-Time
All part-time employees work on an hourly basis. Their schedules may vary according to the demands of the department and they are paid only for the exact amount of time worked.

Part-time employees are not eligible for longevity. Part-time employees may be granted merit increases upon recommendation of the Director with the approval of the Board. Such increases shall be recommended only in cases of talent of a special nature.

VIKING LIBRARY SYSTEM
(Fergus Falls, Minnesota)

Employees generally begin at the entry level salary within their classification. They proceed with merit to the ceiling level for their classification. The ceiling level for the classification is a percentage increase of the base salary.

The base salary (entry level) will be adjusted annually, effective July 1, to reflect the actual rate of inflation. The ceiling will be adjusted proportionally. The Board of Directors will, in consultation with the Director, determine the rate of increase, subject to budgeting restraints, based upon reliable figures for the index of the rate of inflation.

Merit increases of 0-9% may be given annually on the employment anniversary date of each employee and subject to formal evaluation.

A percentage increase, determined by the Director and the employee's supervisor, is applied to the employee's gross salary effective the next pay period.

All salary increases are subject to VLS budgetary restraints.

All positions are classified according to (1) complexity and level of duties, (2) level of responsibility, (3) qualifications required for adequate job performance, and (4) relative value to the System operation as a whole. Positions will contain in the job description the range of classifications deemed appropriate for that position, i.e., LAI-LAII. An employee may be promoted to the next classification, when appropriate, based upon merit as evidenced by the acceptance of extra responsibilities or exceptional service. If that employee's salary is equal to or greater than the entry salary in the next classification, then this employee's salary will increase by the difference between the two base salaries.

MAUDE SHUNK LIBRARY
(Menomonee Falls, Wisconsin)

Organization Chart

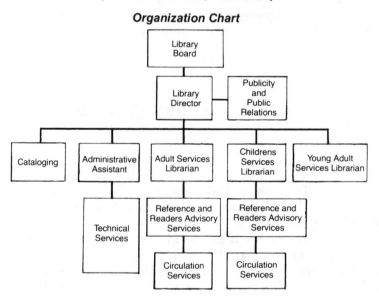

VIKING LIBRARY SYSTEM
(Fergus Falls, Minnesota)

Organization Chart

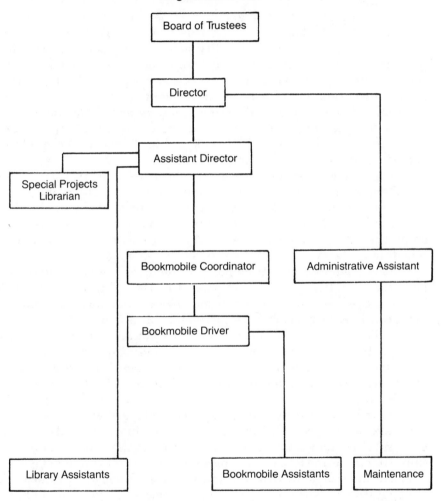

UNIVERSITY OF MISSOURI–ST. LOUIS LIBRARIES
(St. Louis, Missouri)
Permanent Part-Time Employment Policy

In recent years the question of part-time employment and flexible scheduling have become major issues in the labor market. For a variety of reasons both men and women no longer find it feasible to work a 5-day, 40 hour week. At this time the Thomas Jefferson Library recognizes the desirability of providing opportunities for part-time employment, and indeed can recognize the advantages to the Library in such an arrangement. Therefore, the following policy governing permanent part-time employment is set forth.

Permanent part-time employment is defined as any amount of time worked less than full-time (which is accepted to be 40 hours per week) with a minimum of 16 hours per week, unless the specific needs of the department require otherwise.

If a job-sharing situation were deemed feasible, two part-time positions, which total 40 combined hours, would be equivalent to one full-time position. The duties and responsibilities of the single position would be divided so as to provide total coverage by the two employees. For shared positions the Library may require a change of schedule in the event one individual left his/her job.

The creation of a part-time position requires the approval of the Director, the Personnel Committee, the Division Head, and the immediate supervisor. Any staff member or candidate for employment could request a part-time position. If job assignments need to be changed to accommodate the request, this would be at the discretion of the Library. An employee desiring to change his/her status from full-time to part-time should submit the proposal to his/her supervisor and Division Head at least two months prior to the desired starting date.

Permanent part-time non-academic employees would serve the same six month probationary period as full-time non-academic employees. Formal evaluation for all part-time staff would occur on the same timetable and follow the same procedure as full-time employees.

The number of hours to be worked would be agreed upon at the time of appointment. The scheduling of part-time employees would be in accord with department needs and approval of the supervisor. Any changes desired by the individual would be subject to Library approval. Hours worked would not have to be within the normal 8 hour day blocks. For example, 16 hours could be worked in 4 days, 4 hours a day. This flexibility would be especially important in public service positions.

The part-time non-academic employee would be required to keep a bi-weekly timesheet for payroll purposes. The employee would be paid an hourly rate in accord with the University matrix for that position classification. For the part-time academic employee, the immediate supervisor would be responsible for insuring maintenance of schedule. The employee would be paid on an annual salary, pro-rated according to the percentage of full-time hours worked.

Permanent part-time employees would be eligible for annual salary increases on the same basis as a full-time employee.

If a University holiday, or absence due to illness, falls on a day the part-time employee was scheduled to work, the non-academic employee could make up the time within the two-week pay period or lose the hours not worked. The academic employee would have to make up the time missed.

In the event a part-time employee were asked to temporarily work hours above his/her regular schedule, the non-academic employee would be paid for these additional hours at the regular hourly rate. The academic employee would be given compensatory time, at a time agreed upon by the supervisor and the employee.

The University policies on sick leave, paid holidays, insurance benefits, and leave of absence apply only to full-time non-academic employees. Vacation policy ... of the Business Policy and Procedure Manual states ... that paid vacation is not paid to a non-academic employee who works less than 40 hours a week. The Library will adhere to any changes in the present University policy.

In the event the part-time position were eliminated in favor of a full-time position, the part-time employee would be given every opportunity to apply for the position provided he/she met the requirements of the position. This policy would extend to any other full-time position of an equal level within the library. If the part-time employee did not want to apply for the full-time position, the library is under no obligation to retain the part-time employee.

The responsibilities of a permanent part-time employee could be realigned to meet the needs of the library, however such changes could not result in a reduction in rank or salary. Frequent transfers would be avoided.

The part-time employee would not have final responsibility for supervision of other employees, i.e., signing timesheets.

The part-time employee could be allowed to exercise professional responsibilities by attending meetings and conferences. When applicable, travel funds could be appropriated. Excused absence with pay would be granted. The part-time employee would also be encouraged to participate in library committee work to further his/her professional responsibilities.

BOISE STATE UNIVERSITY
(Boise, Idaho)
Longevity

The Second Regular Session of the Forty Third Idaho Legislature authorized a system of longevity bonus payments for state employees effective July 1, 1976. Senate Bill 1494 provides a longevity bonus based upon months of service as outlined in the following table:

0-59	months of service	no longevity bonus
60-119	months of service	2½% of base salary
120-179	months of service	5% of base salary
180-239	months of service	7½% of base salary
240 plus	months of service	10% of base salary

For purposes of computing longevity prior to July 1, 1976, a month of service is defined as any calendar month in which an employee is carried on a state payroll. The following types of appointments and service will count towards the longevity bonus: classified, exempt, permanent, part-time, provisional, temporary, seasonal exempt, WIN, CETA, PIER 62, military leave, emergency, project exempt, student, and intermittent. One full month of service in any of the above can be counted for longevity regardless of the number of hours worked during any month prior to July 1, 1976 . . . .

UNION THEOLOGICAL SEMINARY IN NEW YORK CITY
(New York, New York)
Classification for Librarians

Definition of Librarian

For purposes of this personnel classification system, a professional librarian is defined as a person who possesses a special background and education on the basis of which library needs are identified, problems are analyzed, goals are set, and original and creative solutions are formulated for them, integrating theory into practice and planning, organizing, communicating, and administering successful programs of service to users, the professional librarian recognizes potential users as well as current ones, and designs services which will reach all who could benefit from them.

The title "Librarian" therefore should be used only to designate positions in the library which utilize the qualifications and impose the responsibilities suggested above. Positions which are primarily devoted to the routine application of established rules and techniques, however useful and essential to the effective operation of the Library's ongoing services, should not carry the word "Librarian" in the job title.

Rationale of the System

This classification system, designed for librarians in the UTS Library, is intended to cover all professional positions except highest administrative position. In brief, this system is meant to cover all librarians from the beginning professional grade (Librarian I) through positions that require a higher order of accomplishment. To qualify for positions at the upper levels, an incumbent must demonstrate progressive development in either 1) distinction in a specialty of substantial benefit to UTS apart from any administrative or supervisory responsibility, or 2) supervisory and administrative responsibilities up to and including the level of division or departmental supervisor. This is explicitly a two-track system that is meant to create opportunities for advancement in non-supervisory as well as supervisory positions to equally high level.

It is important to keep in mind that supervisory and administrative positions are determined by organizational requirements and related needs of the Library. A staff member cannot expect to be considered for such a position unless a vacancy exists. This requirement is less restrictive in the non-administrative track. There is enough flexibility in the system to accord the Librarian III grade to an individual when his/her level of accomplishment is both fully evident and sufficiently sustained quite apart from the occurrence of a specific vacancy. It is essential, however, that distinction be achieved in a field like reference work, cataloguing, theological literature, etc., that is meaningful in the UTS context.

If a system of this kind is not to be debased, it calls for rigorous decision-making at all levels beginning with Librarian I. We must endeavor to appoint candidates who show great promise whatever the level of appointment. There may be a very few positions that are inherently Librarian I and not intended to accommodate incumbents at a higher grade: it is expected that normal turnover will make possible the recurring appointment of beginning professionals to such positions. The Librarian I grade as it relates to an individual (in contrast to its place in the organizational structure) is not meant to be a career grade. A Librarian I who is not good enough to be promoted to Librarian II should not have his appointment renewed. Except in the case of termination for cause, the Library should give as much notice as possible (hopefully 3-12 months) in such cases and usually within three years of initial appointment.

Time alone does not guarantee growth in a person's usefulness or distinction. Nonetheless complete disregard of time in determining advancement is also unwise. To assert that a person has held a certain grade for x years and therefore should be advanced a grade is completely uncompelling. Conversely, the UTS Librarian must give some weight to length of experience in determining a person's worthiness to be considered for promotion.

A great research library needs many skills and much knowledge that cannot be learned in library school. Staff members with non-librarian specialized backgrounds may be appointed to such positions as bibliographers or archivists; other staff members may lack formal training but have acquired experience on the job which justifies their appointment to a position graded at the professional level. While there is no predisposition to exclude from the librarian ranks persons who, by reason of background and experience, are fully useful in what is narrowly denominated as "librarian" work, nonetheless such appointments will tend to be exceptions, and it would be misleading to convey the impression that such appointments will be numerous or casual. Persons so appointed will tend to have a relatively limited field for advancement, it being unlikely that a cataloguer so appointed would progress to an advanced position. Granted these reservations, there is no intention to put insuperable barriers in the way of appointing the occasional outstanding person to a librarian position without formal training.

The UTS Seminary Library has only a limited number of regular professional librarian positions. The usual are the Head of Technical Services (who also serves as the professional cataloguer), the Head of Access Services (who also serves as the professional reference librarian) and the Library Director. Each of these persons is responsible for training and directing associated personnel. From time to time another term professional position is opened for special projects. Because of the size of the Library the positions Librarian IV and V (usual in large academic libraries) are not normally foreseen.

The titles Librarian I, II, III are drawn from current academic/research library administrative practice and as described here, are reasonable equivalent to the understandings operative in university libraries of the area, e.g., Columbia University. Thus, a librarian leaving UTS with such a title would be recognizable in other institutions.

UNIVERSITY OF NEW MEXICO
(Albuquerque, New Mexico)
Employee Classification

Employee Designation

The term "Staff" refers to any employee who is in a position other than teaching and who does not have faculty rank.

The term "Professional Staff" refers to personnel holding positions classified as "exempt" under the Fair Labor Standards Act as amended. These include such positions as directors, managers, supervisors, engineers, accountants, systems analysts and counselors. Professional staff employees are on the monthly payroll.

The term "General Staff" refers to personnel holding positions classified as "non-exempt" under the Fair Labor Standards Act, as amended and include such positions as secretarial, clerical, maintenance and service workers. General Staff employees are on the bi-weekly payroll.

Employee Definitions

Permanent Full-Time. An employee hired for an indefinite time, scheduled to work 40 hours or more per week over a minimum period of nine (9) months per year.

Permanent Part-Time. An employee hired for an indefinite time, scheduled to work less than 40 hours per week over a minimum period of (9) months per year.

Temporary Full-Time. An employee in this classification is employed for a workweek of 40 hours or more for a limited period of time with a designated ending date. Normally, the limited period of time does not exceed nine (9) months, extensions must be approved by the concerned Dean or Director and the Director of Personnel.

Occasional. An employee in this classification is hired for ninety (90) days or less or on an on-call basis.

If a student is employed into a Permanent position (full or part-time) the primary classification will be considered Staff Employee.

Multiple Positions

An employee working two (2) Permanent Part-Time positions, totaling 40 hours or more per week, will be considered a Permanent *Full-Time* employee. If the total hours regularly worked are less than 40, the employee will be considered Permanent *Part-Time*.

An employee working two (2) Temporary Part-Time positions, totaling 40 hours or more per week, will be considered a Temporary *Full-Time* employee. If the total hours regularly worked are less than 40, the employee will be considered Permanent *Part-Time*.

An employee working a Permanent Part-Time and a Temporary Part-Time position will be considered a Permanent Part-Time employee.

An employee may not be on more than one payroll (e.g., Payrolls 20 and 50). If employed in two positions, one being exempt and one non-exempt, the employee will be considered non-exempt, and both positions would be on payroll 20.

Fair Labor Standards Act Exemptions

Executive Employee: An employee whose primary duty consists of the management of the enterprise, who must regularly direct the work of at least two (2) full-time employees therein, who has the authority to hire or fire other employees or recommend hiring or firing, who customarily and regularly exercises discretionary power, who receives a salary of at least $155 a week [1978], who does not devote more than 20% of his hours in non-exempt work or non-supervisory activity shall be considered an Executive employee.

Administrative Employee: An employee whose primary duty must be either the performance of office or non-manual work directly related to management policies of general business operations, or responsible work that is directly related to academic instruction or training carried on in the administration of a school system or educational establishment; who customarily and regularly exercises discretion and independent judgement; who regularly and directly assists a bona-fide executive; who performs under only general supervision work along specialized or technical lines requiring special training, experience, or knowledge; who executes special assignments and tasks under general supervision; who receives a salary of at least $155 per week [1978]; who does not spend over 20% of his workweek in non-exempt work shall be considered an Administrative employee.

Professional: A professional employee is one whose primary duty must be: work requiring knowledge of an advanced type in a field of science or learning usually acquired by a prolonged course of specialized intellectual instruction and study; or work that is original and creative in a recognized field of artistic endeavor and the result of which depends primarily on the invention, imagination, or talent; or work as a teacher certified or recognized as such in the school system or educational institution by which he is employed; and whose work requires the consistent exercise of discretion and judgement; whose work is mainly intellectual and varied as distinguished from routine or mechanical duties; who is compensated for his services with a salary of at least $170 per week [1978]; who does not devote more than 20% of his hours worked in the workweek to activities which are not an essential part of and necessarily incident to the work [as "Professional"] shall be considered a Professional employee . . . .

Change from Temporary to Permanent

When a position is changed from Temporary to Permanent, the position is considered a new position and shall be treated consistently with the policies governing new positions or vacancies. The incumbent of the Temporary position may be considered along with other applicants for the Permanent position.

WEST GEORGIA COLLEGE LIBRARY
(Carrolton, Georgia)

Organization Chart

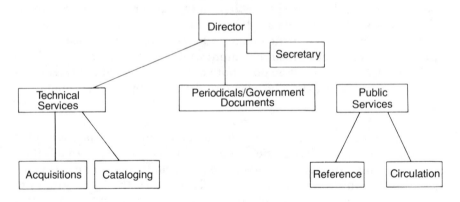

Working Conditions

MINNESOTA VALLEY
REGIONAL LIBRARY
(Mankato, Minnesota)

Hours of Work

Headquarters' Staff

The work week for permanent employees is set by the Board of Trustees upon recommendation by the Director. Unless otherwise authorized by the Board or necessitated by a temporary or emergency situation, the work week will be five (5) days and total forty (40) hours.

Employees may be required to work Saturdays and evening hours as a part of their regular schedule. Insofar as possible, permanent employees will not generally be required to work more than two evenings a week on a regularly scheduled basis.

Scheduled overtime (over 40 hours per week) will be compensated at the rate of one and one half times the hourly rate.

Employees volunteering to work overtime, will be given compensatory time off; the time off must be taken within two weeks of the overtime worked. Such arrangements must be approved by departmental Supervisor.

Branch Libraries

Branch libraries are open specific hours each week, as determined by the Director, with consideration to the convenience and needs of the community where the branch library is located.

VIKING LIBRARY SYSTEM
(Fergus Falls, Minnesota)
Hours of Work

The regular work schedule for full-time employees is a 37½ hour work week Monday thru Saturday. All variations from this schedule will be approved by the Director. The System will attempt to offer "flex-time" scheduling for all employees provided it meets with the objectives of their positions and the overall goals of the System. What is meant by "flex-time" scheduling is the assumption that a 37½ hour work week is required of all employees. It can be of mutual benefit to the employee and the System to allow some flexibility in the time and length of the work day, provided the employee's schedule reflects the needs and objectives of his/her position and promotes a greater overall efficiency for the System operation as a whole. The Director or supervisor has a right to schedule working hours to meet System needs; however, employees should be asked their preference and schedules must be approved by the Director or supervisor.

Administrative and Support Personnel may find it necessary to work beyond the normal work week in order to discharge their duties and responsibilities. Compensatory time may be taken at the convenience of the System. No employee will carry more than 15 hours or work less than 15 hours in any given pay period.

Staff members are allowed a relief period of fifteen minutes during each three hour consecutive work period per day. The purpose of a work break is to provide a short rest period enabling employees to perform their work more effectively. They may be taken in conjunction with the half-hour meal period, joined together for an additional half-hour period.

TOLEDO-LUCAS COUNTY PUBLIC LIBRARY
(Toledo, Ohio)
Time Regulations

Work Week

A full-time work week is made up of five 7½ hour days, or 37½ hours a week. Employees working fewer than 37½ per week (or 75 hours per pay period) will be paid at an hourly rate for all hours worked during each pay period.

Absence Slips

Full-time and regularly scheduled part-time employees who do not work their full schedule will fill out an absence slip to account for time used for sick leave, or leave with or without pay.

Time Cards

Part-time staff, who do not work a regular schedule, and pages will complete time cards on every other Friday covering the previous two-week period. Time cards are signed by the appropriate supervisor and forwarded to the Accounting Office by the agency head.

Time Sheets

Time sheets will be filled out every other Friday covering the previous two week period for every employee in the agency. The time cards and the absence slips will provide the details needed.

Emergency Closing

The closing of all or part of the Library system may be required by natural, mechanical, or other emergencies. The following will apply in such instances:

1. In the event of an emergency closing of a full day, *all* employees scheduled to work will be considered to have worked and will be paid for the hours scheduled. Should the closing exceed one day but not more than five days, employees (except pages) regularly scheduled half-time or more will be paid for time after the first day. The extent

to which staff shall be paid should an emergency closing extend beyond five days will be determined by action of the Board of Trustees.

2. During an emergency if the system is open for any part of a day, employees scheduled for work during those hours will be expected to do so (see exception under paragraph 3). Anyone unable to do so will have to charge lost time to annual leave or to sick leave.

3. If an employee is late because of hazardous road conditions, supervisors may use their own judgment as to the necessity for making up the time missed. When threatening weather conditions cause an employee to feel that his/her ability to get home safely requires an early departure, the supervisor should allow such departure if possible. Time lost may be made up by arrangement of the supervisor or may be charged to annual leave.

4. Under certain circumstances staff members may be directed not to report for work even though the system is open. For example, when an early closing is to take place, those employees due to report at noon may well be notified that they need not do so. In such cases those staff members will be paid for their scheduled number of hours as defined in paragraph 1.

5. The closing of all or part of the library system may require certain employees to report for work and not others. For example, by the nature of their assignments, custodial and maintenance staff members have an inherent responsibility to perform duties of snow removal, building checks, etc., when other operations are closed down. In such cases, there will be no premium pay for any regular hours worked. When only part of the system is affected by a closing, staff from the areas so affected may be temporarily assigned elsewhere in the system.

6. Staff on sick leave, annual leave, or otherwise not scheduled during the period of emergency closing are not affected.

Schedules

Working schedules are arranged by the agency head or other designated personnel. Employees in public service agencies may be scheduled for two evenings and a fair distribution of Saturdays. Copies of the schedule are forwarded to the appropriate supervising office as well as Personnel.

Split Days

If an employee is asked by a supervisor to work a split day, the employee is entitled to transportation. If the employee asks to work a split day, transportation will not be paid. (Transportation would be bus fare or [by the] mile.)

Reporting Absences

Any illness or other inability to report for work as scheduled should be reported to the agency head before the opening hour. Any employee who *fails to report* to the supervisor will *not be paid for time not worked*, i.e., this will not automatically be treated as sick leave or annual leave. If for some reason it has been impossible for the employee to report to the supervisor, consideration will be given to the circumstances involved.

Any employee who fails to notify the supervisor giving an acceptable reason for not appearing for three working days will be assumed to be uninterested, and his/her employment will be terminated.

Reporting Tardiness

If late for work, the employee should report to the agency head immediately and arrange to make up the time.

Meal Hours

Lunch and dinner hours are normally 60 minutes, or 30 minutes if "minus" time is to be made up, when approved by the supervisor. Meal hours are taken on the employee's own time.

Rest Periods

Any employee may take a 10-minute rest period for each continuous work period of 3 ¾ hours. Rest periods may not be taken consecutively nor at the beginning or end of a work period.

Overtime

Overtime is granted only to meet emergency situations with the supervisor securing the prior approval of the Director. In those emergencies when it is impossible for the supervisor to seek prior approval, the Director should be notified as soon afterwards as possible. Mechanical maintenance crisis or excessive snow removal are two examples of when overtime might be used.

Under the 1974 Fair Standards Act overtime is computed on the basis of a 40-hour week. Since our work week is 37 ½ hours only compensatory time returned on a one to one basis will be received for the hours worked beyond 37 ½ up to 40 hours. Any employee required to work more than 40 hours in a week will receive compensatory time at a rate of time and a half. Compensatory time should be taken in the same pay period if possible, or in the very next pay period. When the situation in the agency makes it impossible to arrange for time returned at the rate of time and a half within the prescribed pay periods, then the individual should be financially reimbursed.

Executive, administrative, and professional categories of staff are exempt from these regulations. Exemptions are based on both salaries and responsibilities. The minimum salary for the exempt executive and administrative staff is $160 a week.

The executive exemption is available to employees whose primary duties are the management of the institution, or of a recognized department or subdivision. The executive must direct the work of at least two fulltime employees and have the authority to effectively recommend the hiring and firing of employees. Furthermore, the executive must regularly exercise discretionary powers and devote no more than 20 percent of his hours of work to activities not directly and closely related to his managerial duties. Such activities include performing the same tasks as those performed by those he supervises. The 20 percent rule does not apply to employees whose weekly salary is at least $200 or if the employee is in sole charge of an independent establishment or a physically separated branch establishment . . . .

Staff Facilities

All libraries are provided with staff rest areas and kitchen facilities where simple meals or light refreshments can be prepared and eaten. Eating and/or drinking is not permitted in other parts of the buildings.

Lockers or designated space is allotted to each employee and should be kept in orderly condition. Employees should observe local agency regulations governing the use of staff facilities.

ROCKFORD PUBLIC LIBRARY
(Rockford, Illinois)
Staff Lounge

A lounge, with cooking, refrigeration, and dishwashing units, is provided for the staff. Those who prepare meals are responsible for washing the dishes, silver, and utensils they use. Rules regarding the storage of food are posted on the refrigerator door. Staff members are permitted to smoke in the lounge only and are expected to empty ash trays they use. All are asked to help keep the room in order. The telephone provided in the staff lounge is for local calls only, limited to three minutes.

Volunteers working in the library and official visitors are welcome to use the staff lounge. Personal friends or relatives of staff members, or former staff members, are welcome only on an infrequent basis, due to lack of space and for security reasons. Such visitors should be accompanied by a staff member.

PARAMUS PUBLIC LIBRARY
(Paramus, New Jersey)
Working Conditions

Staff working hours shall be 9 a.m. to 9 p.m., Monday through Friday. Saturday hours are 9 a.m. to 5 p.m. Sunday from 1 p.m. to 5 p.m. October through May.

The standard work week for full-time employees shall be a 5 day week consisting of 35 hours. No staff member may leave the Library building during working hours except with approval of the Director or authorized delegate.

Full-time staff members shall be required to work no more than two evenings a week, preferably only one evening if scheduling permits.

Full-time staff shall be required to work no more than every other Saturday. Personnel required to work Saturday shall receive Friday as their day off that week.

The Library is open on Sundays from 1 p.m. to 5 p.m., October through May. Every effort shall be made to staff the Library on a voluntary basis. However, staff members may be required to work if necessary, on a fair rotational basis. Full-time staff working Sundays in addition to regular 35 hours will be remunerated at time and a half rate. Part-time personnel and pages will generally be paid a per hour bonus above their regular hourly rate.

The Director, within limitations of the budget, is authorized to request overtime for any employee in cases of emergency, unusually heavy workloads and during vacation periods when hiring of suitable substitutes is impossible or impractical. All employees will be paid in compensatory time or pay at straight time rate up to 40 hours of work a week, and one and one half time rate for work in excess of 40 hours a week.

Compensatory time should be taken as soon as possible within the scheduling needs of the Library but shall be taken within 30 days or within the calendar year for which it was earned and may not be added to vacation time.

Any employee working more than 5 consecutive hours on a single day shall take one hour, without pay, for meals.

Each staff member is allowed a relief period of 15 minutes of paid time for each 3½ hours of continuous work, provided it does not interfere with service to the public. Break time begins from the time the employee leaves his/her post until the time he/she returns. Rest periods may not be added to lunch time or used to shorten the work day.

An employee who deviates from his/her schedule shall make up the missed time only with authorization of the department head and to the benefit of the Library's schedule, or pay for said time shall be deducted from salary. Records on vacations, absences, and tardiness shall be kept by the Administrative Assistant and reported to the Board on a monthly basis. All discretionary actions taken by the Director shall be reported to the Board of Trustees at their next meeting.

JEFFERSON MADISON REGIONAL LIBRARY
(Charlottesville, Virginia)
Working Conditions

Work Week

Each full-time staff member works 37½ hours per week according to a schedule arranged by the department head.

Weather Emergencies

In cases of inclement weather, supervisors shall have the authority to allow staff members who live in outlying areas to leave early from work. In the event of extreme weather conditions or other emergency, the Library Director may order the library to be closed. In his absence, the person in charge of a library agency may close it if an emergency exists. Any such closing will be reported to the Board of Trustees at the next regular meeting. During inclement weather, staff members are expected to report to work unless informed otherwise.

Breaks

Staff members may take a break from their duties for fifteen minutes in the morning and fifteen minutes in the afternoon provided such breaks do not interfere with the operation of the library. In no case may a staff member skip his or her break and leave early from work.

ATLANTIC CITY FREE PUBLIC LIBRARY
(Atlantic City, New Jersey)
Work Week, Breaks, Overtime

Full-time Library and clerical staff members work an average thirty-five (35) hour per week schedule. Custodial employees work an average forty (40) hour per week schedule. One hour of the staff member's own time is allowed for lunch or supper and staff members are usually required to take the full hour. Schedules are prepared under the supervision of the Director. No staff member may change his/her schedule without advance permission from the Director.

Breaks of fifteen (15) minute periods *may* usually be given in the morning and afternoon under the direction of the supervisor. Employees are not to leave the building at these times without permission of the Director. On payday an employee may, with the permission of his/her supervisor, go to the bank in Atlantic City instead of taking a fifteen (15) minute break. Break time may not be used to shorten working hours or counted as overtime if not taken.

All employees may be requested to work at least one night per week. Such work is considered a part of the regular schedule. Saturday may be arranged on a rotating basis so as to distribute assignments among employees qualified for the duties involved. Such work is considered a part of the regular work schedule.

Normally, there is no cash payment for overtime, but equivalent time off shall be granted during the same pay period or during the next pay period and shall be approved by the Director. One half hour or more, in addition to seven hours, may be considered overtime. Less than one half hour at a time should not be considered overtime and compensatory time will not be granted. Time lost for which pay is not granted under stated policy must be made up within one pay period if possible. Failure to do so without special permission from the Director will result in deduction from salary. A differential payment of 20% will be given for each scheduled hour worked after 5:00 p.m. and all day Saturday or Sunday for all full time non-professional employees.

WINNETKA PUBLIC LIBRARY DISTRICT
(Winnetka, Illinois)
Hours of Work

The library is open for service Monday–Friday, 1:00 a.m.–9:00 p.m.; Saturday, 9:00 a.m.–5:00 p.m.; Sunday, 2:00 p.m.–5:00 .p.m. The library is normally closed on Sundays during the summer months, June, July, and August. Except as may otherwise be assigned by the Library Director, normally hours worked must fall within the hours the library is open, with the exception of the custodian.

The normal work week for full time employees shall be 40 hours, but the Library Director, with the approval of the Board of Trustees, may establish schedules which require fewer than 40 hours within the normal work week. Currently full time employees are scheduled 37 ½ hours of work per week.

Hourly paid employees are paid their regular rate of pay for each hour worked. Salaried employees (full time employees and part time permanent employees) will be paid for their hour of lunch or dinner when they work seven hours in a day which includes an evening or on Saturday.

WEST GEORGIA COLLEGE LIBRARY
(Carrollton, Georgia)
Flex-Time

All staff members have a positive attitude toward their jobs and are committed to the concept of providing the best possible service to patrons. No one would voluntarily be away from his/her post if it meant disruption of this service.

By the nature of their responsibilities and expertise, some departments and staff members are more involved in direct patron service than are others and, therefore, are bound to more rigid schedules.

With the above percepts as guidelines, [it is] agreed that "flex-time" (such as shortened lunch hours, skipping breaks, etc., in order to arrive later or leave earlier) would have to be decided on an individual basis and any change in regular hours approved by the department/division head in charge.

THE UNIVERSITY OF TENNESSEE LIBRARY
(Knoxville, Tennessee)

WORK SCHEDULES

The basic work schedule for full-time personnel is an eight-hour day and forty-hour week with a one-hour meal break near the middle of an eight-hour shift and rest breaks near the middle of each four-hour work period. Technical Services and Administrative Services (except Duplication) personnel may work between 7:30 a.m. and 6:00 p.m. after consulting with the appropriate department head.

Schedule adjustments may be made to accommodate attendance at classes or for other important reasons. Public Services staff may have variant schedules depending upon the requirements of the department involved. A work schedule once arrived at for a department should be regularly followed with exceptions made only at the discretion of the department head.

Should a staff member be delayed in arriving at work for unavoidable reasons, the time lost may be made up by remaining after the customary departure time or arriving before the customary beginning time on another day within the same work period at the discretion of the department head.

When repeated infractions such as regular tardiness occur, the employee may not be granted the opportunity to make up the time lost. Instead, the loss of time will be charged to annual leave.

A copy of the departmental work schedule should be posted in each department as stipulated by the University's work schedule policy . . . .

WORK WEEK

Six-Day Work Limit

University and federal regulations specify a 40-hour work week, preferably accomplished in five days. The library operation may require a six-day week for some employees on some occasions, but the supervisor should avoid this whenever possible. A seven-day week for any employee is to be considered as contrary to library policy.

OVERTIME AND COMPENSATORY TIME

All employees of UTK, except those specifically exempted by law, are subject to the basic provisions of time-and-one-half compensation for all hours worked in excess of 40 hours per week. For purposes of weekly time reporting, the University work week is from midnight Sunday to midnight the following Sunday. *Supervisors must organize work so that no employees will be permitted or required to work in excess of 40 hours in any week except in emergency situations.* An employee may be given compensatory time at one-and-a-half times the time worked in lieu of time-and-one-half pay. Such adjustment must be made within the same pay period.

Employees exempt from the Fair Labor Standards Act may work more than 40 hours in a single week and are not eligible for a pay rate adjustment or compensatory time at a premium rate. Included in the exempt category are those with faculty rank, department heads without faculty rank, and those earning $10,400 or more per year . . . .

Employee Relations

TOLEDO-LUCAS COUNTY PUBLIC LIBRARY
(Toledo, Ohio)

RESPONSIBILITIES OF THE STAFF TO THE PUBLIC

It is the responsibility of the staff to provide the individual patron with efficient service in a friendly and cordial manner. Each staff member's attitude must always be one of intelligent, courteous and interested service. No staff member should be so engrossed in his/her routines that a patron receives only superficial attention. Every patron should receive the same standard of service without regard for social standing, sex, race, creed, or age.

COMMUNITY INVOLVEMENT

The Library Administration encourages staff members to participate in community activities and to become members of civic and educational organizations. While encouraging such staff involvement in and awareness of current issues in the community, no staff member should presume to speak for the Library when taking a private stand on a public issue. Staff members are urged to contribute through the Library to the annual drive of the Crusade of Mercy, as a demonstration of their responsibility to the community.

RESPONSIBILITIES OF A SUPERVISOR

It is the responsibility of the supervisors to make the members of their staffs aware of the overall objectives of the library system and how the work of the agency contributes to the achievement of these goals. It is also the supervisors' responsibility to keep staff members informed of proposed changes in the system and to encourage involvement in local, state, and national library activities.

When changes in operations or techniques are being contemplated within individual departments, divisions, or branches, it is the supervisor's responsibility to involve the staff in discussions regarding such changes, giving the staff ample opportunity to discuss such proposals and to make useful and meaningful suggestions.

It is a key responsibility of a supervisor to see that all staff members learn how to do their work, accept the responsibility of the job, and be happy and interested in doing it. Good work habits and the proper attitude toward the job are the supervisor's responsibility.

It is the supervisors' responsibility to listen to the complaints of their staffs and to resolve those questions which they can.

The procedure for handling complaints not resolved by the supervisor is outlined under "Grievance Procedure" [found elsewhere in this collection].

RELATIONSHIPS WITH SUPERVISORS

Each staff member is responsible to someone else. One of the key responsibilities of a supervisor is to help staff members learn their work, accept responsibility and be happy and interested in doing it. All of us must learn all we can about our job and perform efficiently and well to do credit to ourselves and to the Library.

Inevitably each of us will make mistakes. When a mistake is made your supervisor will talk the problem over with you and make suggestions. Should you feel that your supervisor fails in obligations to you, please express that feeling to him/her before discussing the matter with others. While other library officials will be willing to help you, they will not want to weaken the authority of the supervisor by having you consult them before you have tried to solve the problem with the supervisor. Supervisors are held accountable for good management, and it is demoralizing when their authority is bypassed.

When you and your supervisor cannot agree on a solution to a problem or on a point of conduct, the supervisor or you can arrange to discuss the problem with the supervisor's supervisor.

RELATIONSHIPS WITH OTHER STAFF MEMBERS

Generosity, tolerance and understanding toward each other will make possible a good working relationship. One's relations with other staff members are similar to relations with supervisors. Good conduct and good work habits are essential for the smooth functioning of the individual departments as well as the Library as a whole. Here are a few other points that should help:

• Within the hearing of Library patrons it is preferable that fellow workers not be called by their first names. Personal telephone calls and personal conversations should be avoided as disruptive to the flow of work, inconsiderate of co-workers, annoying to the supervisor, as well as poor public relations. Maintaining neat work space speeds work, and neatness is also appreciated in staff rooms, lounges or lunch rooms. Observing the time limitation on breaks is not only courteous and considerate of fellow employees, but disregarding the time is cheating the Library of working hours. Punctuality and dependability are important to the public, the supervisor and fellow workers. It is important to keep one's supervisor and the Personnel Office informed of any change in personal data such as address, phone number, etc., since it is essential that all files be current.

• It is essential that the Library's property, buildings, materials, equipment and supplies be carefully protected by the individual and by reporting any abuses observed.

• Avoid conducting personal business while at work, for it creates an unbusinesslike impression with the public, the supervisor and other staff members. In emergencies, personal mail, phone calls and visitors may be received. When pay phones are available, use these during breaks or meal hours if at all possible. Always ask permission of the supervisor when it is necessary to use the Library phone for a private call, and keep the call brief.

WORTHINGTON PUBLIC LIBRARY
(Worthington, Ohio)
Employee Relations

To the Community

All staff members are expected to give a high standard of service to all patrons regardless of social standing, sex, creed, race or age. Staff members are encouraged to take an active interest in the concerns of the community in which they work.

Towards Supervisors

Employees are expected to cooperate with their supervisors in attaining the common goals of the library for which they work. In resolving problems between employee and supervisor, the established chain of command should be followed.

Supervisors

Supervisors welcome inquiries and suggestions from employees. The employee has the right to expect direction from a specific supervisor, thus avoiding conflicting directions.

Staff Rooms

A staff room is maintained for the use of employees. Employees who avail themselves of the facilities are responsible for maintaining the general cleanliness of the room.

Special Responsibilities

Each employee is responsible for providing the supervisor with current address, telephone number, and an emergency contact. The staff member is also responsible for all keys and/or equipment given in trust and the return of same upon termination of employment.

SONOMA COUNTY LIBRARY
(Santa Rosa, California)
Philosophy of Library Service

The free public library is crucial to a democratic society. It is a communication center for the community—a source of knowledge and ideas that an enlightened populace must use if it is to govern itself wisely and develop its full potential.

The public library has special importance for the individual. Each one approaches it with a unique background, utilizes it at one's own pace, and derives benefits from it to the full extent of one's needs, desires and capacities.

As a member of the American Library Association and the California Library Association, Sonoma County Library contributes to the development of principles, standards and concerns of the American public library generally.

Sonoma County Library is committed to providing the widest diversity of views and expressions, without restriction, and to upholding the *Library Bill of Rights* and related policies of the American Library Association.

Sonoma County Library believes in a policy of affirmative action to reach all members of the community with its services, through its selection of material and in its staffing practices.

Sonoma County Library has primary responsibility to its own constituency, but it is also committed to cooperative sharing of resources and services with other agencies, inside and outside the county and the state, for the mutual benefit of all. The Library accepts the Basic Concepts and Goals statement of *The California Library Network: A Master Plan.*

ROCKFORD PUBLIC LIBRARY
(Rockford, Illinois)
Standards of Service

It is the aim of the library to bring people together with the library's resources, and all library processes and operations exist for the sake of the individual patron who comes into the library, or whom the library seeks to attract. A staff member must never be so engrossed in routines or other work that a patron is given only superficial attention. All requests are to be regarded as important to the patron. The same standard of service is to be granted all patrons, regardless of social standing, race, age, or any other potentially segregating characteristic. The employee's attitude is at all times to be one of intelligent, courteous, and interested service, and all conduct which would interfere with this standard must be avoided.

ELA AREA PUBLIC LIBRARY DISTRICT
(Lake Zurich, Illinois)

The Librarian and the Library Staff Should:

1. Provide for the reading and research needs of the citizens by meeting the information needs of all in so far as possible, and by willingly assisting all patrons in availing themselves of other library services and materials available to them.
2. Encourage creative use of leisure time by providing books and materials, library facilities and services, for all ages and for people of widely divergent interests.
3. Provide assistance and encouragement to local groups and organizations in locating materials for program planning.
4. Be instrumental in providing the means for self-education for all citizens.

PUBLIC LIBRARY
(Anonymous)

Meeting rooms on the lower level and one conference room on the ground level are available for community groups at a small fee. Bulletins of community events are posted on the bulletin boards on either side of the circulation desk. Both the reading room and the reference room try to keep information available on local activities, classes, shows, school programs, etc. All employees are expected to act as interested members of the community and to treat patrons with courtesy and friendliness. As this is a small community, personal relationships are particularly important.

JEFFERSON MADISON
REGIONAL LIBRARY
(Charlottesville, Virginia)
Relationship with the Community

As a tax-supported institution, all activities of the library are motivated by the idea of public services. Paramount in each staff member's mind should be the idea that he is a public employee and that the activities of the institution in carrying out its objectives are of first concern.

EASTERN MICHIGAN UNIVERSITY
(Ypsilanti, Michigan)
Professional Responsibilities

Agreement between Eastern Michigan University and the Eastern Michigan University Chapter of the American Association of University Professors, October, 1978.

EMU and the Association agree that the primary professional responsibility of Faculty Members is teaching or professional library service supported by active participation in scholarly activities (e.g., research) and academic advising. Further, EMU and the Association agree that Faculty Members have additional professional responsibilities in such areas as participation in committee activities and keeping posted office hours which are scheduled at times most beneficial to students, and participation in such activities as orientation, registration, and in ceremonial academic functions such as convocations and commencement.

WESTERN ILLINOIS UNIVERSITY LIBRARY
(Macomb, Illinois)
Professional and Community Service

Professional and community service play an important role in advancing the profession and the visibility of Western Illinois University. Those areas listed below are some of the ways that one can contribute to this goal. This list is not intended to be inclusive. However, a faculty member has the obligation to participate in professional and community service in a meaningful way that will enhance the profession, the university, and the individual:

1. Committee work at all levels within the university.
2. Officer, committee member, or member in a professional organization.
3. Consultant work (written proof).
4. Coordinator, speaker, or attendee in convention programs, institutes, seminars, etc.
5. Advisor or sponsor in officially recognized student or other university organizations.

The Community service area comprises a wide variety of activities that are too numerous to list. However, community service should be conducted in addition to those organizations and services that one is a member of for reasons of longstanding personal choice.

Due to the inherent difficulty in measuring the participative effort in professional and community service, it is incumbent upon the individual that the effort be appropriate and of sufficient quality to be seriously considered for purposes of promotion and tenure.

Employee Benefits

TOLEDO-LUCAS COUNTY PUBLIC LIBRARY
(Toledo, Ohio)
Employment Benefits

Pension Plan

All full-time employees of the Toledo-Lucas County Public Library are required by law to join the Ohio Public Employees Retirement System. However, a membership is optional for employees who work fewer than 20 hours per week and students who work fewer than 800 hours per year. Applications for exemptions must be filed in the Accounting Office within 20 days of date of employment.

The employee's share of payment (8% of earnings) is deducted from his salary. The library contributes funds equal to or better than the employee's payment. Read *PERS; A Handbook for Members*, Public Employees Retirement System of Ohio, 1974.

Ohio Public Library employees are not eligible for Social Security, unemployment insurance, or Civil Service.

Insurance

Blue Cross of Northwest Ohio: Any or all of the following coverage is available to all employees (except pages) working half-time or more, with the Library paying full costs for *single* coverage: Blue

Cross Hospital Services, Blue Shield Surgical-Medical Services, and Supplemental Medical Expense (Major Medical).

Prudential Life Insurance: Life insurance at Library expense is provided to all staff working a *regular full-time* schedule who have completed their first or probationary year of employment. The amount of the insurance is equal to one times the annual salary to the nearest thousand, with a maximum of $10,000.

Washington National Accident and Income Protection Insurance: Voluntary group membership is available to all employees, except substitutes and pages, who work a regular schedule of 28 or more hours per week. Premium deducted from employee's check.

Workmen's Compensation of Ohio: The Library contributes to the Ohio State Workmen's Compensation Fund, and accidents causing injury to any staff member while on duty are covered by Workmen's Compensation as described in the Ohio Revised Code, Chapter 4123. Such injuries should be reported to the Accounting Office and the proper claim form completed.

Materials for Personal Use

Library employees must have their materials properly charged to their identification cards. No fines will be charged regular employees on overdue materials until the first notice is issued when the normal fines will be charged. When 60 days has elapsed the employee will be billed for the cost of the materials as well as the fine. Supervisors are urged to see the material is returned. PAGES ARE TREATED AS REGULAR PATRONS.

New materials should be in the collection a month before staff members borrow them unless they are needed for reviews or other professional reasons. If a staff member pays for a reserve it should be treated as a regular reserve.

Book Purchase

The T-LCPL Staff Association has formulated a policy affording staff members and trustees the opportunity to purchase library materials at the library discount . . . . The person wishing to purchase library materials is responsible for the correctness of the bibliographic citation. The request must be submitted to the Head of Order Department on the standard library multiple order form and be accompanied by a cash deposit for the list price of the item(s) wished ordered . . . . The staff member will be given a receipt for the full amount of money deposited. The Head of Order Department will keep a separate record of all transactions and will place the order marked STAFF through the appropriate dealer and specify that a separate billing is required for those items ordered by staff.

MINNESOTA VALLEY REGIONAL LIBRARY
(Mankato, Minnesota)
Benefits

Workmen's Compensation/Unemployment Compensation

Each employee in the system shall be covered by workman's compensation insurance and unemployment compensation in accordance with state law regulating such coverage.

Public Employees Retirement Association

All permanent employees who earn $250.00 or more per month are required to become members of the Public Employees Retirement Association. Any member who ceases to be a public employee by reason of termination of public service, shall be entitled to a refund of his accumulated deductions . . . .

Health Insurance

All permanent employees are covered by a medical program. The library pays the premium cost for the individual. If family coverage is desired, employee is responsible for additional premium.

Upon termination of employment, an employee may continue coverage under the library's policy for six months providing employee makes the monthly payments in advance to the bookkeeper.

Life Insurance

All permanent employees are eligible for a $4,000.00 term life insurance policy of which the entire premium is paid by the library.

Accumulated Benefits

Accumulated benefits acquired under a prior personnel policy of the Minnesota Valley Regional Library shall not be lost to the employee by the adoption of this policy . . . .

CHAMPAIGN PUBLIC LIBRARY AND INFORMATION CENTER
(Champaign, Illinois)

STATUTORY BENEFITS

Illinois Municipal Retirement Fund (I.M.R.F.) Social Security (F.I.C.A.) Employees of the library are covered under I.M.R.F. and Social Security retirement programs. Employees and the City of Champaign make monthly contributions to IMRF and FICA. Employee's share is deducted from his/her pay check monthly. . . . IMRF provides benefits in the event of retirement, disability or death.

Retirement
Employees classified as permanent and who work 600 or more hours a year are eligible for IMRF retirement benefits. Employees who terminate their employment before retirement may be refunded the contributions they paid into the fund . . . .

Disability
Employees covered by IMRF may receive disability benefits at 50% of annual rate of pay for the year ending on the date of the disability. A disability is any physical or mental impairment which makes an employee unable to perform the duties of any position which might reasonably be assigned . . . .

Death Benefits
There are eight different types of death benefits under the IMRF law. The kind received by supervisors depends on an employee's status at time of death . . . .

Workmen's Compensation Insurance
This form of insurance provides coverage for employees who receive job related injuries. The library pays the premiums for this

insurance which covers benefits and other compensation required by the workmen's compensation act . . . .

HOSPITALIZATION INSURANCE

A city sponsored hospitalization group insurance plan is available to all full-time employees. The Library pays for the cost of staff member's personal coverage. The Library will also pay fifty (50%) per cent of the premium coverage of a staff member's dependents. Employees become eligible for coverage on the first of the month following one month of continuous service . . . .

PARAMUS PUBLIC LIBRARY
(Paramus, New Jersey)
Benefits

Social Security

The Library, as employer, matches contributions of the employee to the Social Security System.

Workmen's Compensation

The Library contributes to Workmen's Compensation for the benefit of the employee in cases of disability.

Health and Hospitalization Insurance

The Library pays for coverage by Blue Cross and Blue Shield for all employees regularly scheduled to work 20 hours or more a week.

Pension Plan

Regularly scheduled employees earning $500 or more per year are required to enroll in the Public Employees Retirement System (P.E.R.S.), with all other employees given the option to enroll. The Library matches employees' contributions . . . .

ST. JOHN'S UNIVERSITY
(Collegeville, Minnesota)
Faculty and Administrative Fringe Benefits

Social Security

Saint John's University and each employee contribute monthly to
the retirement program established under the Federal Social Security Act (FICA). Beside retirement benefits, this program includes
disability, survivor and dependent benefits . . . .

Workmen's Compensation Insurance

All members of the faculty and administration are protected under
the Minnesota Workmen's Compensation Act. This insurance covers
any accidental injury occurring while at work. In case of accident,
even slight, the department head shall be notified immediately.
Within twenty-four (24) hours, the injury sustained, as well as treatment received, should be reported to the personnel office . . . .

Unemployment Compensation

Saint John's University provides unemployment compensation coverage as established under the Minnesota Department of Unemployment Services . . . .

Tax Sheltered Annuities

Saint John's offers the possibility of payroll reduction for the purpose
of a tax sheltered annuity. All employees may participate in the Tax
Sheltered Annuity Program if they wish. The TSA program is available only to persons employed by non-profit organizations. It allows
individuals to transfer amounts of up to one-sixth of their gross
income to a TSA fund. The amount deducted is not subject to State
and Federal income tax at the time it is earned. It is subject to
taxation at the time it is withdrawn from the plan. The number of
TSA or similar funds which Saint John's participates in is limited to
eight (8).
    The TSA program is intended to provide a means by which employ-
ees may supplement their retirement income. After retirement, regular monthly payments are made back to the employee. The amount
of the payments takes into account the earnings on the money depos-

ited by the employee. If you would like additional information about the TSA plan, please contact the Business Office.

Educational Benefits for Faculty, Administrative Employees and their Spouses

Educational benefits for a full-time faculty and administrative employee and spouse are available within the scope of the following policies and procedures. The benefits provide for free tuition. The payment of special fees is the responsibility of the employee or spouse . . . .

Saint John's University Faculty Sons' and Daughters' Tuition Remission

Full-time faculty and administrative employees are entitled to educational benefits for the undergraduate education of their sons and daughters . . . .

Group Health and Life Insurance

A low cost Group Insurance Plan is offered to full-time members of the faculty and administration. This plan provides coverage for medical and surgical care, hospitalization, and term life insurance, and is offered as a benefit with Saint John's University paying the full premium. The Health Insurance benefits are available to the employee and his dependents with the life insurance benefit being reserved for the employee alone.

Banker's Life of Des Moines, Iowa, is presently the carrier of the Saint John's group health insurance . . . .

Group Total Disability Insurance

A low cost Group Total Disability Insurance Program is offered to full-time members of the faculty and administration. This program is subject to a one-year waiting period and benefits paid are coordinated with Social Security benefits . . . .

Pension . . . .

Use of Facilities

Children of administrators and faculty may attend athletic and cultural events and make use of recreational facilities on campus according to published procedures . . . .

Services which the Library performs for students are also available to employees.

In case of on-the-job illness or injury, the Health Service is available during regular working hours for your convenience and security.

Campus Parking

Free parking on campus is provided as a fringe benefit to all employees. A staff parking permit is to be properly displayed on employees' cars . . . .

UNION THEOLOGICAL SEMINARY IN NEW YORK CITY
(New York, New York)
Benefits

Salaries

Salaries are set annually by the Library Director in consultation with the President. The Seminary's financial position and ambient salary and benefit structures inform this meeting of the Library Director and the President.

Medical Insurance

Blue Cross/Blue Shield individual insurance coverage is provided by the Seminary. Major Medical insurance coverage is provided by the Seminary for the individual and dependents. Long term Total Disability insurance is provided the professional librarian by the Seminary.

Life Insurance

$30,000 of life insurance for the individual is provided by the Seminary for professional librarians under 55; 55 and over, $5,000.

Travel

When on official business for the Seminary, a professional librarian is covered by a travel accident insurance which can reach the level of five times the annual cash salary. (The employee should request in writing before traveling approval for the official nature of the trip.)

Statutory Benefits

Statutory Benefits as provided by applicable Laws: Social Security; workmen's compensation; unemployment insurance; disability insurance.

Retirement Plan

The Seminary contributes 15% of the value of the professional librarian's annual salary to either TIAA/CREF or a denominational retirement plan.

Absences

Academic Non-Regular Vacation and Leave Policies

Vacation

Amount: 24 work days of vacation per year, effective from the initial day of employment. Vacation days are earned at the rate of 2 days for each month worked; for record keeping purposes the total annual 24 days are credited to the librarian each September 1st. These 24 days may be used any time during the year, subject to consideration of the library needs, scheduling of personnel, etc. Supervisors and/or the Library Director shall decide if a requested vacation is appropriate because of library scheduling. The employees shall have the right to request the length of vacation periods, i.e., one day, two weeks, etc.

Accumulation: Employees may accumulate up to ten working days of vacation to be carried into the following year's vacation period (determined by anniversary date of employment). Such carry-over time must be used during the subsequent period into which it is carried over, or it shall be forfeited. Exceptional situations which may involve longer vacations (e.g., 3 months of overseas travel) shall be approved at the discretion of the supervisor and director. It is recommended that employees use up their vacation on a continuing basis, rather than accumulating, since the basic idea of vacation is to provide time away from work for employee's well-being and/or personal interests.

Cessation of employment: Upon resignation, termination, or interruption of employment, paid terminal vacation time will be computed on a pro rata basis.

Holidays: Holidays recognized by the University shall not be counted against vacation time. Employees who are required to work on official holidays when the library is open for business shall be granted compensatory time off. Holidays are: New Year's Day, the Friday of Spring break, Independence Day, Labor Day, Thanksgiving Day and the following Friday, Christmas Day, and two additional "floating" days.

Planning Vacations: Employees are requested to inform supervisors of vacation plans as much in advance as possible so the schedules may be pre-arranged.

Funeral Leave

In the event of a death in the employee's immediate family, he/she may take up to 3 working days as funeral leave without a deduction from the employee's salary or accrued vacation time. The immediate family shall mean husband, wife, mother, father, stepmother, stepfather, son, daughter, brother, sister, mother-in-law, father-in-law or foster children or grandparents.

Jury Duty, Witness Service, Etc.

Any employee who is served with a subpoena to appear as a witness for jury service or who is a party in any legal proceedings and is required to be absent from his/her duties for the purpose of attending a trial or hearing shall report this to his supervisor. The employee shall be entitled to retain all compensation received for his/her participation and no deduction will be made in his/her regular compensation for the reasonable time he/she is absent from duty to attend such legal proceedings.

Maternity Leave

An academic non-regular employee may take up to 20 work days for maternity purposes after one year of service. Any time taken beyond these 20 days must be subtracted from vacation time or counted as a leave of absence without pay.

In cases of medical complications caused by or related to the pregnancy, sick leave may be considered appropriate beyond the 20 days.

Military Leave

It is the policy of the University to grant any full time, permanent employee who is or shall become a member of the Armed Forces of the State or of the United States, a leave of absence for military service, voluntary or involuntary, during which time the employee is engaged under official orders in the performance of duty or training subject to limitations as stated in Paragraph 5.000.12 of the University of Missouri Collection of Rules and Regulations. Armed Forces shall include the Air Force, Army, Marines, Navy, Coast Guard or any reserve component.

Sick Leave

Academic non-regular staff members do not receive any set number of sick days. Sick leave shall include reasonable time for the purpose of medical or dental appointments if it is not possible for the employee to schedule the appointment on his/her own time.

Sick leave is for the purpose of attending to the medical needs of the employee. An employee may take up to ten days sick leave in order to attend to full medical needs of his/her immediate family. In all other illness related instances time must be deducted from vacation or taken as leave without pay.

In case of an extended illness the employee is entitled to sick leave until such time as the University of Missouri Long Term Disability Program becomes effective. This time period applies to an employee regardless of his/her participation in the disability program.

LIBERAL ARTS COLLEGE
(Anonymous)
Faculty and Administrative Absences

For a full-time member of the faculty or administration not on tenure who is incapacitated by an accident or major illness [the college] shall assume the salary for ten academic days per year of service at [the college] up to a maximum of 60 days for six years of service. The fringe benefits shall continue in effect for this period with the understanding that the medical ones shall be extended through the coverage of the policy if the illness lasts longer than the maximum length of salary coverage.

For a full-time member of the faculty or administration on tenure, [the college] shall assume the salary for ten academic days per year of service at [the college] up to a maximum of 120 days with the fringe benefits assumed on the basis as explained in the above paragraph.

For part-time lecturer or teacher in the day session, [the college] shall assume one salary payment for ten academic days after three years of service at [the college].

If short absences occasioned by minor illnesses become excessive and interfere with teaching effectiveness, the institution reserves the right to charge a reasonable number of days of illness against the number of days of accrued leave available for prolonged illness.

The policy will be implemented by record keeping in the appropriate offices. In the event of absence because of illness of whatever duration, the member of the faculty or administration will notify his dean or department head who will make a notation. Such notations will be used in determining the absence status of the particular faculty member or administrator.

Academic Leave and Leave of Absence

The program of academic leaves is designed to foster the professional development of the faculty and to produce research and service which will be consonant with the mission of the college.

Eligibility

A faculty member on tenure is eligible to apply for academic leave after six full-time years of service at [the college]. Academic leave shall not be considered automatic. The recipient of an academic leave is obligated to return to [the college] for one year. If the recipient uses his leave to work toward an advanced degree, he must return to [the college] for three years. If in either case the faculty member does not return to [the college], he will be expected to reimburse the school for the salary incurred during his leave. A faculty member is not eligible for academic leave if, upon completion of the leave, he will reach retirement age before he can give two more years of service to [the college].

Application Procedure

Academic leave is not automatically approved for faculty members who are eligible in years of service. Application for academic leave must be made in writing, with a detailed description of the planned activities and an evaluation of the benefits which will be produced. The application should be presented to the Vice President for Academic Affairs by December 15 of the year prior to the proposed leave. The recommendation of the division chairperson will be required. Satisfactory arrangements must be made for covering the instructional activities of the faculty member during the period of academic leave. The Vice President for Academic Affairs may seek the advice of the Faculty Personnel Committee or the Committee of Professors to assist him in developing a recommendation to the President. Academic leave is granted by the Board of Directors upon recommendation of the President.

Leave of Absence Without Pay

In addition to the regular academic leaves here described, special leave of absence, without salary, may be granted if such leave is considered to be in the best interests of the institution. Such special leave of absence does not affect the terms of eligibility for regular academic leave.

WESTERN MICHIGAN UNIVERSITY
(Kalamazoo, Michigan)
Sabbatical Leave Policy

[Agreement between Western Michigan University and the Western Michigan University American Association of University Professors Chapter.]

Sabbatical leaves are intended primarily to encourage and promote the professional growth of the faculty and to enhance their scholarly and teaching effectiveness. Such leaves contribute to the accomplishment of these ends by enabling the faculty to undertake specific, planned activities involving study, research, scholarship, and creative work of mutual benefit to the faculty member and the University.

Eligibility for Sabbatical Leave

A sabbatical leave may be granted to any tenured faculty member at Western. Such leave may not be awarded to the same person more than once in every seven years, and sabbatical leave time shall not be cumulative. For part-time tenured faculty, the sabbatical leave shall be at the same FTE proportion as the faculty member's appointment. The granting of a sabbatical leave shall be without distinction as to rank, department or college affiliation, full-time or part-time status, or total years of service at Western.

One year in any six-year period spent on approved leaves of absence from Western for purposes of professional growth shall count toward the sabbatical eligibility period.

Requirements for Sabbatical Leaves

The Sabbatical project shall require a lengthy period of continuous release from normal faculty responsibilities—at least one full semester—and shall not be accomplishable in shorter intervals and with other forms of assistance already available for professional growth (e.g., the Spring or Summer Sessions, faculty research grants, released time, etc.).

Applicants for sabbatical leaves shall inform Western of other salaries, grants, fellowships, or financial support they expect to receive (or do receive) during the period of leave. The combined income from such sources and the sabbatical grant shall not exceed the faculty member's salary, research expenses, travel, and relocation costs associated with the leave.

A person granted sabbatical leave shall agree to return to his/her University duties for at least one academic year or the equivalent following the leave. A faculty member who fails to return to his/her employment at the expiration of his/her sabbatical shall be deemed to have voluntarily resigned his/her position unless unable to return by reason of injury or illness.

By the end of the first semester following their return to the campus, recipients of sabbatical leaves shall file a written account of their sabbatical activities and accomplishments with their chairperson, their dean, and the University Sabbatical Leave Committee.

Selection Process

Department and College Review:
Each department shall establish and set forth in its Departmental Policy Statement the procedures and criteria by which department

recommendations for sabbatical leaves shall be made. The criteria shall include the proposal's merits: (a) in its own right, (b) for the individual, and (c) for the University.

Applications and proposals for sabbatical leave shall be submitted by the faculty member to the department according to established deadlines. The appropriate department committee shall review all applications and proposals and forward its recommendations in priority order to the department chairperson. The department chairperson shall review all departmental recommendations and forward them to the dean, indicating in each case his/her recommendation on each proposal. The department chairperson shall also submit to the dean a specific written proposal for reallocation of the workloads of faculty members recommended for sabbatical leaves.

It shall be the responsibility of the dean to: (a) review all recommendations received; (b) determine whether the granting of the approved leave(s) would seriously impair the department's effectiveness; and (c) forward to the University Sabbatical Leave Committee each proposal which he/she approves with concurrent notice to the applicant and the department chairperson regarding said approval; and (d) return to the faculty member any proposal which he/she does not approve with concurrent notice to the department chairpersons regarding said non-approval.

The University Sabbatical Leave Committee:
The University Sabbatical Leave Committee shall be a standing committee consisting of one faculty member elected from each College, and one representative of the unaffiliated units, serving staggered three-year terms to assure continuity . . . .

The committee shall evaluate all proposals submitted as approved by both departments and deans to assure that they meet established University criteria and that the total number granted in any one year would not adversely affect the institution's academic program. They shall then submit their recommendations to the Vice President for Academic Affairs for his/her decision, which shall be forwarded to the Board of Trustees.

The committee shall inform each applicant whether the committee is or is not recommending that his/her application be approved, with concurrent notice of said decision to the department chairperson and the dean. Appeals to the committee shall be in accordance with procedures developed by the committee and approved by the Office of Academic Affairs.

The committee shall publish annual reports to the faculty, the Vice President for Academic Affairs, and the Chapter on the results of the selection process, and shall keep on file a cumulative record of those reports.

The committee shall be responsible for reviewing and recommending revision of sabbatical leave policies and practices.

Starting with the 1979-80 academic year, applications and proposals must be filed with the department not later than September 1 of the year preceding the fiscal year in which the applicant wants leave. Proposals approved by the department, the department chairperson and the dean should reach the University Sabbatical Leave Committee not later than October 1; the committee's recommendations should reach the Vice President for Academic Affairs not later than November 1. Final recommendations shall be submitted to the Board of Trustees at its December meeting. Sabbatical leave proposals submitted in the Fall semester of 1978 shall be handled under the October/January time schedule.

Funding

A faculty member may apply for a two-semester or a one-semester leave. In either case, if the leave is granted, the faculty member shall receive 75% of his/her salary for the period of the sabbatical.

[The following statement is based on the preceding Agreement between Western Michigan University and the Western Michigan University American Association of University Professors Chapter.]

WESTERN MICHIGAN UNIVERSITY LIBRARIES
(Kalamazoo, Michigan)

SABBATICAL LEAVE POLICY STATEMENT

Eligibility and requirements for sabbatical leave shall be those as stated in the *Agreement.*

Procedures

The "appropriate department committee" for review of all applications and proposals in the University Libraries shall be the Tenure and Personnel Committee. The Tenure and Personnel Committee may request input from those Library Faculty who can best assess the merit of the sabbatical project. The Tenure and Personnel Committee shall forward its recommendations to the Director of Libraries in accordance with the Agreement. The Committee will inform the sabbatical applicant in writing whether or not the proposal has been favorably recommended to the Director of Libraries.

The proposal shall include the following: (1) A clear, concise statement of the proposed activity; (2) Background information to assist the Committee in judging the merit of the proposal and the competence of the applicant to accomplish what is proposed; (3) The expected benefits to be derived from the sabbatical.

The proposal shall meet several of the following criteria:

1. In Its Own Right
   Deals with a significant problem, area, or issue.
   Shows promise of making contribution to the subject under study, or to the solution of a problem.
   Is especially appropriate at this time.
   Utilizes newly-available facilities or concepts.

2. Relative to the Individual
   Utilizes his/her expertise in a way not otherwise possible.
   Develops new capabilities for research, teaching, or professional services.
   Allows a synthesis or development of prior efforts or experiences.

3. Relative to the Institution
   Enhances the capabilities of the faculty member in his/her professional performance.
   Enhances the stature of the Department of the University.

[The agreement between WMU and the WMU-AAUP Chapter continues.]

LEAVE OF ABSENCE

Annual Leave

Accrual: Western shall provide annual leave to those unit faculty on full-time fiscal year appointments according to the following schedule:

Length of Service	*Accrual Rate Yr.*	*Max. Accrual*
0-5 yrs. (0-60 mos.)	20 days (160 hrs.)	30 days (240 hours)
6-10 yrs. (61-120 mos.)	22 days (176 hrs.)	30 days (240 hours)
11-20 yrs. (121-240 mos.)	24 days (192 hrs.)	30 days (240 hours)
20 or more yrs. (241 or more mos.)	25 days (200 hrs.)	30 days (240 hours)

Use of Annual Leave: The following conditions will obtain relative to the faculty member's use of accrued annual leave or Western's payment therefore to survivors.

Faculty who retire, who resign their employment, or who transfer from a fiscal year to an academic year position are expected to use all of their accrued annual leave prior to the effective date of retirement, resignation, or transfer . . . .

The surviving spouse or estate of any faculty member who dies shall be paid for all annual leave accrued up to a maximum of two hundred-forty (240) hours. Unit faculty terminated for any reason will be compensated for their accrued annual leave. Unit faculty, any time after being laid off, may elect to be compensated for their accrued annual leave.

Leave of Absence Without Pay

An unpaid leave of absence, for which written request has been made, may be granted to a faculty member upon the recommendation of the department chairperson and the dean, and upon approval of the Vice President for Academic Affairs. When such leaves are granted, Western shall notify the faculty member in writing of all conditions of such leave, including, but not limited to, the leave's effect upon tenure and promotion eligibility, salary increments during the period of leave, fringe benefits, and seniority. Normally, such leaves of absence may be granted for (a) a twelve (12) month period beginning with the commencement of the fall semester, or (b) one semester, either fall or winter. Under exceptional circumstances a faculty member may request a leave for a period longer than twelve (12) months or shorter than a semester. The faculty member shall receive no compensation from Western during the period of such leave but shall have the option of maintaining insurance benefits at his/her own expense to the extent permitted by the policies. If a request for leave is rejected, Western will notify the faculty member in writing of the reasons for rejection . . . .

Leave for Court-Required Service

A faculty member who, during an academic period during which he/she is scheduled to work, is summoned and reports for jury duty or is subpoenaed as a witness in a legal action to which he/she is not a party shall immediately notify the department chairperson of this obligation. Such faculty member shall be paid the difference between his/her regular rate of pay and the amount received for serving as a juror or witness. The foregoing provision shall not apply if the faculty member is a plaintiff or is voluntarily testifying for the plaintiff against the University in a legal action . . . .

Funeral Leave

Western shall grant unit members up to but not to exceed four (4) consecutive University working days of funeral leave with pay to make arrangements for and to attend the funeral of a member of his/her immediate family. The immediate family is defined by University policy to include current spouse and the faculty member's and his/her current spouse's children, parents, grandparents, grandchildren, brothers, or sisters. Request for funeral leave shall be made to the appropriate administrator.

Military Leave

Military Service: The reinstatement of rights of any regular faculty member who enters the military service of the United States by reason of an act or law enacted by the Congress of the United States, or who may voluntarily enlist during the effective period of such law, shall be determined in accordance with the provisions of the law granting such rights.

Annual Military Duty: A faculty member who is ordered to active duty during an academic period in which he/she is scheduled to work, upon his/her written request, shall be granted a military leave of absence, normally not to exceed fifteen (15) working days in any fiscal year (July 1 through June 30), to engage in a temporary tour of duty with the National Guard or any recognized branch of the United States Military Service. Such leave shall be credited as continuous service with the University. The faculty member shall be paid the difference between his/her regular rate of pay and the amount received for military duty.

Sick Leave

Sick Leave Credit: Paid sick leave will be credited to the following categories of faculty as herinafter specified:

All *full-time, fiscal year faculty members* will be credited with available sick leave benefits on the basis of one-half (½) working day for each completed pay period of service or major fraction thereof up to a maximum of two hundred sixty (260) days provided that the accumulation for any fiscal year shall not exceed thirteen (13) days nor shall the total accumulation of unused sick leave exceed two hundred sixty (260) days.

Sick leave for *full-time academic year faculty* shall be credited on the basis of five (5) days per semester (fall and winter) and two and one-half (2½) days per session (spring and summer). Credit for sick leave will be granted at the start of each semester or session. Sick leave will be permitted to accumulate to a maximum of thirteen (13) days per fiscal year but not to exceed a total of two hundred (200) days.

All regular Board-appointed part-time faculty shall be credited with sick leave benefits in proportion to the time worked relative to full-time teaching load.

Fiscal year faculty members absent due to illness entitled to the accumulation of sick leave credits will continue to accrue one-half (½) day thereof per pay period as long as they are on the active payroll even though they are absent from duty because of illness or injury . . . .

Use of Sick Leave Credit: Sick leave may be used in any period of the year in which a faculty member is scheduled to be on the active payroll, but only for the number of days the faculty member is scheduled to receive remuneration, subject to the following provisions:

A faculty member on fiscal year appointment may not use more than two hundred sixty (260) accumulated sick leave days during any fiscal year (July 1 through June 30). A faculty member on academic year appointment may not use more than two hundred (200) accumulated sick leave days during any fiscal year (July 1 through June 30).

All absences of the faculty member due to illness or injury of one-half (½) day or more will be debited against the faculty member's accumulated bank of sick leave regardless of whether his/her department absorbs his/her work load or the University provides a substitute. This applies to the illness or injury of the individual faculty member only.

If a faculty member elects to use sick leave while off duty because of a compensable injury and receives his/her full salary, part of the sick leave credit may be regained by depositing his/her Workmen's Compensation check with the University. Sick leave credit will be computed by dividing the total of Workmen's Compensation payments by the faculty member's rate of pay per day.

Western reserves the right to request a physician's statement or sworn affidavit that the claim for sick leave is *bona fide* as a condition precedent to the allowance of paid sick leave.

When a faculty member has used all of his/her sick leave credit, he/she will be removed from the payroll until he/she returns to duty.

The sick leave provisions herein set forth also shall apply to disabilities resulting from pregnancy and/or childbirth.

Coverage of Sick Leave Absences: Departments may be expected to absorb loss of services owing to illness or injury for a period of two weeks or less during the academic year and one week or less during spring and summer sessions. In the case of a very long absence (of more than a semester or session), a new appointment would presumably be necessary. If, in the case of an absence longer than two weeks but shorter than a full semester, an appropriate part-time faculty member cannot be hired, the services may be performed on an overload basis by a regular full-time staff member, with the approval of the department chairperson. Compensation will be based on the current University funding level for part-time instructors paid on a per-credit-hour basis prorated according to the time involved. The responsibility for funding the individual temporarily performing such services shall be determined jointly by the department chairperson, the dean and the Vice President for Academic Affairs.

Pregnancy and Childbirth Leave: Western regards pregnancy in the same light as other temporary physical disabilities. Accrued paid sick leave may be used for illness or temporary disability associated with pregnancy and childbirth. Absences due to illness associated with pregnancy or childbirth required after paid sick leave is exhausted are to be considered unpaid leave of absence due to sickness. A faculty member who is absent from work for the period of time in which she is physically unable to work due to pregnancy or childbirth is assured that she will be returned to her same position in the same manner as applies to other sick leave absences.

Sick Leave Payoff: [For] fiscal year faculty, one-half (50%) of the accumulated sick leave up to a maximum of 130 days (1,040 hours) is payable at retirement. In case of death, all (100%) of the accumulated sick leave is payable to the beneficiary of the faculty member up to a maximum of 130 days (1,040 hours). [For] academic year faculty, one-half (50%) of the accumulated sick leave up to a maximum of 100 days (800 hours) is payable at retirement. In case of death, all (100%) of the accumulated sick leave is payable to the beneficiary of the faculty member up to a maximum of 100 days (800 hours).

Personal Leave

In case of a personal emergency, a faculty member shall, with the approval of the department chairperson, receive a short-term leave with full compensation of up to four (4) calendar days excluding Saturdays, Sundays and University-recognized holidays. The faculty member's department will be expected to absorb the loss of services for the period of the leave. This leave is non-cumulative.

Leave of Absence for Political Office

In the event a faculty member decides to become a candidate for public office, it is professional courtesy that the faculty member inform the department chairperson or director of this intention. In the case of a candidacy for any office, the faculty member shall either continue to perform all duties, or take a leave of absence without pay. The faculty member shall inform the department chairperson or director and appropriate departmental committee in the event of his/her election or appointment to public office. In the case of appointment or election for a full-time public office, the faculty member shall request a leave of absence without pay. No such leave of absence shall be extended beyond two (2) years. In the case of a part-time office, such as membership on city councils, school boards, boards of supervisors, etc., a leave of absence may not be required.

CHAMPAIGN PUBLIC LIBRARY AND INFORMATION CENTER
(Champaign, Illinois)

HOLIDAYS

New Year's Day, Washington's Birthday, Memorial Day, Independence Day, Labor Day, Veteran's Day, Thanksgiving Day, Christmas Day, or days observed as such shall be recognized as holidays. However, the library will not be closed on Washington's Birthday or on Veteran's Day.

Employees scheduled to work on these recognized holidays, but who perform no work, shall be paid therefore at the employee's regular rate for such days, except to employees on leave of absence or extended sick leave. Work performed on a holiday other than Washington's Birthday or Veteran's Day shall be paid for at one and one-half times the regular straight time rate for the hours actually worked. Where the holiday falls on his regular scheduled day off or during his vacation, an employee shall be given a compensating day off with pay within 30 regular working days following the holiday.

The library will close at noon on Christmas Eve and New Year's Eve and all day Christmas Day and New Year's Day. Whenever Christmas or New Year's falls on Saturday, the library will close at noon Friday and will remain closed Saturday and Sunday. Whenever a holiday falls on a Sunday, the following Monday will be observed as a holiday and the library will be closed Sunday and Monday.

Time off may be given to attend special religious services. Such attendance must be approved in advance by the Library Director.

Employees who are classified as permanent part-time employees will be compensated for holidays in the same ratio as their working hours per week are to the regular full-time employee's working hours per week to the nearest half (½) day.

VACATIONS

Vacations are granted only to permanent and continuous employees who complete the probationary period, unless approved by the Library Director. Vacation schedules will be arranged in accordance with the employees' requests whenever possible, subject to the following regulations, needs of the library and fairness to other employees.

New full-time professional employees will earn 1⅔ days of paid vacation for each month worked from date of employment to the end of the current fiscal year (June 30) subject to meeting requirements for continued employment. Each year thereafter full-time professional staff members will earn 20 working days vacation a year. Vacation schedules may normally not be divided into more than four separate periods.

New full-time non-professional employees will earn one day of paid vacation for each month worked from date of employment. Each year thereafter full-time non-professional employees will earn 12 working days up to a total of 20 working days vacation a year. Vacation schedules may normally not be divided into more than four separate periods.

Vacations should be scheduled at least one month in advance through the supervisor. Departmental vacation schedules will then be approved by the Library Director. This is particularly important for summer vacations and seasonal periods such as Thanksgiving, Christmas or New Year's Day.

Vacations may not be taken in advance or before granted without approval of the Library Director. An employee who resigns before completing his probationary period will not be entitled to vacation pay.

Earned vacation credits may not be cumulative beyond the fiscal year without approval of the Library Director. No salary payment will be made in lieu of vacation not taken except at termination of employment.

Compensatory time for legal holidays falling on days off may be added to vacation time with approval of the supervisor. Notice of compensatory time earned for legal holidays will be given by the Library Director when applicable. Legal holidays falling within a vacation period will not be counted as vacation time used.

Permanent part-time employees will accrue paid vacation time in the same ratio as their working hours per week to the nearest half day. Vacation may be taken at the convenience of the schedule, subject to the needs of the library and approval of the supervisor.

Vacation credits accrued from date of employment will be posted at the end of the probationary period and on the following January 1 and July 1 of each year for all full-time employees. Vacation credits will only be posted July 1 for permanent part-time employees since vacation credits are calculated on the basis of hours worked per year. Vacation credits should be used within the year following date posted.

Employees who have completed the probationary period, and whose employment is subsequently terminated, will be paid unused vacation credits accrued at time of termination.

LEAVES OF ABSENCE

Personal Leave

Full-time employees may be granted up to a total of three (3) days personal leave during the fiscal year. No specific reason need accompany a request of personal leave unless used in conjunction with holidays, weekends, or vacation. Requests for personal leave must have the approval of the supervisor.

Sick Leave

Sick leave for full-time employees is earned at the rate of one (1) day for each month of employment, cumulative to 120 days. Permanent part-time employees earn sick leave at the same ratio as their working hours per week are to the regular full-time employee's working hours per week. Sick leave is to be considered a privilege useable only in case of actual personal illness. In the case of sickness within the immediate family, a limited amount of sick leave may be used with the approval of the Library Director.

An employee who reports for work at the beginning of a work day and who is excused, by the supervisor, for illness after working a minimum of two (2) hours will be charged for one-half (½) sick-leave day only. If an employee works to within two (2) hours of quitting time and is excused for illness, no charge will be made against sick leave earned.

If an employee is ill and has no unused sick leave credits, time off will be deducted from his/her last check unless the employee requests this time be charged against vacation earned.

An employee should call the administrative secretary or supervisor when he/she is ill prior to the beginning of a work day. If scheduled for evening or weekend assignment and neither the secretary nor the supervisor is available, the Information Desk staff should be notified. It is the supervisor's responsibility to report all absences on the weekly time reports.

An occasional emergency appointment of an hour or two with a doctor, dentist or to transact other urgent business may warrant approval by the supervisor without deduction from sick leave earned.

An employee is eligible to receive payment in cash for one-half (½) of his accumulated sick leave upon retirement.

Funeral Leave

Leave with pay, not to exceed five (5) days, is allowed an employee in the case of death of a member of the immediate family. Immediate family is defined as husband, wife, son, daughter, grandchildren, parent, brother, sister, grandparents, or the spouse's immediate family. For other members of the family, leave may be charged against accumulated sick leave or vacation credits earned.

Jury Duty

The library will not request exemption from jury duty for its employees. A staff member will be paid the difference between his basic wage rate and jury pay, but will be expected to give as much time as possible to the regular library work schedule during the period of service on the jury, e.g., Saturdays and days when attendance in court is not required.

Educational Leave

Full-time employees may request to take courses at a recognized institution of higher education to improve their library work skills or effectiveness. If the Library Director determines that funds are available, the Library Board of Directors will approve the payment of one-half (½) of the tuition costs for the course, and one-half (½) the employee's base salary while in attendance of such courses. An employee granted educational leave under the terms of this paragraph shall maintain his/her regular work schedule as class attendance permits. After completion of the course of study, the employee will be required to furnish proof of satisfactory completion of the course of study, or he/she will be required to reimburse the Library for the entire costs incurred by the library in supporting the employee's classroom attendance. If the employee leaves the Library service within one (1) year after completing the course of study, he/she will be required to reimburse the Library for the salary paid the employee during his/her education leave.

Maternity Leave

An employee on becoming pregnant may remain in employment during her pregnancy until such time as the director determines she is unable to maintain the schedule and work level. In most cases the director will rely on the employee's judgment and her doctor's opinion. Permanent employees with one or more years of satisfactory service may make written application to the director for a maternity leave not to exceed three (3) months after birth of the child. Benefits do not accrue during such leave of absence nor can the same position be assured when the employee returns. Leave prior to the birth of a child may be granted for a period not to exceed three (3) months, subject to the discretion of the director. When maternity leave is granted by the Library Director, the non-probationary employee may use all accumulated sick leave and vacation leave for absence due to pregnancy. The employee who expends all such accrued leave may be granted additional leave without pay, subject to the other provisions of the Maternity Leave section.

Records of Leave of Absence

The business office will prepare and maintain a continuous record for each employee showing vacation, and other credits earned and used. A record of the current status of an employee's "earned and used" account is available for examination upon request.

Voting

Employees will be allowed time off to vote if they cannot arrange to do so on their free time. Such absence must be arranged with the supervisor as the schedule allows.

WORTHINGTON PUBLIC LIBRARY
(Worthington, Ohio)

VACATIONS

Professional: 1¾ days per month (156 hours per year).

Clerical: 1 day per month (90 hours per year) for the first 5 years. Same as professional after that.

Though vacation time accumulates monthly, it is not due a staff member until one full year has been completed. Any vacation taken before the end of this period will be considered leave of absence and deducted from the final paycheck if employee leaves before the end of 1 year employment.

PAID LEGAL HOLIDAYS

Eight legal holidays are allowed: New Year's Day, President's Day, Memorial Day, Independence Day, Labor Day, Veteran's Day, Thanksgiving and Christmas. Other holidays may be designated by the board. Though the following are staff holidays, the library will remain open with part-time personnel or full-time people receiving compensatory free time: President's Day and Veteran's Day.

SUNDAY HOURS

Full-time staff who work on Sunday receive double compensatory free time.

SICK LEAVE

Employees earn 10 hours per month for each full month employed. Emergency leave shall be granted to a staff member in the case of serious illness, injury, or death of a member of his immediate family or household. The amount should depend upon circumstances, but normally would not exceed three days and should be deducted from sick leave.

CENTRAL NORTH CAROLINA REGIONAL LIBRARY
(Burlington, North Carolina)
Maternity/Paternity Leave of Absence

On recommendation of the department head and with approval of the Director, an employee may be granted maternity/paternity leave for a period not to exceed six months. That portion of such leave certified by the employee's physician to be medically necessary shall be with pay and charged as part of the employee's sick leave. The remainder of a six month's period may be allotted the employee as leave without pay.

PARAMUS PUBLIC LIBRARY
(Paramus, New Jersey)

HOLIDAYS AND EMERGENCY CLOSINGS

The Library is closed on the following legal holidays: New Year's Day, Lincoln's Birthday, Good Friday, Memorial Day, Independence Day, Labor Day, Columbus Day, Election Day, Veterans' Day, Thanksgiving Day, and Christmas. On December 24 and December 31 the Library will close at 12 noon. When July 4, Christmas or New Year's falls on a Sunday, the Library will be closed on the next day, Monday. If any of the other holidays falls on a Sunday, the Library will be open the next day and the staff will be given a compensatory day off. In cooperation with the Mid-Bergen Federation of Public Libraries, and in order to have at least one member-library open on all but major holidays, the Paramus Library will be open on Washington's Birthday. Staff members will be given compensatory time off at a later date. The three holidays the Government has designated to fall on Mondays, Memorial Day, Columbus Day and Washington's Birthday, shall be observed on those Mondays.

Part-Time Employees

Those employees scheduled to work an average of 20 hours or more per week shall receive paid holiday hours equal to 1.2 times the average number of hours scheduled per week, to the nearest half hour.

Emergency Closings

If the Library is closed for any temporary emergency (snow storms, utilities failure, etc.) not exceeding two days, only full and regular part-time employees shall be paid their regular salaries during such closings..

The decision to close the Library for any emergency shall be made by the Board President and the Director.

VACATIONS

Full-Time Employees

A new employee may not take any paid vacation during the first six months of employment. The employee will then earn one day of paid vacation for each subsequent month worked to the end of the calendar year, to a maximum of 10 days. Professional employees receive 20 days paid vacation each succeeding calendar year. Non-professional employees receive 11 days paid vacation for the next calendar year, and one additional day each year to a maximum of 15 working days.

Vacations must be completed by December 31 of each year, unless circumstances warrant a delay to the following year only, without detriment to adequate staffing of the Library. If a holiday falls during a full-time employee's vacation, compensatory time shall be given. When conflicts arise in desired vacation schedules, priority shall usually be given to the employee with seniority within job classification. During vacation periods, the library shall be covered by the remaining regularly scheduled staff wherever possible. A vacation-time pay check may be advanced to an employee before vacation starts if it is requested from the Director at least 2 weeks before going on vacation. Staff members who retire in good standing shall be entitled to earned vacation. On the contrary, employees who have taken their annual vacation allowances but retire or resign before year-end shall incur deductions for the unearned portion.

Part-Time Employees

Part-time employees regularly scheduled to work an average of 20 hours or more a week shall receive annual paid vacation time equal to 1.75 times the average weekly number of hours scheduled. New part-time employees may not take vacations within the first six months of employment.

SICK LEAVE

Sick leave means the absence of an employee because of illness, accident, exposure to contagious disease, medical or dental appointment, or attendance upon a sick member of his/her immediate family (defined as parent, spouse, child, or sibling, or relative residing in the employee's household). In the case of an absence exceeding 5 working days, the employee shall furnish a doctor's statement, unless the Director indicates otherwise.

All full-time employees shall accrue sick leave at the rate of 1¼ days per month for a total of 15 days each year. New employees may not take sick leave with pay during their first 3 months of employment, although they do accumulate such leave at the stated rate. Unused sick leave may accumulate from year to year to a maximum of 90 days.

The Board may grant additional sick leave upon written application by an employee, such application accompanied by a written statement by the employee's doctor setting forth the nature and extent of the injury or illness and his opinion as to when the employee may reasonably be expected to be ready to resume usual duties.

If an employee becomes seriously ill while on vacation, the days of illness may be charged to sick leave, on submission of proof of illness to the Director.

All submitted documents will become part of the employee's personnel file.

On the job injuries should be reported to the Administrative Assistant within 72 hours for Workmen's Compensation Coverage.

Part-time Employees

Part-time employees scheduled to work an average of 20 hours or more a week shall receive annual paid hours of sick leave equal to 1.5 times the average weekly number of hours scheduled. These hours may accumulate to a maximum of 9 times the average weekly number of hours scheduled.

PERSONAL LEAVE

In addition to the regular holiday and vacation time, full-time employees shall be allowed 3 extra paid days per year to be used for personal business. Requests for personal days must be submitted reasonably in advance whenever possible for the approval of the Director. Personal days shall not be added to sick leave or vacation, nor shall they be cumulative from one year to the next.

EMERGENCY LEAVE

Death in the immediate family may necessitate the absence of any employee regularly scheduled for 20 hours or more a week for no more than 3 days with pay. Additional days, or leave in the event of death other than in the immediate family may be granted from accumulated sick leave, personal days, or vacation time at the discretion of the Director.

JURY DUTY

All employees absent because of jury duty shall be compensated for the difference between jury pay and full salary. This shall also apply to employees required to be witnesses in court trials.

TERMINAL LEAVE

Upon retirement or resignation in good standing, an employee is entitled to remuneration for one half his/her total accumulated sick leave at the rate of the average daily pay over the last 3 years of employment. An employee who resigns or retires in good standing is also entitled to payment for vacation time earned but not used.

LEAVE WITHOUT PAY

Leave without pay may be granted at the discretion of the Board of Trustees for a period not exceeding one year. Requests for a leave of absence without pay must be submitted in writing to the Director. All requests, accompanied by recommendations of the Director, must be submitted for approval to the Board. The Board reserves the right to stipulate any conditions for such leave. During extended leave granted for other than medical reasons, the employee may elect to continue medical coverage at his/her own expense, payable in advance. Leaves without pay up to one month may be granted at the discretion of the Director, within budgetary limitations, since substitutes may be needed.

Terminations

PIKES PEAK REGIONAL LIBRARY DISTRICT
(Colorado Springs, Colorado)

Termination

No permanent employee shall have his services terminated without adequate cause, unless he is being retired or is being separated because of clearly evident financial exigencies of the institution. An employee being dismissed for unsatisfactory work performance [see below] shall have been placed on probation prior to dismissal. An employee dismissed for conduct prejudicial to the best interest of the library [see below] may be dismissed without having been on probation.

End of Temporary Assignment

Employment in temporary positions is usually for a stated period of time. If the employment period is indefinite and if funded from library funds, a two week notice prior to the termination date is required. Employment in a temporary position which is funded from outside sources such as grant money, or federally funded programs will be designated as such and may end without notice if outside funding source is withdrawn.

Lay-off

If, due to necessary organizational changes, lack of funds or other cogent reasons, a position is eliminated, the incumbent may be laid off. If another suitable vacancy exists for which the employee is qualified, a transfer may be effected, but the final decision as to disposition of personnel to best meet the needs of the library ... is the responsibility of the Director. The employee is notified of the decision at least two weeks prior to his effective date of termination, and the letter of notification will contain explanation of the circumstances as a means of assisting the employee in finding other employment.

Resignation

An employee wishing to resign in good standing must submit a letter of resignation in advance through his supervisor to the Personnel Resources Officer. All employees must give at least a two week notice prior to their last working day. A four week notice for librarians and a 2 months or longer notice for members of the Management Team are considered appropriate. Employees who resign without a two week notice will not be paid for terminal leave, except for emergency maternity situations when the supervisor has been notified in advance by the employee that the possibility exists.

Dismissal

Dismissal is the termination of employment for cause. An employee may be dismissed for unsatisfactory work performance or for conduct prejudicial to the best interest of the library.

Unsatisfactory Work Performance: Prior to dismissal of an employee guilty of unsatisfactory work performance, the employee must be placed on probation and given the opportunity to improve his work performance. A performance appraisal should be completed at the time an employee is placed on probation, objectives necessary to retain the job should be agreed upon in writing by the supervisor, employee should be given an adequate time period to reach these objectives agreed to, and follow up evaluation periods set. Evaluations, objectives, and progress will be sent to the Personnel Resources Officer to be included in the employee's personnel file. If the objectives are not attained, dismissal may be recommended by the Director. If another position vacancy exists for which the employee is qualified, ... transfer may be made and the probationary period extended for a reasonable period. If, at the end of the extended probationary period, the employee's work is still unsatisfactory, the employee will be dismissed. The employee will be given a written notice of his termination, including the reasons therefore, two weeks prior to the effective date. The Director may, if circumstances warrant, authorize two weeks pay in lieu of the written notice of dismissal.

Unsatisfactory work performance includes but is not limited to the following: Failure to perform satisfactorily the duties of the position because of unwillingness, incompetence, or physical incapability; habitual tardiness; unauthorized absence; abuse of sick leave privilege; failure to work harmoniously with other employees to the extent of impairing the usefulness of the employee; repeated discourtesy to the public; failure to observe library policies, procedures, rules and regulations; failure to meet required qualitative and quantitative standards of performance; failure or refusal to comply with the reasonable orders and directions of a supervisor; failure to observe established safety regulations; or sleeping on the job.

Conduct Prejudicial to the Best Interest of the Library: An employee charged on the basis of clearly factual evidence with misconduct prejudicial to the best interests of the library will be dismissed immediately. An employee charged with such conduct, but who denies the charges, will be given an immediate hearing before the Director, who will review the case and render a final decision. The employee will be notified of the decision in writing.

Conduct prejudicial to the best interest of the library includes but is not limited to the following: Falsification of records, including false statements on the application form; use of official position or authority for personal gain; drug addiction, use of drugs that effect job performance, intoxication or the effect thereof, while on duty; theft and/or willful destruction or negligent use of library property; conviction of a felony or of a misdemeanor involving moral turpitude; unauthorized release of confidential information from restricted official records; or any other action or activity which tends to discredit the employee or the library or which is proven to be legally or morally criminal, infamous or dishonest.

Retirement

Retirement of library employees is mandatory at the age of seventy. Voluntary retirement may occur at any time after a person reaches age 62.

Death

The Personnel Resources Officer will be notified immediately upon the death of any employee of the library and will: (1) Notify the next of kin, if necessary; (2) Call the Police Department, if death occurs at work; (3) Notify the County offices concerned and the Social Security Office; (4) Adjust and complete pay and other necessary records.

NATRONA COUNTY PUBLIC LIBRARY
(Casper, Wyoming)
Separation and Suspension

The separation of an employee from the Library shall be designated one of the following: disqualification or fraud, end of temporary assignment, layoff, resignation, retirement, or dismissal.

Disqualification or fraud

When information is received, after an employee has been appointed, that such employee is physically or otherwise unqualified to perform the duties of the position to which he has been appointed, or that he obtained his appointment through fraud, he shall be separated immediately. The Library Director shall notify the employee of his separation in writing within twenty-four hours after receipt of information resulting in the separation.

End of Temporary Assignment

When an employee has completed his temporary assignment, he shall be separated.

Layoff

Whenever it becomes necessary to lay off an employee either because of elimination of his position or reduction in force, the Library Director shall, in writing, notify the employee to be laid off at least 15 days prior to the effective date, except that professional librarians must be so notified 30 days prior to the effective date.

Resignation

To resign in good standing, an employee must give the library at least fifteen days prior notice, except that professional librarians must give thirty days notice. The Library Director, because of extenuating circumstances, may agree to permit a shorter period of notice. A written resignation shall be submitted by the employee to the department head giving the reasons for leaving. The resignation shall be forwarded to the Director of Libraries with a statement by the appointing authority as to the resigned employee's service performance and other pertinent information concerning the cause for resignation. Failure to comply with this rule shall be entered on the service record of the employee, may be cause for loss of payment for accumulated annual leave, and may be cause for denying future employment by the Library. The resignation of an employee who fails to give notice shall be reported by the department head immediately. The Director of Libraries may take steps to verify reasons for any resignation.

Retirement

Employees shall retire on the first day of the month following their sixty-fifth birthday, except as provided elsewhere in the rule. The Director of Libraries shall notify persons approaching mandatory retirement age at least ninety days prior to the effective day so that their application for retirement can be processed in time for them to receive retirement benefits during their first months of retirement.

Employees reaching age sixty-five who wish to continue may, at least six months before the employee's sixty-fifth birthday, apply to the Director of Libraries through appointing authority for a continuance of up to twelve months.

Dismissals

The Library Director may dismiss any employee in the Library for misconduct, inefficiency, or other just cause. He shall give such employee a written statement setting forth in substance the reasons therefore and file a copy of the statement with the Board of Trustees. Fifteen days severance pay will be paid to the dismissed employee within one calendar week of the dismissal.

Suspension

An employee may be suspended by the Library Director without pay for a period not to exceed five working days, where the case is not sufficiently grave to merit dismissal.

Reports

In all cases of separation or suspension the Library Director shall place a personnel action form in the personnel folder of the employee, setting forth the type of action taken, reasons therefore, effective date, and period covered in the case of suspension, and any other pertinent information bearing on the case.

TOLEDO-LUCAS PUBLIC LIBRARY
(Toledo, Ohio)

DISMISSAL

Any decision regarding the dismissal of an employee is made with the prior approval of the Director or his delegated authority, upon the recommendation of the employee's supervisor.

Causes for dismissal include incompetency, inefficiency, dishonesty, drunkenness, being under the influence of illegal drugs, immoral conduct, stealing, insubordination, objectionable treatment of the public or fellow staff members, neglect of duty, habitual tardiness, misrepresentation of time worked, sleeping on the job, excessive absenteeism, smoking in non-smoking areas, falsification of application, any act of misfeasance, malfeasance, nonfeasance, or the persistent and willful violation of library rules and regulations.

The supervisor shall have counseled and tried to help the employee achieve an acceptable standard of performance. If counseling does not result in any improvement, then a written notice shall be sent to the employee warning that the performance is not acceptable and that unless there is improvement in the quality of work the employee's services will be terminated. The employee should have a reasonable period of time (to be determined by the supervisor) in which to improve the performance. If there is not sufficient improvement then a written notice of dismissal is sent to the employee giving a minimum of two week's notice.

Should the employee, at any time preceding receipt of the written notice, feel that the supervisor is not being fair or just in the evaluation of the performance, he or she has the right to initiate the grievance procedure developed by the Staff Association Personnel Committee with the administration.

The written notice of dismissal shall inform the employee that should he or she has been treated unjustly, he or she has the right within five working days from the receipt of the letter to request a hearing before the Personnel Committee of the Board of Trustees. The hearing and the Committee's decision shall take place before the date of termination stated in the dismissal letter.

SUSPENSION

A supervisor has the right, should an employee flagrantly violate the library rules, to suspend an employee without pay until a decision is made on dismissal. At the time of suspension, the employee must surrender any library keys to the supervisor until the decision has been made. The supervisor should give the employee a receipt. The supervisor will report the case to the appropriate supervisor and the Personnel Officer.

Some examples of when an employee would be suspended without pay subject to dismissal would be if caught stealing; smoking in a non-smoking area; being under the influence of alcohol or an illegal drug that impaired his performance; physical violence.

Temporary suspension without pay may also be used to warn an employee that certain conduct will not be condoned, but that certain extenuating circumstances may cause one to overlook an initial offense. Some examples of when temporary suspension may be invoked: sleeping on the job; being under the influence of alcohol or illegal drugs which was of a level that did not adversely affect the employee's work or contact with the public or staff.

The Personnel Office as well as the supervisor should be kept informed of any such action, and a written report should be submitted for the Personnel files.

RESIGNATION

Resignations must be submitted in writing to the Personnel Office by way of the appropriate supervisors.

The effective date of the individual's resignation will be the last day for which the employee is paid. This effective date, determined by the Accounting Office, will include all annual paid leave that the individual has accumulated up to the effective date of the individual's resignation. The individual will have the option of receiving all earnings paid in one lump sum or paid as the regular payroll is issued. No PERS service credit is earned nor contribution for PERS taken on any lump sum payment.

The minimum notice customary for professional and semi-professional positions is one month; minimum notice for all other positions is two weeks.

A staff member in an important administrative position should give, if possible, a longer notice to allow sufficient time for the consideration and appointment of a successor.

An employee must turn in the identification card as well as any keys, books, or other library materials or equipment before receiving a final check. The Personnel Office shall notify the Circulation Department when the identification card is terminated.

RETIREMENT

Normal retirement at age 70. Effective at the end of the month in which the 70th birthday occurs.

Continued service of an employee may be requested by the Director according to the needs of the Library. A doctor's certificate of satisfactory physical and mental health will be required on a prescribed library form describing the job of the incumbent.

Retiree has an option of being placed on the Paid Substitute list.

SENIORITY POLICY

Exclusions

Administrative Council members, department heads, branch heads, Circulation Coordinator, Deputy Clerk-Treasurer, Displays Head, Purchasing Agent, Printer, Custodial Head, Main, and secretaries of the Director, Assistant Director, Personnel Officer and Public Information Officer are not covered by this policy except as provided for ... under "Bumping Rights" below.

Definition of Seniority

Seniority shall constitute in time of layoff a right of preference for retention between two or more employees in the same job classification. It is therefore a relative status and does not convey a right to a position.

Seniority shall be in classification and grade based on length of continuous service since last date of hire. If more than one employee were hired on a given day in the same seniority unit then the respective order of seniority shall be based on performance and qualifications. Continuous part-time service of half-time or more will also count towards seniority on a prorated basis. Service as a page does not count towards seniority. Individuals who have been promoted or laterally transferred shall retain seniority rights in previously held classifications. The service accumulated in a higher classification shall count for seniority purposes in a classification formerly held. The service accumulated in a lower classification however cannot count towards seniority in a higher classification except in a position reclassification in which the administration may elect to count the previous classification time towards seniority in the new classification.

Seniority Classification

Grade 1: Clerks-Circulation, Clerks-Technical Services, Menders, Doormen, Matrons, and Delivery-Printer Assistant.

Grade 2: Clerks-Circulation, Clerks-Technical Services, Delivery Assistant, and Dept. Clerk-typists (inc. Child. Coord. Office).

Grade 3: Switchboard Operator, Clerks-Circulation (inc. Sr. Clerks and Tech Ass'ts), Technical Services, Administrative Offices (Extension, Adult Services, Circulation Coord., Local History), Driver-Clerks, Delivery Head, and Custodial Assistants.

Grade 4: Clerks-Circulation, Clerks-Technical Services, Displays assistant, Secretaries (Ass't Director & Public Information), Custodial Heads in Branches, and Accounting Assistants.

Grades 5 or 6: Semi-Prof. Assistants-Adult Services, Semi-Prof. Assistants-Children's Services, and Maintenance Assistants.

Grade 7: Professional Assistants-Adult Services, Professional Assistants-Children's Services, and Professional Assistants-Cataloger.

Grade 8: Professional Assistants-(HeD, Sanger, West Toledo, Social Science-3).

Order of Layoff

Newest employee in terms of seniority in each classification is the first one laid off with two possible types of exceptions. Personnel who have exhibited exceptional performance clearly well above that of other personnel in the classification or who have special qualifications needed for an available job that other personnel with more seniority do not have, may be passed. In both of the above cases the order of layoff shall then move to the next newest employee.

When an individual is to be passed over because of clearly exceptional performance the administration will notify the Personnel

Relations Committee of the Staff Association and give the reasons for the exemption. A committee of the Director, Assistant Director, Head of Main, Head of Extension, Personnel Officer and Children's Coordinator will determine such exemptions on the basis of recorded evaluations and input from appropriate supervisors.

Notice of Layoff

When a reduction in force becomes necessary a listing of the types and numbers of positions to be vacated will be posted four weeks prior to the first effective date of layoff. Notification letters will have first been sent to the individuals on the initial layoff list. In no case will an individual be given less than 30 calendar days notice of layoff.

Bumping Rights

An individual notified of layoff may bump into a lower or equal level classification. An individual who bumps into a lower classification will be appointed within the lower pay grade at a step equivalent (as far as can reasonably be determined) to what he or she would have reached had he or she not been promoted. The bumping is contingent upon having the ability to do the job. The employee bumped shall be the newest employee in terms of seniority unless excepted as described above. Bumping must be within one's own classification or classification series or into another classification series in which seniority is held. The classification series are: Circulation Clerks, Technical Service Clerks, Custodial Assistants, Maintenance Assistants, Adult Service Semi-Professionals and Professionals, and Children's Service Semi-Prof. and Professionals.

A request to bump must be communicated in writing to the Personnel Office listing the desired position within three working days after the layoff notification is received.

If an excluded position as described above is discontinued or the incumbent is displaced by another staff member, an incumbent may bump into previously held classifications in the manner described above. A person in any of the excluded positions however cannot bump into another excluded position.

Order of Recall

After first consideration has been given to qualified personnel who have bumped down into lower positions, laid off personnel who meet the qualifications for an available position will be recalled in reverse order of layoff so that last out is first back in. No outside candidates will be considered until the above process has been exhausted.

Recall Notice

Notification of recall shall be by return receipt requested mail to the last address the employee has given to the Library Personnel Office. An employee who has been recalled must report for work on the scheduled date or show good cause why he or she is unable to do so within three working days after receipt of the notification. Failure to show good cause in writing shall result in a forfeiture of seniority and employment. If the recall is to a position other than that previously held by the employee he or she shall have a right to refuse that recall. If that recall was in the individual's last classification the employee shall then go to the end of his or her seniority unit. If the individual refuses a second recall he or she will be considered to have resigned.

Seniority During Initial Probation

Unless there is a significant difference in level of performance, first year probationary employees shall be subject to layoff according to date of hire.

No Accrual When on Subsequent Probations

An employee shall not accrue seniority when on probation for disciplinary or performance reasons.

No Accrual When on Leaves of Absence or Layoff

Employees shall retain their seniority when on approved leaves of absence or layoff. Their seniority will cease to accrue during the absence or layoff and resume accrual upon return to work.

Loss of Seniority

Seniority shall automatically terminate when (a) an employee quits, (b) an employee is discharged for cause, (3) an employee fails to report for work within three days after a leave of absence expires, (d) an employee is not recalled after 12 months on layoff, (e) see recall notice provision.

CETA Positions

CETA maintenance of effort provisions stipulate that when regular employees are laid off then any CETA personnel in identical positions must also be laid off regardless of the amount of time they have been with the system. If a CETA employee is appointed to the regular staff, his or her seniority shall date from the date of his or her CETA appointment (subject to the same personnel regulations that govern any library employee).

VIKING LIBRARY SYSTEM
(Fergus Falls, Minnesota)
Separations

Retirement

Legal retirement age is 70. Employees participate in the PERA and the Social Security system.

Resignation

Resignations should be submitted to the Director, in writing, far enough in advance to ensure adequate staffing of and continuity in System programs. A one-month period is required of all full-time employees. When an employee is terminated, pay for accrued vacation time and sick leave is calculated on the basis of current monthly salary and is added to the final paycheck.

Dismissals

Made by the Director with the approval of the Board of Directors. The advice and counsel of the legal representative of the Board may be obtained when advisable. No arbitrary discharge shall threaten the security of staff members on permanent appointment. Since the fitness of staff members is carefully tested and reported on during the probationary period, it is expected that the cause for dismissal will not arise except under unusual circumstances or changed conditions. Dismissal for incompetence, insubordination, or inability to perform the job as described by the job description, may be made for the good of the System. Chronic tardiness or absenteeism, if continued after sufficient warning, are grounds for suspension pending dismissal.

If the work of a staff member is unsatisfactory, the staff member shall be so advised in writing by his/her immediate supervisor. If, within a reasonable time and after meaningful attempts at correction by supervisory staff, the employee fails to improve, employment will be terminated with one pay period dismissal pay.

TERMINATION WITHOUT PREJUDICE

Reduction in Force

In the event that a reduction in force becomes necessary, consideration will be given to the quality of each employee's past performance, the needs of the service, and seniority in determining those employees to be retained. In the event of financial exigency or urgently needed retrenchment, it may be necessary to terminate the services of staff members. In such cases, as much notice as possible is given to those employees to be separated from service. Every assistance will be given the employee, and an explanatory statement provided the employee for use in seeking another position.

Discontinuance of an Activity

In those cases where an activity may be curtailed or discontinued, every effort will be made to transfer affected staff members to another position within the System. If a transfer cannot be arranged, a minimum notice of two months for all employees will be given, and every possible assistance in securing another position will be offered.

Right to Appeal

If an employee wishes to appeal his/her discharge before the Board of Directors, a written notice must be submitted to the Director within five working days from the time the employee received dismissal notification from the Director.

UNIVERSITY OF NEW MEXICO
(Albuquerque, New Mexico)

TYPES OF TERMINATION

Each termination must be categorized as falling within one of the following seven official types of terminations.

Resignation

- Employee's request.
- Employee walks off job.
- Is absent for three (3) consecutive work days without permission except when an emergency situation precludes giving notice.

Work days are considered consecutive even when broken by normal non-working days, such as holidays or weekends.

- Fails to return to work within the prescribed time limits following a Military Leave of Absence.
- Fails to return to work within the prescribed time limits following a Leave of Absence for Extended Illness, Injury or Personal Reasons.

Release

- Termination at the end of temporary employment.

Relieved

- Terminated during the six (6) month probationary period. Probationary employees may be terminated any time prior to completion of the probationary period without recourse.

Layoff

- Terminated because of reduction of force due to lack of funds, work or other compelling reasons.

Discharge

- Terminated after corrective discipline has failed or the seriousness of the infraction so warrants. (See Policy on University's Right to Manage, Discipline and Discharge.)

Retire

- Terminated under the New Mexico Educational Retirement Act and/or University's age policy.

Deceased

NOTICE OF TERMINATION

In discharge cases, permanent employees should be given a minimum notice of two (2) calendar weeks, except in cases of immediate discharge for serious infractions or discharge immediately following a suspension for a serious infraction.

Temporary and probationary employees are given as much notice as possible but no minimum notice is required.

PAY IN LIEU OF NOTICE

Pay in lieu of notice may be given at straight time rate when giving notice is not expedient.

Pay in lieu of notice is not given in cases of immediate discharge for serious infractions or discharge immediately following suspension for serious infractions.

Normally, disciplinary action is taken prior to discharge.... Where disciplinary action has failed, an employee may be discharged and given pay in lieu of notice.

Employees terminated during probation should not be given pay in lieu of notice.

TERMINATION OF EMPLOYMENT PROCEDURE

To protect both the employee and the University, and for official records to determine if an employee is eligible for unemployment compensation, the following procedure is to be used for *all terminations* (except deceased): Complete a Personnel Action Notice (PAN) and a Notice of Employee Separation form and submit both to the Personnel Department.

The supervisor is responsible for the following: Confirms that the employee does not take vacation which would extend the termination date beyond the last day actually worked, provides the Personnel Department with a forwarding address, assures that employee has completed the UNM check-off sheet that requires the employee contact each department (i.e., locksmith, cashier) and be cleared....

Layoff Cases

Every effort should be made to place an employee in good standing in another position within the University prior to layoff.

Order of Layoff and Recall from Layoff

The order of layoff shall be based on least performance, ability, training, seniority and other qualifications as determined by the University. When performance, ability, etc., are equal, seniority ... shall be the determining factor. Recall shall be in reverse order.

Probationary, temporary and occasional employees are normally laid off before permanent employees in the same classification and department. All layoff cases should have prior consultation with the Personnel Department.

An employee recalled from layoff within one year will be given credit for prior service in computing accrual rate for vacation, sick leave and other benefits. Such credit will be given by having their anniversary (date in current position) date adjusted by the number of days spent in layoff status. Salary increases and probationary periods will be based on the adjusted anniversary date. Employees rehired at a higher rated job will have the rehire date as their anniversary date.

EASTERN MICHIGAN UNIVERSITY
(Ypsilanti, Michigan)
Layoff and Recall

[Agreement between Eastern Michigan University and the Eastern Michigan University Chapter of the American Association of University Professors, October 1978.]

Requirements

The following procedure shall be followed should EMU determine to reduce the number of Faculty Members [librarians are faculty rank] within a department or program owing to its curtailment or elimination, or owing to a bona fide financial exigency, or owing to an enrollment decline or reasonably anticipated enrollment decline. (Layoffs based upon an enrollment decline or a reasonably anticipated enrollment decline can be made only to the extent that they do not cause the remaining Faculty Members in the affected department or program to exceed the work load norm as specified [elsewhere].)

1. EMU shall notify the Association of its intent to reduce Faculty Members in a department(s) or program(s).
2. Prior to a final decision by EMU to curtail or eliminate a department or program for reasons other than financial exigency, EMU shall seek the recommendations of the Faculty regarding the need for and plan for effecting such curtailment or elimination through the Faculty input procedures specified [elsewhere]. If such recommendations are not made to EMU within twenty-

five (25) days ... of the date they are requested, EMU shall be deemed to have met its responsibility pursuant to this paragraph.

Layoff Procedures

Provided that the Faculty Members being retained can carry out the full range of instruction needed, the following layoff procedures shall be implemented:

1. The adjustment [in work load] shown below shall be utilized before actual release of Faculty Members unless it is agreed not to use either or both [procedures] by a majority of the full time Faculty Members in a department and EMU ...[details of plans omitted].
2. Regular, full-time Faculty Members in the same department shall have priority for retention over temporary and part-time staff and priority for retention for teaching assignments over graduate assistants with similar duties. Such rights shall not extend over graduate assistants who exercise teaching responsibilities in a course for which a Faculty Member has been assigned primary instructional responsibility or graduate assistants in other assignments.
3. Tenured Faculty Members shall have priority for retention over probationary Faculty Members in the same department or program.
4. Between probationary Faculty Members, the Faculty Members with the higher rank shall have priority for retention.
5. Between probationary Faculty Members with equal rank, retention priority shall be based on the following criteria, in sequence: Length of service in rank; Highest relevant academic degree; Total length of service at EMU; Date of highest relevant academic degree.
6. Between tenured Faculty Members the Faculty Member with the higher rank shall have priority for retention.
7. Between tenured Faculty Members with equal rank, retention priority shall be based on the following criteria, in sequence: Length of service in rank; Total length of service at EMU; Highest relevant academic degree; Date of highest relevant academic degree.
8. A change in regular appointment from full-time to part-time service may be offered as an acceptable substitute for layoff. Rank shall be maintained with part-time salary proportionate to the base full-time salary. The Faculty Member shall be retained in the Bargaining Unit and shall receive such fringe

benefits as are provided by EMU policy for part-time faculty. The Faculty Member shall be returned to full-time service in accordance with the recall procedure.

9. Members of the Bargaining Unit subject to or on layoff status shall be given preference over new hires in filling vacant positions in the bargaining unit for which they are qualified. Appointments to such bargaining unit vacancies and rank and salary considerations shall be subject to the provision . . . .Such Faculty Members shall be considered to be on layoff status from their original departments and shall be eligible for recall to their original departments in accordance with the provisions [outlined below].

10. Tenured Faculty Members who are subject to layoff shall receive notice of at least two (2) semesters prior to the effective date of the layoff or pay in lieu thereof. Non-tenured Faculty Members who are subject to layoff shall receive notice of at least one (1) semester prior to the effective date of the layoff or pay in lieu thereof. For purposes of this provision, the spring and summer terms shall constitute one (1) semester.

11. A Faculty Member who held a tenured appointment on the date of termination by reason of layoff may resume the tenured appointment upon recall. The Faculty Member shall receive the same credit for years of service held on the date of layoff.

12. A Faculty Member who is laid-off shall be eligible to continue elected group medical and life insurance coverage if enrolled at the time of layoff, consistent with the terms of the master contracts with the insurance carriers for a period not to exceed one year without University subsidy, provided: The Faculty Member makes written request for continuation of such coverage no less than thirty (30) days prior to the effective date of layoff; and, the Faculty Member pays the full cost of such coverage on a quarterly basis (commencing with the first day of the month in which the laid-off Faculty Member is on the payroll for less than one-half of the month); and payment is made at least fifteen (15) days prior to the beginning of each quarter.

Recall Procedures

Recall shall be in the inverse order of release provided the Faculty Member being recalled is qualified for the available position. It is the responsibility of the released Faculty Member to keep EMU informed of where he/she may be reached readily. Declining or failure to respond within thirty (30) days to an opportunity to return to a former position will result in removal from further consideration under this provision. The released Faculty Member's position shall not be filled by a replacement within a period of three (3) years unless the released Faculty Member has been offered reappointment and has declined or has failed to respond within thirty (30) days.

ST. JOHN'S UNIVERSITY
(Collegeville, Minnesota)
Termination of Administrative Appointments

Unless otherwise specified, administrative appointments are for a term of one year.

Administrators are entitled to written notification of nonreappointment according to the following norms:

- In their first year of service, not less than three months before the expiration of their contract.
- In their second year, not less than six months before the expiration of their contract.
- At least twelve months before the expiration of an appointment after two or more years of service in the University.

This provision for terminal notice need not apply in the event that there has been a finding that the grounds which justified dismissal involved serious personal misconduct, provided that the individual is extended the protection of due process.

An administrator may terminate his appointment effective at the end of an academic year, provided that he gives notice in writing at the earliest possible opportunity, but not later than May 15, or thirty days after receiving notification of the terms of his appointment for the coming year, whichever date occurs later. He may properly request a waiver of this requirement of notice in case of hardship or in a situation where he would otherwise be denied substantial professional advancement or other comparable opportunity.

The regulations concerning academic freedom ... apply to administrative personnel who hold academic rank, but only in their capacity as faculty members. Where an administrator alleges that a consideration violative of academic freedom contributed to a decision to terminate his appointment to an administrative post, or not to reappoint him, he is entitled to the procedures set forth [elsewhere in the personnel document].

In no case will administrators . . . who are not otherwise protected by the regulations which relate to dismissal proceedings be dismissed without having been provided with a statement of reasons and an opportunity to be heard before the Administrative Services and Development Advisory Council. (A dismissal is a termination before the end of the period of appointment.)

Index